# The 22 Mysteries of the Christian Way

## Konstantin Serebrov
## Gouri Gozalov

Serebrov Boeken
The Hague

English translation of a Russian book '22 тайны христианского пути' by Konstantin Serebrov and Gouri Gozalov, Moscow - The Hague, 2009

ISBN: 978-90-77820-23-0

| | |
|---|---|
| Editors: | Gouri Gozalov cs, The Hague, Holland |
| Translators: | Gouri Gozalov and Maria Toonen, The Hague, Holland |
| Illustrations and cover image: | aquarelles by Natalya Komarovskaya-Jumati, St. Petersburg, Russia |

Design of the book: Gouri Gozalov and Maria Toonen

© Serebrov Boeken, The Hague, 2010
Tel./Fax: +31 (0) 70 352 15 65
E-mail: serebrovboeken@planet.nl

All rights reserved. No part of this publication may be reproduced or transmitted in any form or by any means, electronic or mechanical, including photocopy and recording, or stored in a retrieval system, without the written permission of the publisher.

## Contents

Foreword by the authors ......... 5

The First Arcanum. God the Father – Creator of the Universe ......... 8

The Second Arcanum. God the Son ......... 16

The Third Arcanum. God the Holy Spirit ......... 35

The Fourth Arcanum. The Mother of God ......... 44

The Fifth Arcanum. The Baptism ......... 54

The Sixth Arcanum. The Choice of the Path ......... 66

The Seventh Arcanum. The Victor ......... 77

The Eighth Arcanum. Particular Judgement ......... 92

The Ninth Arcanum. Spiritual Guidance ......... 104

The Tenth Arcanum. The Law of ascending to the Kingdom of Heaven and of the fall into the lower worlds ......... 114

The Eleventh Arcanum. The Super-Effort ......... 124

The Twelfth Arcanum. The Sacrifice ......... 135

The Thirteenth Arcanum. Death ......... 148

The Fourteenth Arcanum. Serenity of the Heart ......... 161

The Fifteenth Arcanum. Overcoming Lucifer's temptation ......... 172

The Sixteenth Arcanum. The rules for ascending to the Kingdom of Heaven ......... 184

The Seventeenth Arcanum. Meeting the Theotokos in one's heart ......... 194

The Eighteenth Arcanum. Finding the Lord Jesus Christ in one's heart ......... 205

The Nineteenth Arcanum. Receiving the Holy Spirit ......... 221

The Twentieth Arcanum. Finding God the Father in one's heart ............................................................... 230

The Twenty First Arcanum. The Epoch of the Paracletus ............ 240

The Twenty Second Arcanum. Finding the Holy Trinity in one's heart ............................................................... 250

Enclosure. Breathing techniques ........................................... 260

Books by Konstantin Serebrov ............................................... 268

FOREWORD BY THE AUTHORS

The principal spiritual experience from the times of the Old Testament is represented, amongst other forms, as 22 symbolical pictures, known as Arcana Taro. The comments on them are given the general name 'Arcanology'.

This name consists of the Latin word 'arcanum' which means 'secret', 'mystery' and the Greek word 'logos', one of the meanings of which is 'doctrine, knowledge'. The meaning of the word 'arcanology' is therefore 'the knowledge of mystery'. These are the mysteries, the riddles of being that man has to solve in order to find contact with God.

The apostolic church has inherited its basic forms from the tradition of the Old Testament and has poured into them the contents of the New Testament. As Saint John the Forerunner says 'For the law is given through Moses, while the blessing and the truth came through Jesus Christ.' (John, 1,17). It can be seen in the seven-armed candlestick at the altar, in the way the holy Church Fathers commented and interpreted the psalms of the king and prophet David, and in other parts of the Christian tradition. This work of co-creation with God was started by the apostles and was continued by the holy Fathers, who have been creating the liturgies, prayer services, chants, canons, acathists, icons, exercises of inner praying. All of these contribute to the spiritual treasury of the Christian tradition, and especially of the Russian Orthodox tradition, which is the direct successor of the Byzantine tradition.

Thus, in the spirit of this creative work, and praying to the holy Fathers for help, we attempted to replenish the Major Arcana of Taro with new contents: the mysteries of the New Testament, given to people by Christ. It is a presentation of the Royal Path to find God inside the soul, which was accomplished by thousands and thousands of Christian ascetics, who have left us the description of their spiritual experiences. Their instructions form the basis of this book.

The whole of Arcana forms the ladder of 22 steps leading to heaven. Studying each Arcanum and mastering the practices of prayer and contemplation you climb one step higher. The prayer and contemplation exercises purify and elevate the soul and prepare it to become the temple of the living God.

The 22 Arcana, the 22 mysteries are divided into two categories.

The first four Arcana are the contemplative mysteries, as they explain where the Path starts and where it leads to. The rest of the Arcana are the active mysteries, as they explain in which way man can purify and elevate his soul. The essence of the Path is faithfulness towards God and praying and contemplative exercises, which make the soul crystal-clear and full of the fire of the Holy Spirit. A believer, following as far as possible the example of the holy Fathers, satiating his soul by the light of their teaching and performing prayer exercises, will be able to ascend the spiritual ladder to the Kingdom of Heaven. 'Spiritual ladder' in fact means that there will be growing in the soul of the believer the positive qualities, Christian virtues, until he or she will become worthy of the Heavenly Kingdom and will enter into it.

To write this book the following sources have been used:
1. The Gospel (The King James Version)
2. The Philokalia
3. 'Solovetski Patericon: the holy Fathers of the Solovetski Isles'
4. 'Notes of Elder Silouan'
5. 'The zealous Intercessor' by Hieromonk Philadelph.

Konstantin Serebrov
Gouri Gozalov
Moscow - The Hague, 2009

The First Arcanum

## The First Arcanum. God the Father – Creator of the Universe

The first Arcanum states the following spiritual truth: everything is created by our Heavenly Father, Whose essence is the Divine, spiritual, fire.

The picture of the first Arcanum represents symbolically God the Father, the Creator of the whole Universe and all living beings. He is surrounded by the six-winged seraphims and four-winged thrones.

God inserted in each soul He created, a particle of His light-bearing fire. The Saints perceive the Divine fire to such an extent only that their soul can stand without being burnt in the fire of God's loving heart. The spiritual fire brings with it heavenly blessings and satiates the heart with spiritual warmth, the soul feels stillness and peace.

In order to perceive the heavenly Creator man must undergo a long process of purification and elevation of the soul. He who wants to come closer to the Creator and avoid scorching the wings of his soul, should first purify his body, heart and mind from what are to God impure deeds, feelings and thoughts. Even though they seem to be pure in worldly eyes, for Him they might be unbearably polluted. Radiating invisible light, God Sabaoth abides far away from His creation, but He penetrates by His emanations all the worlds. He contains in His consciousness all the beings that He created and He has an invisible link to all of them. All the created worlds are maintained by the power of His divine will. We are the sons of light, created by our heavenly Father, and the divine sparkle, which is part of His spiritual light, is burning inside of each of us. The Lord Sabaoth has created our souls in His own image. This means that the soul of each person has an immortal nature and the potential to re-unite with God and to co-create with Him eternally. Human souls incarnate on earth in order to have the possibility of ascending to the heavenly Father and acquiring a place near Him. For this, man should endeavour to be a temple of God during his earthly life, which means, to purify his body, heart and mind from passions. At the end of their lives, holy elders, having accomplished a long Path of spiritual development, found God within their heart. God the Father appeared to them in the form of a great spiritual, radiant sun. From the centre of it His indescribable voice reached them. The elders recognized then the One, Who secretly had been instructing them on their spiritual Path, had been sharing with them His love and caring for them. Having met the Lord in all His radiant strength and beauty, they did not wish to see anything else. They realized that all the happiness of the world is in the Creator of the Universe and therefore there can be no greater happiness than communicating and conversing with Him.

Having found God the Father, holy elders received from the great Creator the mission to lead to Him His lost children, who got stuck in the material, worldly life and forgot about their spiritual fatherland. They became identified with their bodies, which are just a temporary shelter for their souls, and they started to think that there is no soul, or life after death but just a material body. Therefore they exchanged spiritual goals for worldly ones. Instead of aspiring towards the heavenly Father, they sought happiness on earth or attempted to build it, being convinced that they are only physical bodies. Being blinded by their passions, concerns and worldly dreams they forgot about their heavenly Father, their divine nature, the eternal life of their souls and thus they became just a part of nature endowed by reason. This part of the incarnate humanity, instead of taming their passions and irrepressible desires, attempts to get out of their physical bodies as much pleasure and enjoyment as possible, without really thinking how they are going to live when their physical body will be taken away from them. For the sake of helping the sleeping part of humanity the Creator of all the worlds sends to them the prophets, spiritual mentors, holy elders who endeavour to wake them up and to teach them how they can return to man's spiritual home. Conversing with the heavenly Father gives an unspeakable bliss and elevates man's soul to heaven.

An unprepared man cannot stand the spiritual radiance of the heavenly Father as he will be burned down by His spiritual fire. Only purified from passions and prepared, can a soul meet the heavenly Father.

God the Father, Creator of all the worlds, appears before the inner eyes of the Saints as a vast radiant, spiritual sun, the purity of which surpasses human understanding. Therefore the holy apostles call God the Son 'the Father's Radiance'. (Kondakion of the Feast of Transfiguration).

Part of the nature of God the Father which is comprehensible to us is a spiritual fire. The Holy Spirit, which comes from the Father, appears as a dazzling, invisible light. Jesus Christ, God the Son, can appear either in His human aspect, as He was incarnated on earth, or in His natural, fiery form, as the essence of Christ is the Divine, radiant spiritual fire.

God the Father is one with His Son, Jesus Christ and with His Holy Spirit. The Creator of all the worlds, God Sabaoth, contains in Himself all the beauty, part of which He gave to His creation. The Lord is Allmighty, He contains in Himself all the love of the world. He grants His love to all humans, He provides the beauty of their body and soul and He does everything so that His creatures will aspire to Him and will become one with Him. For He abides in the souls of all the human beings and they abide in Him. The Lord God grants him, who has become worthy of the honour of conversing with Him, great spiritual bliss. He gives him omniscience and a possibility to merge with the entire universe. A believer, who finds God inside himself, receives the great divine heritage of love, beauty and the eternal bliss of communicating with God. The Lord always appears to the one who found Him, in a new aspect, He is always different and unique. Communication with God comes as a reward for the long lasting and hard inner work. In order to earn this reward one should transform oneself, and for this one should accomplish the path of spiritual perfection. Only after this, can a believer be worthy of meeting God. God could of course transform all people Himself in the twinkling of an eye and make them all perfect beings. However, where then would be the effort of our free will, which God granted to us, for the sake of earning the great reward of communicating with Him? If such a man, who did not make the effort of changing himself, would contact God, he wouldn't be able to hold his ground in God's world of bliss and beauty. Such a man would quickly fall in a world which is even lower than the world he lived in before. Elders say that it is God's will that people learn how to solve their earthly problems themselves and to apply a lot of their own efforts for the sake of ascending to the Heavenly Kingdom. Due to these efforts human beings grow and expand their earthly and spiritual being. And when man walks on the Path of spiritual development and asks God for help, God will always help him. In order to help humanity to purify itself from its sins, God the Father sent down to earth His only-begotten Son. Christ brought people the Message of His heavenly Father so that people could come to know it and to ascend to the Heavenly Kingdom and merge with the Creator and live in His worlds of bliss and beauty. He brought humanity divine mercy and divine love. Here are some fragments of the Gospels where Christ tells us about it.

Jesus said: 'He that believeth on me, believeth not on me, but on him that sent me. And he that seeth me seeth him that sent me.' (John 12:44,45)
The one who will believe in Jesus Christ, will believe in the Heavenly Father, Who sent his only-begotten Son for the salvation of man. He who perceives the divine essence of Christ will perceive the Heavenly Father Who sent Christ. For Christ is one with His Father in His heart, just as God the Father is one with Christ and lives in Him.

Jesus said: 'I am come a light into the world, that whosoever believeth on me should not abide in darkness.' (John 12:46)

## The First Arcanum

Christ bears spiritual light in Himself, which comes from the Heavenly Father, and then through Christ passes onto His disciples. Without the Divine light human souls abide in darkness. Christ is light, He brought the light of His Father, and the souls of those who follow Him, will be filled with this light.

Jesus said: 'And if any man hear my words, and believe not, I judge him not: for I came not to judge the world, but to save the world.' (John 12:47)
It is necessary for us to remember that Christ came to save people from sin, and not to punish them. Man has always an opportunity to turn to Christ and to repent of his sins, and Christ will forgive him, and He will purify his soul with His light which shines in Him eternally. And this light comes from the heavenly Father, for Christ is in the Father and the Father is in Him.

Jesus said: 'He that rejecteth me, and receiveth not my words, hath one that judgeth him: the word that I have spoken, the same shall judge him in the last day.' (John 12:48).
The one who rejects Christ cannot ascend to the Heavenly Kingdom. When at the end of life, the soul parts from the body, then the word by which it rejected the Saviour will become its sentence and it will fall into the dark worlds of atonement.

Jesus said: 'For I have not spoken of myself; but the Father which sent me, he gave me a commandment, what I should say, and what I should speak.' (John 12:49)
Christ speaks not of Himself but He transmits the words, the commandments of the Heavenly Father, Who sent Him into the world. The Lord God gave the commandments to Christ so that Christ would communicate them to the people. The one who rejects Christ rejects in this way the commandments of the Heavenly Father Who sent His Son to save the world. He who does not believe in Christ,

rejects salvation which comes from the Heavenly Father and thus he draws misfortune upon himself.

Jesus said: 'And I know that his commandment is life everlasting: whatsoever I speak therefore, even as the Father said unto me, so I speak.' (John 12:50)
The Heavenly Father gave commandments to the world through His Son Jesus Christ, and these commandments lead those who obey them into the Heavenly Kingdom.

Jesus said: 'Let not your heart be troubled: ye believe in God, believe also in me.
In my Father's house are many mansions: if it were not so, I would have told you. I go to prepare a place for you.
And if I go and prepare a place for you, I will come again, and receive you unto myself; that where I am, there ye may be also.
And whither I go ye know, and the way ye know.' (John 14:1-4)

'Jesus saith unto him, I am the way, the truth, and the life: no man cometh unto the Father, but by me.' (John 14:6)
'Believest thou not that I am in the Father, and the Father in me? The words that I speak unto you I speak not of myself: but the Father that dwelleth in me, he doeth the works.
Believe me that I am in the Father, and the Father in me: or else believe me for the very works' sake.
Verily, verily, I say unto you, He that believeth on me, the works that I do shall he do also; and greater works than these shall he do; because I go unto my Father.
And whatsoever ye shall ask in my name, that will I do, that the Father may be glorified in the Son.' (John 14: 10-13)

## The First Arcanum

**The practice of the prayer 'Heavenly Father, Creator of all the worlds, have mercy on me.'**
Make a small so-called iconostasis, this is a number of icons put together, in the eastern corner (or in the corner, which is the closest to the eastern corner). The icons should be placed on the level of your head or a bit higher. An iconostasis can contain, besides the principal icons, such as icons of the Lord Jesus Christ, The New Testament Trinity and the Theotokos, also icons of the Archangel Michael, the guardian angel, Saint Seraphim of Sarov, Saint Sergius of Radonezh, Saint Nicholas of Myra, your personal Saint protector, whose name you bear and other Saints of your choice, whom you feel are dear to your heart. In front of the icons there should be a small oil lamp: just a small vessel with e.g. sunflower oil and a wick in it, or a shelf for candles. The oil lamp or the candles should be lit during the prayers.

1. Read before your home iconostasis the morning or the evening prayers.
2. Sit on the chair before an icon representing the New Testament Trinity and say aloud for five minutes the prayer 'Heavenly Father, Creator of all the worlds, have mercy on me.'
3. Pronounce this prayer mentally for another five minutes.
4. Focus your mind on the physical heart and then let your mind go into your heart and pronounce as if with your heart this prayer for another five minutes.
5. Say this prayer every day for five minutes longer.
6. When you will be able to repeat this prayer for an hour a day, it means that the prayer has become established in you. Try to perform this prayer rule daily. In addition to it you can say this prayer when you walk on the street or do some simple manual work.

You have learned the first Arcanum if you pray so daily for one hour.

The Second Arcanum

## The Second Arcanum. God the Son

The second Arcanum states the following spiritual truth: mankind, which has fallen following its forefather Adam who sinned, was not able to return by its own power alone to its heavenly Father. Therefore God the Father sent down to earth His only-begotten Son, Jesus Christ, the second Person of the Trinity so that Christ would help people ascend to the Divine spheres again.

The picture of the second Arcanum represents Jesus Christ with seraphim and angels. He is enveloped in the spiritual light which signifies His divine origin.

Jesus Christ brought on earth the seed of the supreme, Divine love: spiritual fire and He wished that this fire would flare up in the hearts of people. 'I am come to send fire on the earth; and what will I, if it be already kindled?' (Luke 12:49) Christ took onto Himself the sins of all people in order to purify and to save their souls, and to take those who repented truly, to the Kingdom of Heaven.

The Jew's clergy had been waiting for the coming of the Messiah, that is the Messenger of God, who would give them, God's chosen people, as Moses had taught them, the supreme spiritual power. There came however not the Messenger, but God Himself, in His second hypostasis of God the Son, in order to give spiritual power to all people, His children, without exception. 'He came unto his own, and his own received him not.

But as many as received him, to them gave he power to become the sons of God, even to them that believe on his name:

Which were born, not of blood, nor of the will of the flesh, nor of the will of man, but of God.' (John 1:11-13). Christ explains to Nicodemus, a Pharisee of high rank, what it means: 'to be born of God'.

'Jesus answered and said unto him, Verily, verily, I say unto thee, Except a man be born again, he cannot see the kingdom of God.

Nicodemus saith unto him, How can a man be born when he is old? can he enter the second time into his mother's womb, and be born? Jesus answered, Verily, verily, I say unto thee, Except a man be born of water and of the Spirit, he cannot enter into the kingdom of God.' (John 3:3-5)

The sacrament of baptism in the water of the baptistery, and anointing, the seal of the Holy Spirit, is God's gift to us: the seeds of the new life. However in order to realise this in our life, in order let these seeds sprout, we should purify our soul, mind and body to such an extent that God can abide in us.

Christ came to earth at the time that the world was approaching its end: the increasing materialism of the soul and the further imprisonment by the prince of this world. Christ reveals His mystery to Nicodemus in the following words:

'For God so loved the world, that he gave his only begotten Son, that whosoever believeth in him should not perish, but have everlasting life.

For God sent not his Son into the world to condemn the world; but that the world through him might be saved.

He that believeth on him is not condemned: but he that believeth not is condemned already, because he hath not believed in the name of the only begotten Son of God.

And this is the condemnation, that light is come into the world, and men loved darkness rather than light, because their deeds were evil.' (John 3: 16-19)

In His Sermon on the Mount Christ gives to people the keys to a life in God, which are the commandments of bliss:

'And the whole multitude sought to touch him: for there went virtue out of him, and healed them all.

And he lifted up his eyes on his disciples, and said, Blessed be ye poor: for yours is the kingdom of God.

Blessed are ye that hunger now: for ye shall be filled. Blessed are ye that weep now: for ye shall laugh.

## The Second Arcanum

Blessed are ye, when men shall hate you, and when they shall separate you from their company, and shall reproach you, and cast out your name as evil, for the Son of man's sake.

Rejoice ye in that day, and leap for joy: for, behold, your reward is great in heaven: for in the like manner did their fathers unto the prophets.

But woe unto you that are rich! for ye have received your consolation.

Woe unto you that are full! for ye shall hunger. Woe unto you that laugh now! for ye shall mourn and weep.

Woe unto you, when all men shall speak well of you! for so did their fathers to the false prophets.

But I say unto you which hear, Love your enemies, do good to them which hate you,

Bless them that curse you, and pray for them which despitefully use you.

And unto him that smiteth thee on the one cheek offer also the other; and him that taketh away thy cloak forbid not to take thy coat also.

Give to every man that asketh of thee; and of him that taketh away thy goods ask them not again.

And as ye would that men should do to you, do ye also to them likewise.

For if ye love them which love you, what thank have ye? for sinners also love those that love them.

And if ye do good to them which do good to you, what thank have ye? for sinners also do even the same.

And if ye lend to them of whom ye hope to receive, what thank have ye? for sinners also lend to sinners, to receive as much again.

But love ye your enemies, and do good, and lend, hoping for nothing again; and your reward shall be great, and ye shall be the children of the Highest: for he is kind unto the unthankful and to the evil.

Be ye therefore merciful, as your Father also is merciful.

Judge not, and ye shall not be judged: condemn not, and ye shall not be condemned: forgive, and ye shall be forgiven:
Give, and it shall be given unto you; good measure, pressed down, and shaken together, and running over, shall men give into your bosom. For with the same measure that ye mete withal it shall be measured to you again.' (Luke 6:19-38)
And Christ also says: 'Come unto me, all ye that labour and are heavy laden, and I will give you rest.
Take my yoke upon you, and learn of me; for I am meek and lowly in heart: and ye shall find rest unto your souls.
For my yoke is easy, and my burden is light.'(Matt 11:28-30)
Christ heals the most terrible illnesses by a single word or touch, he makes the blind see and revives the dead. This is the part of God's message which is understandable for everyone: God's omnipotence. However the message of God's wisdom and love cannot be understood at once by the multitude and Christ chooses twelve apostles,
'Ye have not chosen me, but I have chosen you, and ordained you, that ye should go and bring forth fruit, and that your fruit should remain: that whatsoever ye shall ask of the Father in my name, he may give it you.' John 15:16
to whom He reveals the Path ascending to God:
'Thomas saith unto him, Lord, we know not whither thou goest; and how can we know the way?
Jesus saith unto him, I am the way, the truth, and the life: no man cometh unto the Father, but by me.' (John 14:5-6)
In His answer to Philip, He gives people another overwhelming revelation about God becoming man:
'Philip saith unto him, Lord, show us the Father, and it sufficeth us.
Jesus saith unto him, Have I been so long with you, and yet hast thou not known me, Philip? he that hath seen me hath seen the Father; and how sayest thou then, Show us the Father?' (John 14: 8-9)
When Christ began preaching the Gospel he had more disciples around Him. But when, teaching in the synagogue, he spoke the

## The Second Arcanum

words which received their full extent at the Last Supper and have become the basis of the sacrament of Liturgy, many of his disciples abandoned Him.

'Then Jesus said unto them, Verily, verily, I say unto you, Except ye eat the flesh of the Son of man, and drink his blood, ye have no life in you.

Whoso eateth my flesh, and drinketh my blood, hath eternal life; and I will raise him up at the last day.

He that eateth my flesh, and drinketh my blood, dwelleth in me, and I in him.

As the living Father hath sent me, and I live by the Father: so he that eateth me, even he shall live by me.

Many therefore of his disciples, when they had heard this, said, This is an hard saying; who can hear it?

From that time many of his disciples went back, and walked no more with him.' (John 6: 53,54,56,57,60,66)

Christ had three favourite disciples to whom He revealed the supreme mysteries. He took them with Him to the Tabor mountain where He conversed, in His divine hypostasis, with the leaders of the Old Testament: Moses and Elias, so that the apostles could witness it and proclaim later that there is the hope of transfiguration for all people.

'And after six days Jesus taketh Peter, Jacob, and John his brother, and bringeth them up into an high mountain apart,

 And was transfigured before them: and his face did shine as the sun, and his raiment was white as the light.

 And, behold, there appeared unto them Moses and Elias talking with him.

 Then answered Peter, and said unto Jesus, Lord, it is good for us to be here: if thou wilt, let us make here three tabernacles; one for thee, and one for Moses, and one for Elias.

 While he yet spake, behold, a bright cloud overshadowed them: and behold a voice out of the cloud, which said, This is my beloved Son, in whom I am well pleased; hear ye him.' (Matt. 17: 1-5)

## God the Son

Transforming before the apostles His human nature into the divine one, Christ opens for all people the way to finding their light bearing nature. Thus they can return into the bosom of the heavenly Father as beings of light. It means that they will wake up in the spirit and throw off their bodily clothes.

Christ teaches His disciples how to pray so that they can turn to the heavenly Father by themselves:

'And it came to pass, that, as he was praying in a certain place, when he ceased, one of his disciples said unto him, Lord, teach us to pray, as John also taught his disciples.

And he said unto them, When ye pray, say, Our Father which art in heaven, Hallowed be thy name. Thy kingdom come. Thy will be done, as in heaven, so in earth.

Give us day by day our daily bread.

And forgive us our sins; for we also forgive every one that is indebted to us. And lead us not into temptation; but deliver us from evil.

And he said unto them, Which of you shall have a friend, and shall go unto him at midnight, and say unto him, Friend, lend me three loaves;

For a friend of mine in his journey is come to me, and I have nothing to set before him?

And he from within shall answer and say, Trouble me not: the door is now shut, and my children are with me in bed; I cannot rise and give thee.

I say unto you, Though he will not rise and give him, because he is his friend, yet because of his importunity he will rise and give him as many as he needeth.

And I say unto you, Ask, and it shall be given you; seek, and ye shall find; knock, and it shall be opened unto you.

For every one that asketh receiveth; and he that seeketh findeth; and to him that knocketh it shall be opened.

If a son shall ask bread of any of you that is a father, will he give him a stone? or if he ask a fish, will he for a fish give him a serpent?

Or if he shall ask an egg, will he offer him a scorpion?

## The Second Arcanum

If ye then, being evil, know how to give good gifts unto your children: how much more shall your heavenly Father give the Holy Spirit to them that ask him?' (Luke 11:1-13)

Here Christ mentions for the first time the third Person of the Holy Trinity and He indicates, indirectly, that this is what people should ask first and most of all from the Heavenly Father.

Christ also teaches the apostles how they should pray:

'And when thou prayest, thou shalt not be as the hypocrites are: for they love to pray standing in the synagogues and in the corners of the streets, that they may be seen of men. Verily I say unto you, They have their reward.

But thou, when thou prayest, enter into thy closet, and when thou hast shut thy door, pray to thy Father which is in secret; and thy Father which seeth in secret shall reward thee openly.' (Matt. 6:5-6)

Christ puts to the test the degree of purification and elevation of the apostles:

'When Jesus came into the coasts of Caesarea Philippi, he asked his disciples, saying, Whom do men say that I the Son of man am?

And they said, Some say that thou art John the Baptist: some, Elias; and others, Jeremias, or one of the prophets.

He saith unto them, But whom say ye that I am?

And Simon Peter answered and said, Thou art the Christ, the Son of the living God.

And Jesus answered and said unto him, Blessed art thou, Simon Barjona: for flesh and blood hath not revealed it unto thee, but my Father which is in heaven.

And I say also unto thee, That thou art Peter, and upon this rock I will build my church; and the gates of hell shall not prevail against it.

And I will give unto thee the keys of the kingdom of heaven: and whatsoever thou shalt bind on earth shall be bound in heaven: and whatsoever thou shalt loose on earth shall be loosed in heaven.' (Matt. 16:13-19)

After these words of Peter, Christ, Who as God is omniscient, reveals to the apostles the future events and mentions His second advent:
'From that time forth began Jesus to shew unto his disciples, how that he must go unto Jerusalem, and suffer many things of the elders and chief priests and scribes, and be killed, and be raised again the third day.

Then Peter took him, and began to rebuke him, saying, Be it far from thee, Lord: this shall not be unto thee.

But he turned, and said unto Peter, Get thee behind me, Satan: thou art an offence unto me: for thou savourest not the things that be of God, but those that be of men.

Then said Jesus unto his disciples, If any man will come after me, let him deny himself, and take up his cross, and follow me.

For whosoever will save his life shall lose it: and whosoever will lose his life for my sake shall find it.

For what is a man profited, if he shall gain the whole world, and lose his own soul? or what shall a man give in exchange for his soul?

For the Son of man shall come in the glory of his Father with his angels; and then he shall reward every man according to his works.' (Matt. 16:21-27)

Christ announces the hope and consolation for the apostles when He will no longer be there:
'But the Comforter, which is the Holy Ghost, whom the Father will send in my name, he shall teach you all things, and bring all things to your remembrance, whatsoever I have said unto you.' (John 14:26)

And He gives them the commandment of love:
'I am the true vine, and my Father is the husbandman.

Every branch in me that beareth not fruit he taketh away: and every branch that beareth fruit, he purgeth it, that it may bring forth more fruit.

Now ye are clean through the word which I have spoken unto you. Abide in me, and I in you. As the branch cannot bear fruit of itself, except it abide in the vine; no more can ye, except ye abide in me.

## The Second Arcanum

I am the vine, ye are the branches: He that abideth in me, and I in him, the same bringeth forth much fruit: for without me ye can do nothing.

If a man abide not in me, he is cast forth as a branch, and is withered; and men gather them, and cast them into the fire, and they are burned.

If ye abide in me, and my words abide in you, ye shall ask what ye will, and it shall be done unto you.

Herein is my Father glorified, that ye bear much fruit; so shall ye be my disciples.

As the Father hath loved me, so have I loved you: continue ye in my love.

If ye keep my commandments, ye shall abide in my love; even as I have kept my Father's commandments, and abide in his love.

These things have I spoken unto you, that my joy might remain in you, and that your joy might be full.

This is my commandment, That ye love one another, as I have loved you.

Greater love hath no man than this, that a man lay down his life for his friends.

Ye are my friends, if ye do whatsoever I command you.' (John 15:1-14)

Christ's former apostle, Judas, tempted by the devil, betrays Him and delivers him into the hands of the Jew's clergy. Rabbis envy Christ to such an extent that they want to murder Him at any cost.

'Therefore when they were gathered together, Pilate said unto them, Whom will ye that I release unto you? Barabbas, or Jesus which is called Christ?

For he knew that for envy they had delivered him.

When he was set down on the judgment seat, his wife sent unto him, saying, Have thou nothing to do with that just man: for I have suffered many things this day in a dream because of him.

But the chief priests and elders persuaded the multitude that they should ask Barabbas, and destroy Jesus.' (Matt. 27:17-20)

By their intrigues and threats, the rabbis force Pilate, the governor of Judea, to sentence Christ to the crucifixion:
'When the chief priests therefore and officers saw him, they cried out, saying, Crucify him, crucify him. Pilate saith unto them, Take ye him, and crucify him: for I find no fault in him.
The Jews answered him, We have a law, and by our law he ought to die, because he made himself the Son of God.
When Pilate therefore heard that saying, he was the more afraid; And went again into the judgment hall, and saith unto Jesus, Whence art thou? But Jesus gave him no answer.
Then saith Pilate unto him, Speakest thou not unto me? knowest thou not that I have power to crucify thee, and have power to release thee?
Jesus answered, Thou couldest have no power at all against me, except it were given thee from above: therefore he that delivered me unto thee hath the greater sin.
And from thenceforth Pilate sought to release him: but the Jews cried out, saying, If thou let this man go, thou art not Caesar's friend: whosoever maketh himself a king speaketh against Caesar.
When Pilate therefore heard that saying, he brought Jesus forth, and sat down in the judgment seat in a place that is called the Pavement, but in the Hebrew, Gabbatha.
And it was the preparation of the passover, and about the sixth hour: and he saith unto the Jews, Behold your King!
But they cried out, Away with him, away with him, crucify him. Pilate saith unto them, Shall I crucify your King? The chief priests answered, We have no king but Caesar.
Then delivered he him therefore unto them to be crucified. And they took Jesus, and led him away.' (John 19:6-16)
Jesus Christ died, after terrible suffering, on the cross.
'Now there stood by the cross of Jesus his mother, and his mother's sister, Mary the wife of Cleophas, and Mary Magdalene.' (John 19:25)
One of the beloved disciples of Christ, John, stood by the cross also.

## The Second Arcanum

The two secret disciples of Christ, Josef and Nicodemus, having obtained Pilate's permission, took Christ's body off the cross and put it in the sepulchre in the rock, according to the Jews' custom. But on the third day Christ resurrected, as the Scriptures stated and as He said Himself. Christ appeared first to Mary Magdalene and later to the eleven apostles.

'Then the same day at evening, being the first day of the week, when the doors were shut where the disciples were assembled for fear of the Jews, came Jesus and stood in the midst, and saith unto them, Peace be unto you.

And when he had so said, he shewed unto them his hands and his side. Then were the disciples glad, when they saw the Lord.

Then said Jesus to them again, Peace be unto you: as my Father hath sent me, even so send I you.

And when he had said this, he breathed on them, and saith unto them, Receive ye the Holy Ghost:

Whose soever sins ye remit, they are remitted unto them; and whose soever sins ye retain, they are retained.' (John 20:19-23)

Christ stayed with His disciples for some time and having given them His last commandment, He ascended to heaven. He as if dissolved in the entire Universe in order to save the whole of the fallen world:

'Then the eleven disciples went away into Galilee, into a mountain where Jesus had appointed them.

And when they saw him, they worshipped him: but some doubted.

And Jesus came and spake unto them, saying, All power is given unto me in heaven and in earth.

Go ye therefore, and teach all nations, baptizing them in the name of the Father, and of the Son, and of the Holy Ghost:

Teaching them to observe all things whatsoever I have commanded you: and, lo, I am with you always, even unto the end of the world. Amen.' (Matt. 28:16-20)

Thus these words He spoke have been fulfilled:

'And as Moses lifted up the serpent in the wilderness, even so must the Son of man be lifted up:
 That whosoever believeth in him should not perish, but have eternal life.' (John 3:14-15)
And His other words:
'Heaven and earth shall pass away, but my words shall not pass away.' (Matt. 24: 35)
This is testified by the two thousand-year old and eternal Christian tradition.

**The Commentary on the Gospels**
The Gospel of John
Jesus said: 'Verily, verily, I say unto thee, Except a man be born of water and of the Spirit, he cannot enter into the kingdom of God.
 That which is born of the flesh is flesh; and that which is born of the Spirit is spirit.' (John 3: 5-6)
To be born of the Spirit means to obtain such a degree of purity of heart, mind and body as to become worthy of the Holy Spirit descending into you and of becoming the temple of God.

Jesus said: 'Marvel not that I said unto thee, Ye must be born again. The wind bloweth where it listeth, and thou hearest the sound thereof, but canst not tell whence it cometh, and whither it goeth: so is every one that is born of the Spirit.' (John 3: 7-8)
Christ sent the Holy Spirit onto the apostles. They became born of the Spirit and brought the message of His teaching to all nations. No one can predict when and from where the Holy Spirit comes; He accepts one and He rejects another.

Jesus said: 'And as Moses lifted up the serpent in the wilderness, even so must the Son of man be lifted up:
 That whosoever believeth in him should not perish, but have eternal life.' (John 3:14-15)

Jesus Christ descended from heaven on earth in order to save humanity. After His crucifixion He resurrected like God and He ascended to the heavenly Kingdom so that everyone who believes in Him and follows His commandments will not perish in the outer darkness but will have eternal life.

Jesus said: 'For God so loved the world, that he gave his only begotten Son, that whosoever believeth in him should not perish, but have everlasting life.' (John 3:16)
God loved people so much that He sent His only begotten Son Jesus Christ to them, so that they all could be saved through Him and reach the Heavenly Kingdom.

Jesus said: 'For God sent not his Son into the world to condemn the world; but that the world through him might be saved.' (John 3:17)
Christ was sent to earth not for the condemnation of sinners but for the salvation of humanity which wallowed in sin. Christ showed the path to the heavenly Kingdom and He is the gate. Pray to Christ, call upon His name, and you will be saved.

Jesus said: 'He that believeth on him is not condemned: but he that believeth not is condemned already, because he hath not believed in the name of the only begotten Son of God.' (John 3:18)
God sent Jesus Christ into the world to save people and those who did not have faith in Him are condemned already because they will not see the Kingdom of Heaven and they will perish in the outer darkness.

Jesus said: 'And this is the condemnation, that light is come into the world, and men loved darkness rather than light, because their deeds were evil.
For every one that doeth evil hateth the light, neither cometh to the light, lest his deeds should be reproved.

But he that doeth truth cometh to the light, that his deeds may be made manifest, that they are wrought in God.'(John 3:19-21)
John the Baptist said: 'He that believeth on the Son hath everlasting life: and he that believeth not the Son shall not see life; but the wrath of God abideth on him.' (John 3:36)
Those who will follow Christ and obey His commandments, will see the light, and those who will not obey His commandments, will perish in the darkness.

Jesus said: 'Whosoever drinketh of this water shall thirst again: But whosoever drinketh of the water that I shall give him shall never thirst; but the water that I shall give him shall be in him a well of water springing up into everlasting life.' (John 4:13-14)
'But the hour cometh, and now is, when the true worshippers shall worship the Father in spirit and in truth: for the Father seeketh such to worship him.
 God is a Spirit: and they that worship him must worship him in spirit and in truth.' (John 4: 23-24)
The Divine light will be revealed to those who believe in Christ and obey His commandments. They will be born again, of the Spirit, and they will find eternal life.

Jesus said: 'Labour not for the meat which perisheth, but for that meat which endureth unto everlasting life, which the Son of man shall give unto you: for him hath God the Father sealed.' (John 6:27)
Try to care for the spiritual food: pray to God, follow His commandments for the salvation of your soul for it lives eternally. The body however is liable to decay and its life is temporary.

Jesus said: 'For the bread of God is he which cometh down from heaven, and giveth life unto the world.' John (6:33)
'And Jesus said unto them, I am the bread of life: he that cometh to me shall never hunger; and he that believeth on me shall never thirst.' (John 6:35)

## The Second Arcanum

'All that the Father giveth me shall come to me; and him that cometh to me I will in no wise cast out.' (John 6:37)
'Verily, verily, I say unto you, He that believeth on me hath everlasting life.' (John 6: 47)
Follow God's commandments and you will find eternal life in heaven. Call on the Name of Jesus Christ and your soul will be purified by heavenly fire and it will be saved and will ascend to the Lord.

Jesus said: 'I am the door: by me if any man enter in, he shall be saved, and shall go in and out, and find pasture.' (John 10:9)
'I am the good shepherd, and know my sheep, and am known of mine.
As the Father knoweth me, even so know I the Father: and I lay down my life for the sheep.' (John 10:14-15)
Whoever will believe in Christ and will obey His commandments, will be cleansed from his sins, which darken his soul, and Christ will accept him in the Heavenly Kingdom. For Christ gave His life for him who follows Him truly.

Jesus said: 'A new commandment I give unto you, That ye love one another; as I have loved you, that ye also love one another.
By this shall all men know that ye are my disciples, if ye have love one to another.' (John 13:34-35)
Christ gave a new commandment to the apostles: as Christ loves His apostles spiritually so the apostles should love each other spiritually and transmit this commandment to other people. People recognize the disciples of Christ because of the purity of the spiritual love between them.

Jesus said: 'I am the true vine, and my Father is the husbandman.
Every branch in me that beareth not fruit he taketh away: and every branch that beareth fruit, he purgeth it, that it may bring forth more fruit.
Now ye are clean through the word which I have spoken unto you.

Abide in me, and I in you. As the branch cannot bear fruit of itself, except it abide in the vine; no more can ye, except ye abide in me.
I am the vine, ye are the branches: He that abideth in me, and I in him, the same bringeth forth much fruit: for without me ye can do nothing.' (John 15:1-5)
These are words that Christ spoke to the apostles. If the apostles follow Christ's commandments He will abide in their hearts.
If the apostles spread Christ's message over the world then many will be converted, which means that the apostles, like the branches of the vine, will bear much fruit. And if they don't spread the message over the world, then they will not bear fruit and God will cut them off Christ as dead branches off the vine. Those who do bear fruit, God purifies by the Holy Spirit. Christ says to the apostles that they are cleansed by His word because the words of Christ are full of heavenly fire which burns away all filth.
Christ will abide in the heart of the apostles who will bear much fruit, that is, who will convert many unbelievers and heathens to the Christian faith. If the apostles bear Christ in their hearts, then Christ will also bear them in His heart. Then the apostles will have the Lord's strength in them and they will be able to convert many. However if they do not bear Christ in their hearts, they will not convert anyone because God's strength will not abide in them.

Jesus said: 'If a man abide not in me, he is cast forth as a branch, and is withered; and men gather them, and cast them into the fire, and they are burned.
If ye abide in me, and my words abide in you, ye shall ask what ye will, and it shall be done unto you.' (John 15:6-7)
He who does not follow Christ's commandments, He will not bear in His heart. God will expel such disciples from Christ and will burn them like the withered vine branches. If however the disciples obey His commandments, then Christ will keep them in His heart, and His words and His strength will abide in them. The Apostles will be

able to accomplish many things in the name of Christ and whatever they ask from God, they will receive it.

Jesus said: 'Herein is my Father glorified, that ye bear much fruit; so shall ye be my disciples.' (John 15:8)
If the apostles convert many people to Christianity, they will bear much fruit and they will be called the true disciples of Christ.

Jesus said: 'As the Father hath loved me, so have I loved you: continue ye in my love.
 If ye keep my commandments, ye shall abide in my love; even as I have kept my Father's commandments, and abide in his love.
These things have I spoken unto you, that my joy might remain in you, and that your joy might be full.
This is my commandment, That ye love one another, as I have loved you.
Greater love hath no man than this, that a man lay down his life for his friends.
Ye are my friends, if ye do whatsoever I command you.
Henceforth I call you not servants; for the servant knoweth not what his lord doeth: but I have called you friends; for all things that I have heard of my Father I have made known unto you.
Ye have not chosen me, but I have chosen you, and ordained you, that ye should go and bring forth fruit, and that your fruit should remain: that whatsoever ye shall ask of the Father in my name, he may give it you.
These things I command you, that ye love one another.
If the world hate you, ye know that it hated me before it hated you.
If ye were of the world, the world would love his own: but because ye are not of the world, but I have chosen you out of the world, therefore the world hateth you.
Remember the word that I said unto you, The servant is not greater than his lord. If they have persecuted me, they will also persecute you; if they have kept my saying, they will keep yours also.

But all these things will they do unto you for my name's sake, because they know not him that sent me.
If I had not come and spoken unto them, they had not had sin: but now they have no cloak for their sin.'(John 15:9-22)
As Christ fulfilled all that God the Father commanded Him and transmitted the words of God the Father to the people, they had the choice: to accept the message of God the Father or to reject it. Those who accepted the Good News followed Christ and will reach the Heavenly Kingdom, while those who rejected the message, will be rejected by God the Father. They lapsed into sin and drew God's thorn on them, and their souls after parting from their bodies will undergo torment and suffering, the outer darkness.

**Prayer practice**
Holy elders teach that in order to meet the Lord Jesus Christ the believer should incessantly pronounce the Jesus Prayer in his heart. This is possible by gradually learning the correct manner of praying.
1. Read before your home iconostasis morning or evening prayers.
2. Sit down on a chair in front of an icon of Christ. Pronounce aloud for five minutes the prayer: 'Lord Jesus Christ, have mercy on me.'
3. Pronounce this prayer mentally for another five minutes.
4. Focus your mind on the physical heart and then let down your mind into your heart and pronounce as if with your heart this prayer for another five minutes.
5. Say this prayer every day for five minutes longer.
6. When you will be able to say this prayer for an hour a day, it will mean that the prayer has become established in you. Try to perform this prayer rule daily. In addition to it you can say this prayer when you walk on the street or do some simple manual work.

You have learned the second Arcanum if you will say this prayer daily for one hour.

The Third Arcanum

## The Third Arcanum. God the Holy Spirit

The third Arcanum states the following spiritual truth: the Holy Spirit, the Comforter, is the third Person of God-the Trinity. The Holy Spirit of God the Father gives life to the whole Universe and provides its existence.

The picture of the third Arcanum represents God the Father Who sends God the Holy Spirit, in the form of a white dove, on earth.

The Holy Spirit bears in Him the pure, Divine joy of the Heavenly Father. He can appear in the guise of a wise elder, or a joyful child, or a pure, radiant light. The Holy Spirit bears Divine wisdom in Him and He blows where He wants.

Now the days of the Holy Spirit come: the new times are coming and the new paths of ascension to the Lord God will be revealed. The Holy Spirit bears in Himself the radiant light of the Heavenly Father and he, who will receive Him, will have eternal life in the Kingdom of God.

The beauty of the Holy Spirit exceeds all conceptions. It shines eternally in the boundless depth of the pure heart, It brings a ravishing joy which is not of this world. This joy is pure by nature and does not fade away, but it becomes even more intense the closer man comes to the Heavenly Father. This joy is eternal as it reflects the spiritual joy of the Heavenly Father. This is the joy which the soul feels when it flies, inspired by the Spirit of the Heavenly Father. This is the joy which flows out of the heart by an unbroken stream, like a spring of living water, coming from the Heavenly Father. It nourishes the soul by the highest grace and consolation of the Heavenly Father and gives rest from earthly concerns. It fills the soul with the unfading light of the Heavenly Father. Let us pray the Lord Jesus Christ so that He would send to us the Holy Spirit, and then our hearts will rejoice together with heavenly birds and Angels will

sing praise to the Lord. O Holy Spirit, the Comforter, come and reign in us and cleanse us from impurity and save, O Blessed, our souls.
The heart, crowned by the grace of the Holy Spirit, will shine and the eyes will shine with heavenly fire. The inner eye will open and we will contemplate the Lord God and we will prostrate ourselves before Him, before His might and glory. The heavenly dwellings are indescribably beautiful and the heart will aspire to them and the soul, illuminated by the Holy Spirit of the Heavenly Father, will rejoice and tremble. There is nothing more desirable than ascending to the spheres where the Holy Spirit dwells and there is nothing more elevated than the dream of the worlds of light of the Lord God. Let the grace of the Holy Spirit always be with us. God, the Creator of all the heavens, is enveloped in the radiance of the Holy Spirit. Angels exult when the fallen human soul ascends back to the radiant spheres of the Heavenly Father.

There is in all the created worlds no pursuit more worthy than the one which leads to the knowledge of the Holy Spirit.

Prophets, being inspired by the Holy Spirit, transmitted to people God's commands and the knowledge about the heavenly world.

'By the word of the Lord were the heavens made; and all the host of them by the breath of his mouth,' (Ps.32:6) the king and prophet David says in his psalm.

He says in addition: 'Who maketh his angels spirits; his ministers a flaming fire:

Who laid the foundations of the earth, that it should not be removed for ever.

These wait all upon thee; that thou mayest give them their meat in due season.

That thou givest them they gather: thou openest thine hand, they are filled with good.

Thou hidest thy face, they are troubled: thou takest away their breath, they die, and return to their dust.

Thou sendest forth thy spirit, they are created: and thou renewest the face of the earth.'(Ps. 103:4,5,27-30)

King David when repenting that he sent to his death the commander Uriah, in order to marry his wife Bathsheba, beseeches God: 'Cast me not away from thy presence; and take not thy holy spirit from me.' (Ps.50:11)

The Archangel Gabriel testifies of the Holy Spirit to Josef, who became engaged to the Virgin Mary: 'Now the birth of Jesus Christ was on this wise: When as his mother Mary was espoused to Joseph, before they came together, she was found with child of the Holy Ghost.

Then Joseph her husband, being a just man, and not willing to make her a public example, was minded to put her away privily.

But while he thought on these things, behold, the angel of the Lord appeared unto him in a dream, saying, Joseph, thou son of David, fear not to take unto thee Mary thy wife: for that which is conceived in her is of the Holy Ghost.

And she shall bring forth a son, and thou shalt call his name Jesus: for he shall save his people from their sins.

Now all this was done, that it might be fulfilled which was spoken of the Lord by the prophet, saying,

Behold, a virgin shall be with child, and shall bring forth a son, and they shall call his name Emmanuel, which being interpreted is, God with us.(Matt. 1:18-23)

John the Forerunner testifies to the Holy Spirit, saying: 'I indeed baptize you with water unto repentance. But he that cometh after me is mightier than I, whose shoes I am not worthy to bear: he shall baptize you with the Holy Ghost, and with fire.'(Matt. 3:11)

The Baptism of Jesus is also called Theophany , the Appearance of God, as at the moment of baptizing the heavens opened and God the Holy Spirit manifested Himself: 'Then cometh Jesus from Galilee to Jordan unto John, to be baptized of him.

But John forbad him, saying, I have need to be baptized of thee, and comest thou to me?

And Jesus answering said unto him, Suffer it to be so now: for thus it becometh us to fulfil all righteousness. Then he suffered him.

## The Third Arcanum

And Jesus, when he was baptized, went up straightway out of the water: and, lo, the heavens were opened unto him, and he saw the Spirit of God descending like a dove, and lighting upon him:
And lo a voice from heaven, saying, This is my beloved Son, in whom I am well pleased.' (Matt.3:13-17)
Jesus says repeatedly, many times to the Jews who do not understand and who do not believe Him, that His coming has been already presaged in the Scripture by the Holy Spirit: 'And he came to Nazareth, where he had been brought up: and, as his custom was, he went into the synagogue on the sabbath day, and stood up for to read.
And there was delivered unto him the book of the prophet Esaias. And when he had opened the book, he found the place where it was written,
The Spirit of the Lord is upon me, because he hath anointed me to preach the gospel to the poor; he hath sent me to heal the brokenhearted, to preach deliverance to the captives, and recovering of sight to the blind, to set at liberty them that are bruised,
To preach the acceptable year of the Lord.
And he closed the book, and he gave it again to the minister, and sat down. And the eyes of all them that were in the synagogue were fastened on him.
And he began to say unto them, This day is this scripture fulfilled in your ears.' (Luke 4:16-21)
Jesus continues calling the Jews, but they do not believe Him as they are attached to their interpretations of the Holy Scripture: 'In the last day, that great day of the feast, Jesus stood and cried, saying, If any man thirst, let him come unto me, and drink.
He that believeth on me, as the scripture hath said, out of his belly shall flow rivers of living water.
(But this spake he of the Spirit, which they that believe on him should receive: for the Holy Ghost was not yet given; because that Jesus was not yet glorified.)

Many of the people therefore, when they heard this saying, said, Of a truth this is the Prophet.
Others said, This is the Christ. But some said, Shall Christ come out of Galilee?
Hath not the scripture said, That Christ cometh of the seed of David, and out of the town of Bethlehem, where David was?
So there was a division among the people because of him.
And some of them would have taken him; but no man laid hands on him.
Then came the officers to the chief priests and Pharisees; and they said unto them, Why have ye not brought him?
The officers answered, Never man spake like this man.
Then answered them the Pharisees, Are ye also deceived?
Have any of the rulers or of the Pharisees believed on him?
But this people who knoweth not the law are cursed.
Nicodemus saith unto them, (he that came to Jesus by night, being one of them,)
Doth our law judge any man, before it hear him, and know what he doeth?
They answered and said unto him, Art thou also of Galilee? Search, and look: for out of Galilee ariseth no prophet.
And every man went unto his own house.' (John 7:37-53)
Only the hearts of the apostles and of the secret disciples of Christ are opened to the Holy Spirit and they work wonders with His strength: 'Then he called his twelve disciples together, and gave them power and authority over all devils, and to cure diseases.
And he sent them to preach the kingdom of God, and to heal the sick.
And he said unto them, Take nothing for your journey, neither staves, nor scrip, neither bread, neither money; neither have two coats apiece.
And whatsoever house ye enter into, there abide, and thence depart.

And whosoever will not receive you, when ye go out of that city, shake off the very dust from your feet for a testimony against them. And they departed, and went through the towns, preaching the gospel, and healing every where.' (Luke 9:1-6)

'Behold, I send you forth as sheep in the midst of wolves: be ye therefore wise as serpents, and harmless as doves.

But beware of men: for they will deliver you up to the councils, and they will scourge you in their synagogues;

And ye shall be brought before governors and kings for my sake, for a testimony against them and the Gentiles.

But when they deliver you up, take no thought how or what ye shall speak: for it shall be given you in that same hour what ye shall speak.

For it is not ye that speak, but the Spirit of your Father which speaketh in you.' (Matt. 10:16-20)

And another miracle of the Holy Spirit was manifested to the apostle Peter:

'But the ship was now in the midst of the sea, tossed with waves: for the wind was contrary.

And in the fourth watch of the night Jesus went unto them, walking on the sea.

And when the disciples saw him walking on the sea, they were troubled, saying, It is a spirit; and they cried out for fear.

But straightway Jesus spake unto them, saying, Be of good cheer; it is I; be not afraid.

And Peter answered him and said, Lord, if it be thou, bid me come unto thee on the water.

And he said, Come. And when Peter was come down out of the ship, he walked on the water, to go to Jesus.

But when he saw the wind boisterous, he was afraid; and beginning to sink, he cried, saying, Lord, save me.

And immediately Jesus stretched forth his hand, and caught him, and said unto him, O thou of little faith, wherefore didst thou doubt?

And when they were come into the ship, the wind ceased.' (Matt. 14:24-32)

Jesus Christ promises the apostles that after He will be gone and will come to His Father, He will send the Holy Spirit unto the apostles. He says that the Holy Spirit will teach them all things and He will comfort the souls of those who are grieving for the Lord:

'But when the Comforter is come, whom I will send unto you from the Father, even the Spirit of truth, which proceedeth from the Father, he shall testify of me' (John 15:26)

'I have yet many things to say unto you, but ye cannot bear them now.

Howbeit when he, the Spirit of truth, is come, he will guide you into all truth: for he shall not speak of himself; but whatsoever he shall hear, that shall he speak: and he will shew you things to come.

He shall glorify me: for he shall receive of mine, and shall shew it unto you.

All things that the Father hath are mine: therefore said I, that he shall take of mine, and shall shew it unto you.' (John 16:12-15)

Christ says to the apostles before His ascension:

'And, behold, I send the promise of my Father upon you: but tarry ye in the city of Jerusalem, until ye be endued with power from on high.' (Luke 24:49)

On the eleventh day after the Ascension of Jesus Christ, the Mother of God was with the apostles in a house and at that moment the Holy Spirit, the Comforter, descended onto them in the form of flames of heavenly fire. The Lord sent Him for He would stay with the apostles and would help them to spread the Lord's message further. The Holy Spirit descended first on the Mother of God and He abided on her for a long time and then He descended onto the apostles. He abided longer on her, because the Virgin's soul could receive more heavenly grace than the apostles' souls.

The apostles worked wonders by the strength of the Holy Spirit, but His strength helps also now and eternally the faithful to ascend to God. As Saint Silouan of the Athos writes in his notes: 'Fallen man

becomes clean through repentance and he is renewed by the grace of the Holy Spirit and he becomes like the Lord in all respects.'
Also Saint Seraphim of Sarov tells his disciple Nicolas Motovilov, whom he healed from paralysis by a prayer, the following: 'The true purpose of our Christian life is acquiring the Holy Spirit of God.
Knock, and it shall be opened unto you.(Matt. 7:7)
Seek, and you will find the gate of the Kingdom of heaven. But remember that the Kingdom of heaven is taken by efforts. The believer should practice the prayer every day if he wants to reach the Kingdom of the living God.

**The prayer practice for appealing to the Holy Spirit**
Holy elders teach that in order to meet the God the Holy Spirit the believer should ceaselessly call on Him in his heart. This is possible by gradually learning the correct manner of praying.
1. Read before your home iconostasis the morning or evening prayers and read after that the akathist to the Holy Spirit.
2. Sit on a chair and put an icon of the New Testament Trinity before you. Pronounce aloud the prayer: 'O Holy Spirit, Comforter, Come and abide in us, and cleanse us from every impurity, and save our souls, O Good One.
3. Pronounce this prayer mentally for another five minutes.
4. Focus your mind on the physical heart and then let your mind down into your heart and pronounce as if with your heart this prayer for another five minutes.
5. Say this prayer every day for five minutes longer.
6. When you will be able to say this prayer for an hour a day, it means that the prayer has become established in you. Try to perform this prayer rule daily. In addition to it you can say this prayer when you walk on the street or do some simple manual work.

You have learned the third Arcanum when you can say this prayer daily for one hour.

The Fourth Arcanum

## THE FOURTH ARCANUM. THE MOTHER OF GOD

The fourth Arcanum states the following spiritual truth: Mary, the earthly virgin, gave birth to God and none of His divine qualities were corrupted even in His full incarnation. Therefore she is called the 'true Theotokos'.

The picture of the fourth Aracanum represents the Mother of God surrounded by angels. Above her we see Christ Who blesses her and Who always accompanies her invisibly.

The Mother of God is the main pillar of Christianity and she helps the faithful who want to find God inside themselves.

In the hymn dedicated to her, the Mother of God is called more honourable and glorious than the Cherubim and the Seraphim, the spiritual beings closest to God, for she brought salvation to the whole of mankind and she became the Queen of heaven and earth.

The first person to whom it was revealed was Elisabeth, mother of John the Baptist.

'And Mary arose in those days, and went into the hill country with haste, into a city of Juda;

And entered into the house of Zacharias, and saluted Elisabeth.

And it came to pass, that, when Elisabeth heard the salutation of Mary, the babe leaped in her womb; and Elisabeth was filled with the Holy Ghost:

And she spake out with a loud voice, and said, Blessed art thou among women, and blessed is the fruit of thy womb.

And whence is this to me, that the mother of my Lord should come to me?

For, lo, as soon as the voice of thy salutation sounded in mine ears, the babe leaped in my womb for joy.

And blessed is she that believed: for there shall be a performance of those things which were told her from the Lord.' (Luke 1:39-45)

The Lord said in a parable: 'For unto whomsoever much is given, of him shall be much required: and to whom men have committed much, of him they will ask the more.' (Luke 12:48)

The life of the Mother of God confirms these words to a full extent as the suffering that she suffered during her earthly life is immeasurable and unimaginable for us.

Having reached the Kingdom of Heaven and even being taken there with her physical body, the Mother of God did not abandon us and she helps each one who asks her for help. Most of all she helps those who aspire to God. She possesses truly great strength, given to her by God and she uses it to help all that are in need.

The Most Holy Mother of God is the hope of all those who follow the spiritual path and seek salvation and protection, as it is she who created this new path to God, the path of inner prayer. She prayed with this prayer when in her childhood and early youth she lived in the temple. She helps the faithful and the monks to struggle with their passions and to ward off the demons' attacks.

A hermit of the Solovetski Isle, called Theophanes, was once attacked by demons during his spiritual exercises. He hardly could stand their threats. The Mother of God appeared to him during his sleep and encouraged him, convincing him not to fear the demons' attacks and to continue his spiritual practice. Still during this vision a big horde of demons appeared, who wanted to kill him. However when the demons saw the Mother of God they cried fearfully: 'Woe onto us! His Protectress has come to visit him. But for her, we would have destroyed this believer long ago already!' And with these words the demons disappeared.

The great Russian Saint, Seraphim of Sarov, prayed ceaselessly to the icon of the Mother of God, called 'Eleusa' or 'Tenderness', kneeling on a stone in the forest, day and night for three years. In this way he could overcome the temptations of the devil and find his salvation. The prayer to the Mother of God helps the believer to follow the spiritual path, to overcome barriers on it and the attacks of his own passions; it will save him from illnesses, troubles and misfortunes. The Mother of God illuminates the mind when it is darkened by the devil's temptations: she prays the Lord Jesus Christ for help and she helps also by the Divine strength which is given her by God. The Mother of God helps those who repent from their sins to receive God's forgiveness.

The Mother of God helps not only those who follow the spiritual path, but she helps all the Christians, protecting them from adversities, illnesses and enemies. Saint Andrew, the fool for Christ, together with his disciple, Blessed Epiphanios, had a vision of the Mother of God in the church of the Blachernae Palace in Constantinople. It was a special service which was being held in order to plead God for protection from the Saracens who were invading Byzanthium. They saw the Mother of God high up in the air above the altar, accompanied by John the Baptist and John the Theologian, and surrounded by an assembly of other Saints and angels. The Mother of God was praying kneeling, her face drowned in tears. Then she took her veil off her head and held it over all the people in the church protecting them from all enemies, visible and invisible. The veil was shining brighter then the sun. Then the people saw that the veil spread wide and covered the entire Christian world. At that very moment the attack of the Saracens was warded off and the city was saved from disaster.

The Mother of God protects mothers from all troubles. She also protects warriors during combat, keeping bullets and death away from them. There are many wonderworking icons of the Mother of God, as for example the so called icon 'Increasing of Intelligence' or 'the Mother of God in the burning Bush' which saved or healed many people.

However, the main reason the Mother of God appears is to remind people of the necessity of working for their salvation. The prayers of the Mother of God protect all the followers of the Christian path from the attacks of demons and enemies, as she has reached the Kingdom of Heaven and she helps them who practice the Christian virtues to find Jesus Christ.

During her entire earthly life the Mother of God beseeched God for the salvation of her soul. By means of her prayers she purified her heart, mind and body from passions and her body became a temple of God. And God entered her heart and He abided in her. She abided in God and God abided in her. The Mother of God was an example of piety and holy life and she helped the apostles to spread God's message over the entire world.

On the eleventh day after the Ascension of Jesus Christ, the Mother of God was together with the apostles in a house and at a certain moment the Holy Spirit, the Comforter, descended on them from heaven in the form of fiery tongues. The Lord Jesus Christ sent the Holy Spirit, so that He would abide in His Mother and in the apostles and He would help them to spread the Good Tidings. At first the Holy Spirit descended onto the Mother of God and then He descended onto the apostles. The Holy Spirit abided much longer on the Mother of God as her soul could contain much more heavenly blessing than the souls of the apostles.

When the Mother of God was lying on her death-bed the apostles, except Thomas, gathered around her. She gave each of them her blessing to strengthen them in spreading the Lord's Message. Then she prayed to the Lord, Her Son, to take her soul to His Kingdom of Heaven. Suddenly it was as if the roof of the house was removed and the Lord Jesus Christ had descended from heaven, surrounded by angels. Mary rejoiced, for an unspeakable love for her Godly Son abided in her heart and she gave her soul to Him. Angels sang and Christ ascended to heaven carrying Mary's soul, the most pure of all mankind, with Him.

Next day, the apostles carried the coffin with the fragrant body of the Mother of God to Gethsemane, to bury her next to the graves of her parents and her husband. Many joined the procession. The archpriests and the scribes sent, out of envy and anger, their armed servants with an order to drive away the procession, but holy angels, soaring above the coffin, took away the servants' sight and in addition to it a thick cloud descended on the procession. When the Jews' high priest Athonius appeared, on the Lord's command the protecting cloud disappeared and Athonius saw the coffin of the Mother of God. Full of hatred towards her he rushed to the coffin, wanting to overthrow it. However when he just touched the coffin, his arms were cut off to the elbows by an invisible sword, and they remained attached to the coffin. Athonius, covered in blood, fell on the ground crying: 'I have become aware of my sin; Christ's servants, have mercy on me!' The Apostle Peter said: 'Believe in God and repent of your sins before Him.'

'I believe,' Athonius exclaimed, 'that He is the Saviour of the world, the Messiah, who was foretold by the prophets. Lord, forgive me my transgressions.' The Apostle Peter said: 'Put your elbows to the stumps on the coffin.' Athonius did so and Peter called upon the Mother of God's mercy. In a miraculous way the stumps adhered to the elbows and they became cured. Athonius thanked God and joined the procession.

On the third day after the burial, the apostle Thomas came to the tomb and cried as he could not receive the last blessing of the Mother of God. The Apostles took pity on him and they allowed Thomas to open the coffin to kiss the Virgin Mary's hand. However there was no body in the coffin. During the evening meal, they were discussing the mysterious disappearance of the Virgin's body. Suddenly the angels' choir sounded above them. Looking upwards the apostles saw the Mother of God surrounded by throngs of angels. She said: 'Rejoice, I will always abide with you. The Lord took me to the heavens with my body, on the third day after my passing away.'

In the works of the holy Fathers we find sometimes the story that when believers and monks reached the Kingdom of Heaven they did not find there the Most Holy Mother of God. When they asked where she was, they were given the answer that the Mother of God is the stronghold of Christianity on earth and that she helps those who practice the Christian virtues to ascend to the Kingdom of Heaven.

## The Mother of God

One monastery on Athos had an icon of Mother of God, painted by the founder of the monastery, which hung on the wall by the entrance of the refectory. The monk who was responsible for the refectory walked every night with a burning torch. Once he walked very close to the icon and it became partly blackened. He heard a voice behind him saying: 'Do not spoil my image.' The monk however did not pay attention and the next night he again walked there without minding the icon. Then he heard the voice again: 'You are not worthy of being called 'monk' as you shamelessly blacken my image.' Hearing this the monk became blind. He prostrated himself before the icon and prayed the whole night long for the forgiveness of his sin. His brethren found him there in the morning and after hearing the story they praised the icon. The newly appointed monk responsible for the refectory, had as an extra daily task to burn incense before the icon.

The blind monk spent several days crying and repenting before the icon until he heard the voice saying: 'Your prayers have been heard, I forgive you and I give you your sight back. Announce to all the brethren that I am the Protectress of this monastery. Let them and all the Orthodox Christians come to me with their needs and I will help them. I will pray to God for all who plead for my help, asking Him to forgive their sins. This very icon of mine will receive the name 'Swift to hear'. Many lame and blind were cured by this icon. Through prayers to it many were saved after shipwreck, escaped from imprisonment, survived war-battles.

Saint Sergius of Radonezh daily, after completing his evening prayer rule, spoke in the stillness of his heart with the Mother of God. Suddenly he felt that the Holy Virgin decided to answer his prayers and was approaching him. An Angel's voice sounded: 'The Most Pure One comes.' Saint Sergius went to the entrance of his cell and there he saw a spiritual radiance of incredible intensity. The Mother of God, accompanied by the apostles Peter and John the Theologian stood amidst the radiance. Not being able to stand this radiance Saint Sergius prostrated himself before the Mother of God. The Mother of God touched him and she said: 'Do not be afraid, my chosen one. Your prayers for your disciples have been heard and I came to visit you. From now on your monastery will not be needy anymore, even after your passing away. I will always be here and I will always protect it.' Having said this the Mother of God became invisible.

When the huge hordes of Tamerlan, after conquering many eastern countries, headed for Moscow, the small army of prince Basil, the son of Prince Demetrius Donskoi, came forward to fight them. The army of Tamerlan was many times stronger and he had no doubts that he would win. However in the night just before the battle he had a dream which frightened him: a priest with a golden crozier came down from the top of the mountain. A radiant goddess walked in the air above the priest. A huge army of warriors of light, armed with swords, spears and bows followed her. The goddess commanded Tamerlan to go back as otherwise his army would be destroyed. Next day Tamerlan gathered his advisers and he told them his dream. Advisers told him that the Mother of God Jesus Christ, great Protectress of the entire Christian world and, especially, of Russia, appeared to him. Tamerlan did not dare to disobey the command of the Mother of God, and he retreated.

In the time of the Tartar yoke there appeared on the big stone on the slope of the Pochaev mountain the Mother of God, amidst flames of spiritual fire. The monks of the Kiev-Pecherskaya Lavra found on this stone the imprint of her right foot. They recognized it as a sign and they founded the Pochaev monastery on that place.

In 1675 the Tartars made an attempt to rob and to destroy the Pochaev monastery. In the morning, just before the Tartars' assault, the monks gathered in the church and they sang the akathist to the Mother of God. She appeared suddenly in the air high above the church, radiating dazzling light and she was surrounded by an army of angels with swords. The Tartar army was seized by panic and horror and they ran away, killing each other.

The Mother of God is the protectress of Russia and the stronghold of the Orthodox faith. Many churches in Russia appeared due to a wondrous indication coming directly from her. She defended Russia against Mongols and Tartars, she saved many cities and monasteries from the invasion of enemies. She protected the best warriors of Russia from swords and bullets, and she endowed with Divine grace the zealous believers who followed diligently the commandments of Christ.

By her grace the gates of the Heavenly Kingdom open for the true believers in Christ. The Most Holy Mother of God is always present with the faithful who pray to her daily and she sends them the blessing of her Son, the Lord Jesus Christ. She visits those who are in need and she heals the monks who are sick. She appears enveloped in Divine radiance to those who deserve this honour by his or her righteous life. She appears there where it is necessary to establish a new cloister or a church. She often pleads Christ not to abandon Russia and to continue caring for it.

At the end of our morning prayers we say, following the example of the Archangels: 'O Theotokos and Virgin, rejoice, Mary, full of grace, the Lord is with thee; blessed art thou among women, and blessed is the Fruit of thy womb, for thou hast borne the Saviour of our souls.'

And we complete them with another prayer, given also by the Archangel,: It is truly meet to bless thee, the Theotokos, ever-blessed and most blameless and Mother of our God,' and with
the praise of Cosmas, Archbishop of Maium: ' More honorable than the Cherubim, and beyond compare more glorious than the Seraphim, who without corruption gavest birth to God the Word, the true Theotokos, thee do we magnify.'

## Prayer practice

Holy elders teach that in order to obtain contact with the Mother of God, a believer should ceaselessly pronounce the prayer to the Mother of God inside his heart. It is possible to do this by learning gradually the correct manner of praying.

## The Fourth Arcanum

1. Read aloud before your home iconostasis morning or evening prayers and after that read aloud an akathist to the Theotokos.
2. Sit down and put before you the icon of the Theotokos, which speaks most to your heart. Pronounce aloud for five minutes the prayer: 'O most Holy Theotokos, have mercy on me.'
3. Pronounce this prayer mentally for another five minutes.
4. Focus your mind on the physical heart and then let down your mind into your heart and pronounce as if with your heart this prayer for another five minutes.
5. Say this prayer every day for five minutes longer.
6. When you will be able to say this prayer for an hour a day, it means that the prayer has become established in you. Try to say it aloud before the icon of the Theotokos for an hour daily. In addition to it you can say this prayer when you walk on the street or do some simple manual work.

You have learned the fourth Arcanum when you can say this prayer daily for one hour.

The Fifth Arcanum

## The Fifth Arcanum. The Baptism

The fifth Arcanum states the following spiritual truth: the path to finding Christ in one's heart starts with baptism, which is one of the seven church sacraments. Its foundation lies in the baptism by water which John the Baptist was preaching and doing.
On the picture of the Arcanum we see a priest who executes the sacrament of baptizing a man and a woman. Christ is present above, as He invisibly takes part in each sacrament.

'And he came into all the country about Jordan, preaching the baptism of repentance for the remission of sins;
  As it is written in the book of the words of Esaias the prophet, saying, The voice of one crying in the wilderness, Prepare ye the way of the Lord, make his paths straight.
  Every valley shall be filled, and every mountain and hill shall be brought low; and the crooked shall be made straight, and the rough ways shall be made smooth;
  And all flesh shall see the salvation of God.'(Luke 3:3-6)
'The voice of one crying in the wilderness, Prepare ye the way of the Lord, make his paths straight.
  John did baptize in the wilderness, and preach the baptism of repentance for the remission of sins.
  And there went out unto him all the land of Judaea, and they of Jerusalem, and were all baptized of him in the river of Jordan, confessing their sins.
  And John was clothed with camel's hair, and with a girdle of a skin about his loins; and he did eat locusts and wild honey;
  And preached, saying, There cometh one mightier than I after me, the latchet of whose shoes I am not worthy to stoop down and unloose.
  I indeed have baptized you with water: but he shall baptize you with the Holy Ghost.' (Mk.1:3-8)

## THE BAPTISM

John testifies the descending of the Holy Spirit during the baptism of Christ.

'And it came to pass in those days, that Jesus came from Nazareth of Galilee, and was baptized of John in the Jordan.

And straightway coming up out of the water, he saw the heavens opened, and the Spirit like a dove descending upon him:

And there came a voice from heaven, saying, Thou art my beloved Son, in whom I am well pleased.' (Mk.1:9-11)

The water in the baptistery, which is consecrated by the descent of the Holy Spirit, symbolizes the water of the Jordan; the anointment is the seal of the Holy Spirit. The baptism is the spiritual birth, about which Christ tells Nicodemus:

'Jesus answered, Verily, verily, I say unto thee, Except a man be born of water and of the Spirit, he cannot enter into the kingdom of God.' (Jn.3:5)

Jesus instructs the apostles just before His ascension:

'And he said unto them, Go ye into all the world, and preach the gospel to every creature.

He that believeth and is baptized shall be saved; but he that believeth not shall be damned.

And these signs shall follow them that believe; In my name shall they cast out devils; they shall speak with new tongues;

They shall take up serpents; and if they drink any deadly thing, it shall not hurt them; they shall lay hands on the sick, and they shall recover.

So then after the Lord had spoken unto them, he was received up into heaven, and sat on the right hand of God.

And they went forth, and preached every where, the Lord working with them, and confirming the word with signs following. Amen.'(Mk.16:15-20)

Jesus says: there is no salvation without baptism, and the apostles baptize their disciples. This is what the apostle Peter says: 'And as I began to speak, the Holy Ghost fell on them, as on us at the beginning.

Then remembered I the word of the Lord, how that he said, John indeed baptized with water; but ye shall be baptized with the Holy Ghost.
Forasmuch then as God gave them the like gift as he did unto us, who believed on the Lord Jesus Christ; what was I, that I could withstand God?
When they heard these things, they held their peace, and glorified God, saying, Then hath God also to the Gentiles granted repentance unto life.' (Acts 11:15-20)
Baptism is preceded by one's inner conversion. It means that one has become aware of the weakness of one's soul and its enslavement by sin. No matter how hard man tries, he cannot avoid sinful thoughts, feelings and deeds and his soul dies gradually.
'For, lo, the wicked bend their bow, they make ready their arrow upon the string, that they may privily shoot at the upright in heart. If the foundations be destroyed, what can the righteous do?' (Ps.10:2-3)
The 'wicked' ones are the dark servants of the devil, the demons, who try to destroy the souls by their poisoned arrows, which arouse the passions: hatred, envy, lust and such like. The human soul has by itself not enough strength to repel these arrows.
'Put not your trust in princes, nor in the son of man, in whom there is no help.' (Ps. 146:3)
says the Prophet David. And Jesus says: 'Verily, verily, I say unto you, Whosoever committeth sin is the servant of sin.

And the servant abideth not in the house for ever: but the Son abideth ever.

If the Son therefore shall make you free, ye shall be free indeed.' (Jn.8:34-36)
From ancient times water was considered in the spiritual traditions as a symbol of purification. Therefore John the Baptist had been immersing into the water the repentant, after they had confessed their sins to him. By this immersion, the sins they confessed were washed away.

## The Baptism

In Christianity the baptism by water is preceded by a reconsideration of one's entire life in the light of Christ's commandments, one's conscious decision to work for the salvation of one's soul, confession of all one's sins and renunciation of the devil and all his works. Then the anointment takes place which is a material expression of the seal of the Holy Spirit. The seal of the Holy Spirit signifies involvement with Him and His protection.

During the baptism by water which comes next, there takes place a threefold immersion into the water with the sacred formula: 'In the Name of the Father, amen, and the Son, amen and the Holy Spirit, amen' said three times and the lecture of special prayers. The sacrament of baptism expels the Satan from our heart and installs there the blessing of the Lord Jesus Christ. Before baptism man is the slave of sin. That is, that as he cannot restrain himself from sinning and therefore he cannot regain the purity of his soul, Satan controls such a person. However, through baptism the sting of the primordial sin of Adam is taken out of man's heart. Man, in his immeasurable, spiritual depth, becomes clean, exactly as God has created him. Satan loses his power over the baptized one and he can only attempt to seduce him from outside. Therefore every Christian should struggle manly for the purity of his soul and try to establish it firmly in the faithfulness to God. A Christian should not give in to the feeling of despondency if he lapsed into a temptation, but he should repent and strive again to receive Christ's grace.

During the preparation for baptism, men and women become acquainted with the principal dogmas which are combined in the Creed and with its daily practice. This practice includes an at least weekly attending of the liturgy, confession of sins and communion, daily morning and evening prayers for oneself and one's relatives, prayers for the forgiveness of enemies and reconciliation with them. Thus the Lord starts participating in a more direct way in the life of a man and a woman, helps them to bear the burden of the material existence, protects them from temptations and helps them, in a gentle, motherly manner to discover the higher purpose of the incarnation.

Men and women can gradually realize the fact that although they endeavour to lead a life according to the Christian norms and values, they still miss the main purpose of Chrisitian life. It was the great Russian ascetic and Saint, Seraphim of Sarov, who once said briefly and clearly to a Russian landowner, Nicholas Motovilov, whom Saint Seraphim healed by prayer of paralysis: 'The true purpose of our Christian life is acquiring the Holy Spirit.' In the light of these words the worldly life, even lead according to the strict rules which the holy church has established in order to keep a certain spiritual and moral level of society, do not lead man towards acquiring the Holy Spirit, to the blossoming of the inner, spiritual qualities of the soul, which God gave us.

Read the fragments of the Gospel according to Matthew, that tell us about the message that Christ received from His Father to transmit to people.

'And when the tempter came to him, he said, If thou be the Son of God, command that these stones be made bread.

But he answered and said, It is written, Man shall not live by bread alone, but by every word that proceedeth out of the mouth of God.' (Matt.4:3-4)

It is our body which is nourished by bread, but the soul is attracted to God and is nourished by God's word which is spiritual nourishment, Divine light, spiritual joy, love and Divine purity.

Jesus said: 'The disciple is not above his master, nor the servant above his lord.

It is enough for the disciple that he be as his master, and the servant as his lord. If they have called the master of the house Beelzebub, how much more shall they call them of his household?

Fear them not therefore: for there is nothing covered, that shall not be revealed; and hid, that shall not be known.

What I tell you in darkness, that speak ye in light: and what ye hear in the ear, that preach ye upon the housetops.' (Matt.10:24-27)
What Christ tells the apostles in secret, hiding Himself from those who want to murder Him, the apostles must tell publicly, so that people can receive the message of the Heavenly Father, Who sent Christ on earth.

Jesus said: 'And fear not them which kill the body, but are not able to kill the soul: but rather fear him which is able to destroy both soul and body in hell.' (Matt.10:28)
Do not fear your enemies who can take the life of your body, but who cannot destroy your soul and deter you from the Lord. Fear most your real fiends who can deter your body and soul from the Lord and from the Heavenly Father and cause you to lapse into unbelief and destroy you by this and cause you to fall into hell for long-lasting torments and suffering.

Jesus said: 'Think not that I am come to send peace on earth: I came not to send peace, but a sword.
 For I am come to set a man at variance against his father, and the daughter against her mother, and the daughter in law against her mother in law.' (Matt.10:34-35)
If, in a family, the children will come to believe in Christ, while the parents will be against it, they will walk different paths: the children will follow Christ, while the parents will turn against Christ, but the truth will be on the side of the children.

Jesus said: 'And a man's foes shall be they of his own household.' (Matt.10:36)
If, in a family, the son or the daughter, will come to believe in Christ, while the parents will turn against Christ, they will become each others enemies, and the truth will be on the side of the children.

Jesus said: 'He that loveth father or mother more than me is not worthy of me: and he that loveth son or daughter more than me is not worthy of me.
And he that taketh not his cross, and followeth after me, is not worthy of me.' (Matt.10:37-38)
Christ is God and He preaches the message of His Father, Who sent Him. God is love. The first commandment says that first of all man should come to love Christ. The one who cannot love Christ most of all, who loves someone, even if it were one's son or daughter more than Christ, is not worthy of Gods love. He will never experience the highest, divine love.
He who came to believe in Christ but does not struggle with his passions, does not strive to become worthy of the Kingdom of Heaven and does not perform prayer- and contemplative practices, this man does not take his cross which is to struggle with his passions. He will not follow Christ on the path to the Heavenly Father and he is not worthy of Christ's love.

Jesus said: 'He that findeth his life shall lose it: and he that loseth his life for my sake shall find it.' (Matt.10:39)
He who cares for the earthly life more than for the heavenly life, will lose the eternal life. He who gives up earthly concerns and follows Christ's teaching and the Lord's commandments, will find eternal life.

Jesus said:'He that receiveth you receiveth me, and he that receiveth me receiveth him that sent me.' (Matt.10:40)
Those who receive the teaching of Christ from the apostles, will find Christ Himself also. Those who found Christ will find the Heavenly Father, Who sent Christ on earth, also.

'Then said Jesus unto his disciples, If any man will come after me, let him deny himself, and take up his cross, and follow me.

For whosoever will save his life shall lose it: and whosoever will lose his life for my sake shall find it.

For what is a man profited, if he shall gain the whole world, and lose his own soul? or what shall a man give in exchange for his soul?

For the Son of man shall come in the glory of his Father with his angels; and then he shall reward every man according to his works.' (Matt.16:24-27)

While gaining earthly riches, man wallows so much in sin, that his soul darkens and it no longer shines. It becomes heavy, gloomy and dark and these are the signs of death drawing nearer to the soul.

'And after six days Jesus taketh Peter, Jacob, and John his brother, and bringeth them up into an high mountain apart,

And was transfigured before them: and his face did shine as the sun, and his raiment was white as the light.' (Matt.17:1-2)

On the top of the mountain Christ appeared before the apostles in His Divine hypostasis: He united with God the Father and He shone with spiritual light. He did not wish to reveal His Divine countenance to all people to convince them that He is God; people must believe Christ's words, that He is the messenger of the Heavenly Father.

'And, behold, there appeared unto them Moses and Elias talking with him.

Then answered Peter, and said unto Jesus, Lord, it is good for us to be here: if thou wilt, let us make here three tabernacles; one for thee, and one for Moses, and one for Elias.

While he yet spake, behold, a bright cloud overshadowed them: and behold a voice out of the cloud, which said, This is my beloved Son, in whom I am well pleased; hear ye him.' (Matt.17:3-5)

In order to strengthen the apostles' faith, God the Father appeared before them and He testified that all Christ's words are truth.

## The Fifth Arcanum

Jesus said: 'Verily I say unto you, Except ye be converted, and become as little children, ye shall not enter into the kingdom of heaven.' (Matt.18:3)
If you will not come to believe in the Lord God Who sent Christ, and you do not become pure in soul and body as children are, and if you don't open your heart, like a child, for God, you will not enter the Kingdom of Heaven.

'Woe unto the world because of offences! for it must needs be that offences come; but woe to that man by whom the offence cometh!'(Matt.18:7)
Woe unto the world because of temptations and passions which the devil sends on earth in order to deter people from God and to cause them great suffering. But the people through whom the temptation comes, will suffer even more in the outer darkness.

'Then came Peter to him, and said, Lord, how oft shall my brother sin against me, and I forgive him? till seven times?
Jesus saith unto him, I say not unto thee, Until seven times: but, Until seventy times seven.' (Matt.18:21-22)
Jesus explains to Peter that it is necessary to forgive his brother as many times as he repents. Man is weak and is often tempted and lapses into sin. Man can defeat temptations and sin by calling upon the Name of the Lord. Therefore no matter how often man sins, he should be forgiven if he repents.

Jesus said to the young man: 'but if thou wilt enter into life, keep the commandments.
 He saith unto him, Which? Jesus said, Thou shalt do no murder, Thou shalt not commit adultery, Thou shalt not steal, Thou shalt not bear false witness,
 Honour thy father and thy mother: and, Thou shalt love thy neighbour as thyself.

## The Baptism

The young man saith unto him, All these things have I kept from my youth up: what lack I yet?
Jesus said unto him, If thou wilt be perfect, go and sell that thou hast, and give to the poor, and thou shalt have treasure in heaven: and come and follow me.'(Matt.19:17-21)
'Then said Jesus unto his disciples, Verily I say unto you, That a rich man shall hardly enter into the kingdom of heaven.
And again I say unto you, It is easier for a camel to go through the eye of a needle, than for a rich man to enter into the kingdom of God.
And every one that hath forsaken houses, or brethren, or sisters, or father, or mother, or wife, or children, or lands, for my name's sake, shall receive an hundredfold, and shall inherit everlasting life.' (Matt.19:23-24,29)
Jesus says that one should honour one's father and mother and love one's neighbour as oneself. But He says also that he, who wants to obtain eternal life, should give his possessions to the poor, love God most of all, more than parents and more than himself and follow Christ. And he will find hundreds of times more in heaven than he lost on earth, as he will find Christ inside his heart, he will find eternal comfort in the Kingdom of God. The Kingdom of God is within, inside the pure heart.

'Then one of them, which was a lawyer, asked him a question, tempting him, and saying,
Master, which is the great commandment in the law?
Jesus said unto him, Thou shalt love the Lord thy God with all thy heart, and with all thy soul, and with all thy mind.
This is the first and great commandment.
And the second is like unto it, Thou shalt love thy neighbour as thyself.
On these two commandments hang all the law and the prophets.' (Matt.22:35-49)

## The Fifth Arcanum

**The practice of morning and evening prayers**
When you wake up, preferably early in the morning, light the candle or the oil lamp in front of your iconostasis, and read aloud the morning prayers, focusing your mind on the meaning of the prayer and try to feel it with your heart. This should be done first thing in the morning, before you have breakfast and go about your daily concerns.
In the evening, before you go to sleep, light the candle in front of the iconostasis again and read aloud the evening prayers.
No matter how tired or unwilling you are, you should try with all your might never to omit your 'prayer rule' and read aloud daily all the morning and evening prayers. By these prayers you call upon the help and protection of God the Father Sabaoth, our Lord Jesus Christ, the Holy Spirit, the Most Holy Theotokos, Angels' and Archangels' hierarchies and great Saints. Day and night they will invisibly guard you and favourably influence your pursuits. It is necessary also to read aloud every day a chapter of the GospeTry to think of God, 'to remember Him', as Christian ascetics used to say, also amidst your daily concerns. Remember the Theotokos and the Saints, and pray to them, sometimes with just a short prayer, so that they will help you not to lapse into temptation and sin, and they protect you from enemies and their attacks: temptations and delusions.

You have learned the fifth Arcanum if you perform daily the practice of morning and evening prayers.

The Sixth Arcanum

## THE SIXTH ARCANUM. THE CHOICE OF THE PATH

The sixth Arcanum states the following spiritual truth: man after baptism has the choice between three paths: the first is the so-called 'narrow path' of the priest and of the monk; the second is the 'middle path' of a Christian believer, who stays in the world; and the third one is the 'broad way', as the holy Fathers used to say, of the worldly life.

On the picture of the sixth Arcanum we see an angel, who gives a special blessing to the followers of the first and the second path.

The canonical path of the so-called 'white priesthood' can be described briefly as studying in the seminary, marriage, receiving holy orders, and serving in a parish church. In order to become a monk or a nun, a man or a woman should take the monastic vow in a cloister and dedicate their life to God, which is the most elevated task, as the most important for a Christian is to follow the teaching of Christ. At the same time, it is the most difficult task.

The second path is called the middle path, following which there is no necessity to renounce the world. It is necessary on this path to find an experienced spiritual elder and to become his disciple-apprentice.

The third path for a Christian is the 'broad way' of a worldly life, where he or she will try not to forget God completely. It is then sufficient for them to visit church on Sundays, to repent regularly their sins, to have communion once a month and to try to read regularly the morning and the evening prayers.

Jesus said: 'Let the dead bury their dead: but go thou and preach the kingdom of God.' (Lk.9:60)

Jesus called those, who live in the world and do not wish to listen to God, dead. It is their soul which is dead, as it does not bring forth spiritual fruit. But those, whose souls are alive, will follow Christ, will try to observe His commandments and they will see the Kingdom of Heaven.

He who has decided to follow the spiritual path should be on his guard concerning worldly people. For the worldly atmosphere quickly dissipates God's grace, it consumes the believer's soul and the spiritual warmth of the heart which he receives from God.

If a man and a woman choose the narrow and arduous path of spiritual development it would not be wise to fall back onto the broad way of life as it is impossible to serve the Lord and the prince of this world.

If a man or a woman choose the path of the monk and the nun and they dedicate their life to finding God inside their heart, they give the love of their hearts only to the Lord Jesus Christ and the Theotokos, the Queen of heaven and earth.

The broad way of a worldly life allows man to experience all its pleasures, successes and sufferings. The souls of people who follow this path are attached to the values of the material existence: money, power, material comfort, carnal love, family, continuation and strengthening of the family tree. Such people ponder very little on where exactly they will go after the death of their bodies, and on the necessity of finding God Who created them and of following His commandments. As regards religion, they find it sufficient to follow, within their power, the generally accepted codes and charity.

For some secular people, who have lapsed into complete materialism, even the notions of God and of life after death of the physical body are absent. They have no fear of God and they live in such a way as if their deeds will not be judged in court in afterlife. They just do their best to enjoy a worldly life and they suffer when the circumstances are unfavourable for this. Such souls are immature, being in the state of infanthood. They should grow up and ripen, and experience repeatedly suffering, successes and failures, before they can realize finally that true happiness is finding God in your heart. An elder of Solovetzki Monastery, whose name was Nahum, used to call the worldly life a 'state of enslavement'.

## The Sixth Arcanum

The second path which leads to God, is a narrow and arduous path. Only a mature soul is able to seek God, having renounced the pleasures of life. The path to God is called 'narrow' because only a few try to follow this path and even amongst them the majority stray off it. For a believer on this path undergoes hardship and suffering, struggles with the mortal sins and with the sinful part of his soul, endeavouring to transform it and to make it noble, clean and pleasing to the Lord. This struggle takes place inside the human heart and therefore it is the most heavy and painful battle in which man can be engaged. A believer, following the arduous and narrow path, works on himself, which causes him to suffer bodily and inwardly, until his heart and his soul become purified from sins. Our heart is an accumulation of various negative emotions and temptations. However when the heart is purified, it shines with an invisible light and the ascetic can see God in its depth as in a mirror. 'Blessed are the pure in heart: for they shall see God.'(Matt.5:8)

Both man and woman are created in God's image and the sparkle of the Heavenly Father shines in their soul. Therefore both man and woman can find God inside them. When they choose the narrow and arduous path to God, they become ascetics. It is better for them to follow the path separately or to enter a cloister, for they might be an insuperable temptation to each other. If however they choose to remain together, then they should restrain themselves from the usual family life and dedicate themselves to God. The man-ascetic should love with all his heart first of all God and the heavenly Queen. Then his love for his female companion will support her on her spiritual path. The woman-ascetic dedicates the love of her heart to the Lord Jesus Christ and the Theotokos: then her love for her male companion will inspire him to make spiritual efforts.

The Script says that first of all man should love God, and only then come father, mother, husband, wife and children. Man should consider God and serving Him, the most important. We serve God when we struggle with the seven mortal sins, which darken our heart, mind and body. If man- and woman ascetics choose to live together they should do inner work together, helping and supporting each other. They may then have sex very seldom, and better not at all, but they should purify and transform their sexual energy with the help of fasting, prayer, special physical exercises. They should also practice Tao techniques and the spiritual breathing technique, which were especially adjusted to the needs of the followers of the Christian spiritual path, in combination with the prayer to the Mother of God. If, on the contrary, they give in to the patterns of a usual family life, they will not be able to find God inside themselves and reach the Kingdom of Heaven. God reveals Himself to those whose mind, heart and body are clean.

The couple who follow the spiritual Path, should overcome many temptations and difficulties. They must learn how not to condemn each other, not to be angry in general or angry with each other, respect each other, give each other time for personal inner work and guard each other against falling into laziness and depression. They should try to always remember that they should love God more than each other, not to be carried away by passion of gain, material success, nice clothes and other earthly pleasures, as their main purpose is to find God inside themselves. There are many examples of couples in history where both husband and wife obtained sanctity. Such couples had observed strictly the rules of the ascetic life.

A couple can follow the spiritual path if they observe the following five rules:

- husband and wife should be friends and they should help each other to follow the path: friendship.
- they should love each other: love.
- they should sacrifice their passions and interests, within reasonable limits, for the sake of their mutual advancement on the path: mutual, reasonable sacrifice.
- they should follow one and the same spiritual path.
- they should try to find a mentor who could guide them on the path, an experienced elder. In addition to it they should endeavour

to practice the contemplative and prayer rules and to curb their passions together.

Commentary:

1. The friendship of ascetics differs from the friendship of secular people. The secular friendship is based on the mutually profitable exchange of earthly values. The friendship of those who practice the Christian virtues, is based on the unselfish help and support to each other on the Path to God. Friends forgive each other their mistakes, because mutual affection and the rules of the spiritual path keep them together. Friends are prepared to understand each other and accept each other as they are, without embellishments. Friends to not condemn each other.

2. Love of husband – and wife ascetics for each other differs from secular, selfish love. Secular love is psychic or carnal love and there is no place for love to God in it. The love of husband- and wife-ascetics for each other has its source in their love for God and therefore it inspires them to work on their spiritual perfection. Such love, contrary to earthly love, does not turn into hatred, it does not exhaust either man or woman, and provides them with strength for concerted work and creativity on the spiritual Path.

3. Mutual, reasonable sacrifice.

In order not to stray off the spiritual path and preserve their union, husband and wife should regularly sacrifice something of their own. As fire cannot burn without firewood, so the union of the husband and wife-ascetics is held together by regular sacrifice. Ascetics can sacrifice their habits and their passions and they should bear firmly in mind that they never should sacrifice the principles of the spiritual path, and the goal of finding God for the sake of preserving their union. Jesus said: 'And every one that hath forsaken houses, or brethren, or sisters, or father, or mother, or wife, or children, or lands, for my name's sake, shall receive an hundredfold, and shall inherit everlasting life.' (Matt.19:29)

4. Following one and the same path to God.

The path won't be beneficial, if the wife is e.g. a Buddhist or a moslim, while the husband is a Christian, or the opposite case. It is necessary for husband and wife both to be baptized and to follow one and the same path to God.

5. In order to find God inside, the believer should find an elder, who has found God and abides in communication with Him, and to become the elder's disciple. Only such an elder, who is experienced and skilful in the spiritual warfare, who successfully passed through all the traps and perils of the path, can guide believers in their prayer and contemplative practices and the struggle against their passions. An ascetic will not be able to find God without such an elder.

In order for you to realize the necessity for man to follow the spiritual path, read attentively the short quotations from the Gospel by Mark.

Jesus said: 'Whosoever therefore shall be ashamed of me and of my words in this adulterous and sinful generation; of him also shall the Son of man be ashamed, when he cometh in the glory of his Father with the holy angels.' (Mk.8:38)

The one who will be ashamed of Christ before those who do not believe in Him, Christ will be ashamed and He will not open for them the gate of the Kingdom of Heaven.

Jesus said: 'And whosoever shall offend one of these little ones that believe in me, it is better for him that a millstone were hanged about his neck, and he were cast into the sea.' (Mk.9:42)

The one who would deter children from believing in Christ, had better have died, for deterring children from Christ is a big sin, for which a severe punishment is reserved after the soul has parted from the body. Children, because of their inner purity, are worthy of the Kingdom of Heaven.

## The Sixth Arcanum

Jesus said: 'Salt is good: but if the salt have lost his saltness, wherewith will ye season it? Have salt in yourselves, and have peace one with another' (Mk.9:50)

By salt is meant the strength of the faith in Christ. If the faith of the apostles is weak they will not be able to transmit the message of Christ to other people.

Jesus said: 'Go thy way, sell whatsoever thou hast, and give to the poor, and thou shalt have treasure in heaven: and come, take up the cross, and follow me.' (Mk.10:21)
In order to find spiritual treasures one needs to leave behind earthly treasures and to follow Christ. For finding spiritual treasures means finding Christ and the spiritual bliss that He carries with Him, inside your heart. This spiritual bliss is more elevated than any earthly wealth, pleasure and enjoyment. The earthly concerns and pleasures make the path to the Kingdom of Heaven still less visible, they pollute the heart and deter from Christ.

Jesus said: 'For even the Son of man came not to be ministered unto, but to minister, and to give his life a ransom for many.' (Mk.10:45)
Christ came into the world and brought the Message from the Father in Heaven, not to make people serve Him and build a paradise on earth, but to call them to return to the Father in Heaven. For this, Christ is prepared to suffer and even sacrifice His life for the sake of the spiritual salvation of many, to become for them a door, through which they can enter the Kingdom of Heaven.

Jesus said: 'The first of all the commandments is, Hear, O Israel; The Lord our God is one Lord:
And thou shalt love the Lord thy God with all thy heart, and with all thy soul, and with all thy mind, and with all thy strength: this is the first commandment.

And the second is like, namely this, Thou shalt love thy neighbour as thyself. There is none other commandment greater than these.'(Mk.12:29-31)

The Lord is the supreme spiritual light, who pours His love over His entire creation. As the Lord has created us after His own image, our soul is weaved of spiritual light. However being born on earth, we forgot our spiritual nature and became identified with our physical body. We live life as if we were not the spiritual children of God, but children of the earth who at the death of the material body vanish forever. We are children of God, our souls are weaved of spiritual light and our task is to become fully aware of it and to find the Kingdom of Heaven again.

In order to return to heaven it is necessary to come to love the Lord with all our mind, heart and soul. Then He will give us back our lost spiritual richness, for God is love.

As our souls are weaved of spiritual light, we all are brothers in spirit and we all are one. Therefore the second command says: 'Thou shalt love thy neighbour as thyself.'

However it is impossible to come to love our neighbour mechanically. If we find Christ in our heart He will reveal us what is the divine love of our neighbour. Then, in every man that we love spiritually, we will see the Lord. However do not mistake carnal love for spiritual love, as carnal love darkens the soul and is considered to be carnal sin.

### The practices of the 6th Arcanum

If you have chosen the middle path, you should then start practising the prayer of forgiveness and regaining the energy of your soul that you have lost in the past. These are the practices of purification and after some time your soul will become purified of the worldly life and it will become as pure as it was in the days of your youth. Your eyes will shine, your life will be easier again, your heart will be clean and a sense of life and hope will appear in it again. However it will take at least a year if not more.

## The prayer of forgiveness

Each person with whom we have had contact left his or her imprint in our body, heart and mind. We remain connected forever with people of our past because of these imprints, which are caused mostly by our passions. One of the means to free yourself from these imprints is to ask them for forgiveness and, in your turn, to forgive them. This practice works better during a church service, as the atmosphere is filled with the energy of love and forgiveness. Saying this prayer mentally, one should focus at the same time on one's heart. In this way the heart will feel the beneficial effect of prayer and it will be cleansed from passions. All passions have their seat inside the heart and this is how they take a hold on us. The prayer runs as follows:

1. Lord Jesus Christ, standing before Thee, I ask (name) to forgive me all offences I caused him (her) in word, in deed and in thought, voluntary and involuntary, in knowledge and in ignorance.
2. Lord Jesus Christ, standing before Thee, I forgive (name) all offences that he (she) caused me by word, by deed and by thought, voluntary and involuntary, in knowledge and in ignorance.
3. Let me not condemn him (her) but let Thee judge me.

After saying this prayer you might feel that a heavy, dark clot gets out of your head and you will feel lighter. It is necessary to say this prayer for each person repeatedly until you feel that the imprint of this person has disappeared from your mind and heart.

Divide your life into periods of seven years. Write down in a notebook the names of all the people whom you came to know in each of these seven year periods. Mark the names of people, whom you let free, in your list, for a clearer awareness of the working of the prayer. Nodding acquaintances require at least three prayers. With regard to the persons, with whom you have had an intensive relationship, as parents and relatives or the persons who offended you seriously or vented plenty of their negative emotions on you, it is necessary to say this prayer at least fifty times in succession. With regard to your sexual relations it is necessary to say this prayer at least hundred times in succession.

After you have said the prayer of forgiveness you should get back the energy of your soul from these very persons and return to them their energy which got stuck in you. In this way you will be freed from their subconscious influence, while they – from yours.

Learning the Sixth Arcanum might take several years, depending on the heaviness of your sins and the degree of pollution of your soul, your body, your mind and heart.

The Seventh Arcanum

## The Seventh Arcanum. The Victor

The seventh Arcanum states the following spiritual truth: Christ is the true Victor, as He defeated the devil and primordial sin and He brought the fallen humanity back to God.

'These things I have spoken unto you, that in me ye might have peace. In the world ye shall have tribulation: but be of good cheer; I have overcome the world.' (John.16:33) Hereafter I will not talk much with you: for the prince of this world cometh, and hath nothing in me. (John.14:30) 'Now is the judgment of this world: now shall the prince of this world be cast out.' (John.12:31) A prayerful believer, who follows Christ and struggles manly during the spiritual battle, takes part in Christ's victory and therefore he becomes also a victor at a certain stage of his spiritual development.

We see on the picture of the seventh Arcanum, an elder, who with the help of prayer, fasting and heavenly angels-warriors, has defeated the inner dragon which contains all the human passions. The elder pierces the dragon, that tries to seduce him with the pleasures of this world, with his spiritual spear. The two angels in the picture help the elder to keep the dragon in confinement so that he can ascend into the Kingdom of Heaven. The elder always has the choice: to listen to the angels and ascend on the path of finding God, or to fall, if he gives in to the temptations of the dragon, to forget God and to strive for the pleasures and enjoyments of life.

The dragon whispers constantly that there is neither strict Judge nor hell after death. Perhaps, whispers the dragon, even God does not exist, and the Kingdom of Heaven is just a fantasy of those who want distract people from living a 'real' life, to lead them astray from the right path and push them into the world of dreams and delusions of their own imagination. And the main reason behind it, the dragon whispers, is that man does not want to live a real life, he is afraid of it and tries to escape it through this fairy tale about the Kingdom of Heaven. At first glance, the reasoning of the dragon is logical, but this is the logic of the dark side of the mind. The logic of the light part of the mind, with which light angels attempt to find contact, is totally opposite, as it serves the purpose of growing and opening the light side of the elder' soul and finding God inside. The light angels call the elder to the spiritual battle, pointing at the example of the Lord Jesus Christ, while the dragon tempts him, in millions of different manners, to follow the broad path of life, promising material abundance and sinful pleasures.

The seventh Arcanum explains the methods of struggling with the temptations of the inner dragon.

A novice who follows the Path should follow the example of the holy elder, who defeated his passions and found God in his heart. The novice should follow his instructions. The elder-victor has become passionless and in the depth of his heart he converses with Jesus Christ. The elder defeated the following passions and the demons, which instigate them:

1. The passion of fornication. Fornication causes a slackening of the wish to find God, losing spiritual strength, it pollutes body, mind and heart.

2. The passion of anger, jealousy, irritation; discontent with one's neighbour and the wish to re-fashion the world and its people according to one's own selfish design. One's anger pollutes one's own soul instantaneously and the Lord cannot abide in a polluted heart.

3. The passion of avarice. This passion makes people mad, they forget God and the necessity to aspire to Him. The ascetic should amass imperishable spiritual richness, which are virtues, for the sake of conversing with God.

4. The passion of gluttony, which is a strong attachment to the enjoyment of food and alcohol. It makes it impossible for the believer to fast and to pray to God in a correct manner. '...there cannot possibly be any truthful knowledge about God's mysteries when the stomach is full,' Saint Seraphim of Sarov said in his teaching.

5. The passion of sadness and depression. Sadness and depression are caused by attachment to the worldly life and also from using drugs. It is in fact a longing for worldly pleasures and amusements. Depression causes in its turn a loss of interest in the spiritual Path and forgetting of God. With this passion comes a false feeling of senselessness of one's work on oneself; one feels that there is no need for prayer and contemplative practices and one feels attracted to the realm of passions.

6. The passion of vanity. The expression of the passion of vanity is that the ascetic works on himself and performs the prayer and contemplative practices not for the sake of finding God, but for the sake of the praise of his or her fellow ascetics and the respect of laymen.

7. The passion of pride and self-extolling. The ascetic feels superior to his fellow-men: he feels proudly that it is *he* who conquered the passions of fornication, gluttony, sadness and depression. He is proud of himself for holding nightly prayer vigils. The proud forget that the blessing comes from God alone and that God can take it away if man ascribes to himself what he has received from God.

The nature of passion is a strong, uncontrolled and insatiable desire, which is stirred inside the soul by a demon, the enemy of the human race. Each passion is stirred by a particular sort of demon. The whole of the passions form what is called 'the dark side of the soul', which hinders the passage to the Kingdom of Heaven. The light part of the soul however wishes to follow the spiritual path in order to find God inside it.

The elder-victor has gained a firm hold in the light part of his soul and he has full control over its dark side, that is his passions. As holy fathers say, the centre of all passions is the heart.

For the ascetics the elder is an example which they can follow in their spiritual struggle. The fact of his existence is an evidence to them that, with the help of God and the Theotokos, and practicing the spiritual exercises, they can open and develop the light part of their soul and conquer its dark part, which is imprisoned by the passions of the soul and the body. The ascetics, with the help of work on themselves, conquer their passions and keep them under the control of their enlightened will and reason.

## On obedience

An ascetic, in order to conquer his or her passions, should indispensably find an experienced elder, who has a special blessing from God, and become his novice. The ascetics who deny this rule and who attempt to follow the path to God, entrusting themselves to their own understanding of the Script and to their own ability to withstand temptations and delusions, will not succeed. Their very initial motivation is poisoned by the main sin: pride, which made Lucifer fall. The more efforts such ascetic makes and the more he reads Holy Scripture, the more will he be proud of himself and his achievements, and the less objective will he be able to evaluate his advancement on the Path. He might even become a worse person in comparison to how he was before he attempted to find God. For the sin of pride is the greatest sin and its origin is the demon of pride, who manages to outwit the beginner-ascetic by convincing him that he is wise enough to fight passions by himself. And as the holy fathers say, the lecherous can be corrected by their fellow-men, while it is God alone Who can correct the proud ones (John Climacos, 'The Ladder', 26, 180). Christ said: ' I am the vine, ye are the branches: He that abideth in me, and I in him, the same bringeth forth much fruit: for without me ye can do nothing.' (John 15:5)

Therefore no one has enough strength to find the Lord Jesus Christ, and one should plead the Lord for His help. The Lord will then send His help in the form of an experienced elder. And if an ascetic rejects the elder, then again he is rejecting the help of the Lord. For it is excessive boldness and pride to think 'I will obey only the Lord's instructions, and I will accept nothing from man.' The Lord restrains such proud persons by letting them lapse into temptation and delusion. Obedience to an elder is necessary as a novice is spiritually blind, deaf and mute, and without guidance he or she would fall into the very first trap on the Path.

He is blind for his mind is polluted, his inner eyes are closed, he doesn't percieve the Lord and he doesn't understand anything.

He is deaf for his heart is polluted, cooled off and shut off with regard to the Lord's message. The Lord will never reveal Himself in an impure heart. He is deaf also, because even though he should listen to the admonitions of an elder, he could not put them in practice, and he remains exactly as he was before, as if he heard nothing.

He is mute because he cannot say anything about the Lord and he cannot transmit any message from the Lord to other people for he doesn't know Him.

The meaning of obedience is, on the one hand to listen to the instructions of the elder about the spiritual path and to follow them, and on the other hand to help the elder to maintain his existence. If the novice doesn't help the elder by fulfilling practical tasks, he won't be able to learn anything from him. According to a cosmic law there should be an exchange of energies: a novice can learn and fulfil his own elder' spiritual instructions only if he helps his elder to carry his life's burden and accomplish his duties.

The elder, the spiritual mentor, will teach the novice how to follow the spiritual Path and how
to find God inside himself. He will point out the novice's faults and will help him correct them. He will work at improving the novice's character and will teach him how to struggle with the seven main passions which drive us into seven deadly sins, not only theoretically but by his own example. The elder will teach the novice how to pray, how to perform prayer and contemplation practices; how to purify the body, the mind and the heart from sinful thoughts and desires and how to purify the soul from the consequences of his sinful past. He will teach the novice how he can make himself worthy of God's visit, and then how to turn his soul into a worthy temple of God, where God can abide. Learning from an elder lasts long, in fact a whole life, as the positive changes in the soul come after ten, twenty, thirty years only. Those who believe that they will find God inside them within a year or two, are in delusion. If one has lived

without even thinking of God for many years, and polluting one's soul, then purifying the soul will also take many years.

Faint-heartedness and fear for the future are the obstacles to becoming the novice of an elder. Fear actively influences the imagination and an ascetic starts to fantasise about various horrible things the elder could force him to do if he were to become his novice. He might imagine such a gloomy situation that fear would eat up all his soul's energy, and would prevent him turning to an elder.

The point is, that behind the fear, there lurks a cunning demon, who bewitches the novice with horrible fantasies about the narrow Path. The demon instils doubts, fears, a feeling of the senselessness of seeking God, and he praises the material side of life. The demon steels from the novice his faith in God, his hope of finding God inside his heart and of reaching the Kingdom of Heaven, and finding divine love.

As holy elders say, obedience is cutting off one's own will and fully surrendering to the will of one's spiritual mentor. According to them, it is obedience which helps to conquer passions in the quickest and most reliable manner, for the Lord himself curbs the novice's passions because of his obedience to his elder. Obedience means acquiring humility, restraining the passions and rejecting self-will. As a reward for obedience, the elder transmits to the novice practical knowledge about following the spiritual path to find God in his heart. A novice doesn't have enough willpower to struggle with his passions, perform his personal prayer rule daily and hold vigils. Therefore the elder gives his own willpower to the novice, with the help of which the novice has an opportunity to conquer himself and to complete the Path.

In a monastery, it is the Father Superior who appoints an elder for the novice, and the novice should humbly accept the Father Superior's choice. As Elder Silouan of Mount Athos writes in his notes '... And if an elder has a bad temper then, even if this is a great misfortune for a novice, the novice should be resigned in spirit and pray God for his elder, and then God will have mercy on both, the elder and the novice. (Elder Silouan, Writings, ch. 14). However, an ascetic who doesn't enter a monastery, but practises his prayer rule in the world, should himself take the initiative of trying to find an experienced elder, who found God inside himself and communicates with Him. Otherwise, instead of salvation he will find just outer darkness.

Having become the novice of an elder, the ascetic has no right to judge him, while the elder has the full right to judge and to criticise the novice. The criticism is in fact both a tool to overcome the proud self-will of the novice and an admonition to show him the right direction. As soon as the demon of pride starts instilling in the novice critical and condemning thoughts about his elder, the novice should pray God asking Him to help him cut off the demon of condemnation and backbiting.

The novice should not listen to the demon's criticism about his spiritual mentor, for the elder, in the depth of his heart, converses with God, while the novice doesn't. And if the Lord doesn't condemn the elder, if the Lord doesn't turn away His countenance from him, it means the elder did not commit the sins that the novice ascribes to him. Pride and self-conceit in the novice prompts him to condemn his spiritual mentor and then his obedience becomes fruitless.

Holy Script says that in order to find God the believer should renounce all worldly pleasures, so the believer should dedicate many hours every day to work on himself, on inward prayer and prayer and contemplation exercises.

It is useless to renounce the world just taking vows, while the worldly desires and designs still occupy the mind and the heart. In such a case it would be better to remain in the world, but not to react to its temptations. Saint Silouan the Athonite quotes in his notes the words of an ascetic from the Caucasus, Father Stratonic: 'the time will come when monks will strive for their salvation wearing worldly clothes.' There is another example of this kind, from the life of the Roman-Catholic monastic orders: the monks of the order of Discalced Carmelites, who observe very strict rules, nowadays live just in ordinary flats in the city, still keeping the monastic way of life. The most important is to arrange life in such a way that one can live in solitude and silence and fulfil the prayer and contemplation rule for 3-5 hours a day. It is difficult to find God, while still being in the world, but for some who renounced the world, it turned out to be perhaps even more difficult to find God. Those who renounced the world and chose the spiritual Path because they feared the difficulties of life, will fail also on the path to God. For they are afraid of difficulties and they seek not God, but an easy way of life; however on the Path to God it is necessary to work even more than in an ordinary life in order to conquer one's sinful passions, and, having purified one's body, heart and mind, to become a temple of God.

Starting on the Path, many experience mostly afflictions and disappointments. They work on themselves without joy, compelling themselves by their will and feeling a lot of inner discomfort and suffering. The prayer of beginners doesn't reach God and they do not receive His support. In this period they therefore need the support of their spiritual mentor. However, the higher the believer ascends on the Path, the more it becomes pleasant and easy, for God hears his prayers and He sends him His grace and support. Also the protection and support of the holy Theotokos will fill the believer's soul with a special, heavenly joy.

In order to find God, the believer should indispensably purify his body, heart and mind from passions, because these are exactly the passions which cause the pollution of the soul. God manifests Himself as a most pure, radiant spiritual sun, which cannot shine in an unclean soul. The soul that is darkened with passions and wallows in sin, is like a glass, covered with soot, and the light of the sun cannot shine through it. Only when the soul is purified, can God abide in it. 'Jesus answered and said unto him, If a man love me, he will keep my words: and my Father will love him, and we will come unto him, and make our abode with him.' (John 14:23)

Passion is a strong and insatiable desire, which consumes the mind and the heart of the believer. Passion is that very agent which drives us into the seven deadly sins, which were the subject of the sixth Arcanum. The characteristic of a passion is that man constantly has this particular desire, whether he wants it or not, and he strives to satisfy it. Such a desire is aroused by the demons, the enemies of the human race.

The believer should learn therefore to be watchful with regard to his passions. The first step is to find out which particular passions are active in him or her. The Holy Fathers teach that man has two kinds of passions: the passions of the body and the passions of the soul. The principal passions are: pride, vanity, wrath, avarice and amassing of riches, lechery and fornication, gluttony, jealousy, verbosity, condemnation of our neighbour and backbiting, depression and sadness.

## A practice of observation of the way passions occupy one's mind and heart

In order to struggle with the passions successfully, a believer should become aware of the way passions penetrate into his soul.

1. The first stage: appearing of the sinful thought. Firstly the demon instils into the believer a particular sinful design, connected with one or other passion. The demon does it every day, with certain regularity, until the believer's conscience is defeated and the believer gets used to this sinful design.

2. The second stage: the sinful design takes residence in the believer's soul. This happens when the believer accepts the sinful design, which comes from demons, in his mind and starts conversing with it. At this stage the passion starts to pollute the mind, to distract it from prayer and to lead the believer astray on the Path.

3. The third stage: capture and imprisonment of the believer. Having conquered the mind, the passion goes down into the heart and imprisons it. Now it is the passion which possesses and controls the believer, his time, and no longer he himself. When the heart is captured by a passion it loses interest in prayer.

4. The fourth stage: working out a plan how to satisfy the passion.

5. The fifth stage: realization of this plan.
Thus on the fifth stage the believer gives in to the passion and he lapses into sin, which pollutes his mind, heart and body even more. The mind, when the passions are conquered, is healthy, chaste and light.

To conquer the passions of the body, means to purify oneself from lechery, fornication and gluttony and to fulfil prayer and contemplation exercises during the day and the night.

To conquer the passions of the soul, means to purify the mind and the heart from dark designs and feelings. By working on himself the believer conquers passions and subjects them to the control of will and mind.

Having become passionless, the believer can find contact with God with the help of prayer and contemplation practices and defeat the demons which lurk deep inside the soul.

**Meditation practice: recalling of the passions that the believer has experienced in his life**

Make a list of all the passions that are active in you, in order of size: write down first your most strong passions, then the less strong and so on.

Then divide your lifetime into periods of seven years, and try to recall and to write down in a separate column for each seven years period, the following:

1. At what age was the passion of pride, arrogance, self-conceit, contempt and disregard for the opinion of others aroused in you? What was its original cause? When did you start to consider yourself a chosen one, the first among equals, someone special who is allowed to do anything at all? When did you start to consider yourself an exceptional case, to whom God will forgive transgressions that He wouldn't forgive in others. In what kind of situations does this passion manifest itself?

2. At what age was the passion of vanity aroused in you: the desire to receive honour and praise from other people, a dependence on

the opinion of others? What was its original cause? In what kind of situations does it manifest itself?

3. At what age was the passion of anger, irritability, impatience, jealousy and envy aroused in you? What was its original cause? In what kind of situations does it manifest itself?

4. At what age was a passion for amassing money aroused in you? What was its original cause? In what kind of situations does it manifest itself?

5. At what age was the passion of lechery, masturbation and fornication aroused in you? What was its original cause? In what kind of situations does it manifest itself? How exactly is the passion of fornication activated in you in the presence of an attractive woman or man?

6. At what age was the passion of avarice aroused in you? What was its original cause? In what kind of situations does it manifest itself?

7. At what age was the passion of depression, boredom and sadness aroused in you? What was its original cause? In what kind of situations does it manifest itself?

8. At what age was the passion of verbosity, condemnation of others, slander and backbiting aroused in you? What was its original cause? In what kind of situations does it manifest itself?

It is very important that you recall when and why one or other passion appeared in you for the first time. Try to recall which events preceded it. We often become 'contaminated' by passions from people in our close surroundings. There lurks on the subtle level behind each passion a demon or a so-called 'larva'.

Try to recall who passed the demon of a certain passion to you: were this your parents, your friends, school mates and so forth? Or perhaps that demon grabbed you when you watched porno and horror movies and other infernal garbage of this kind?

Do not despair if you cannot remember all your passions: when you will repent of the passions you could recall and write down, then the forgotten ones also will come to light in your memory.

**Struggle with the passions with the help of prayers to the great saints, to the Most Holy Theotokos and the Lord Jesus Christ.**
After having studied the behaviour of one or other passion and having determined when it starts manifesting itself in your soul, try not to allow the sinful designs which precede it, to penetrate your mind. A rising passion must be stopped the very moment that you notice it: do not let it penetrate into your soul otherwise the passion will enslave you. Do not trust its sweet voice as it will always deceive you.

However, if you have struggled with your passions for a while, you will realize that you cannot control them, especially the chronic ones that have rooted in your soul, and you always lapse in the same sins.

Therefore the believer should seek the help of the Lord Jesus Christ and the Theotokos, pleading Them to save him from these passions. In the rich Orthodox tradition, the faithful also pray to the saints who are known to have received from God a special blessing for the healing of the souls from certain passions. For example, in order to get rid of the passion of pride, people pray to Saint Sergius of Radonezh and to Saint Alexis, the Man of God. In order to get rid of the passions of depression and anger, believers pray to Saint Ephrem the Syrian and the righteous King David, the Psalm singer.

If you did not manage to stop the passion at an early stage and you lapsed into sin, do not despair and do not become depressed, as this is just the passion of depression trying to seize you after you fell in the traps of other passions, its 'sisters'. Confess your sin to a priest, repent it before him, and then pray to the Lord Jesus Christ and the Theotokos and thank Them that they prevented you from lapsing into an even heavier sin, and continue working on yourself.

It is impossible to satiate a passion: no matter how often you satisfy it, it still demands all your attention. The believer, who is possessed by passions, cannot think of the Lord, he can think only of how to satisfy these passions.

As passions are insatiable, it is useless to spend time trying to satisfy them: they will torture man until he loses his mind or dies. A passion is not something natural for the soul, it is steered from outside. There is at least one demon lurking behind each passion. He feeds the passion and arouses in man an irresistible desire to satisfy it. As the demons are insatiable, they torture man until he perishes. When the demon of a certain passion becomes active, he tempts the believer and causes his fall. Therefore we sin when we satisfy one of our passions.

Repentance is the most powerful weapon in the struggle with the demons behind our passions. After having sinned, you should go to church and repent before a priest that the demon of a passion took hold of you and you sinned. If you are not able to defeat him and you sin again, then go again to church and repent of your sin again. Sin is a single staining of the soul. Passion resembles a chronic disease, and bouts of passion repeat themselves regularly like the bouts of malaria, and they are difficult to cure. The passion manifests itself in you as long as the demon of this particular passion lurks in the depth of your soul.

It is impossible to defeat the demon of passion on your own, and therefore it is necessary to go to church and to pray there before the icons to the Lord Jesus Christ and the Theotokos, pleading for help in your struggle with some demon of passion.

It is also impossible to defeat at once all the demons of all your passions. You should start with the smallest one and then fight the stronger ones. However, before a believer can fight the demons of passions, he must purify himself from the passion according to the following method:

1. Describe all the manifestations of a certain passion in the periods of seven years.
2. Confess and repent before the priest all the sins you have committed while satisfying that particular passion.
3. It is recommended to repent not more than seven sins of one certain passion at a time, mentioning the name of the person who was

involved in your sinful action, the time and the place where it happened. Then your repentance will be real and not just a formal one.
4. If you repent the sins of fornication, then repent not more than three sins during one confession, mentioning the name of the person who was involved in your sin, how much time you spent sinning and the name of the place where it happened.

It is absolutely necessary to mention the place, the time and the name(s) of person(s) who were involved in your sin. This process of purifying your soul from sins can last for years. It resembles somehow the work for our daily bread. Just as we go every day to our job, we should go every day to church in order to work on ourselves, and not just once a month, when you have a free minute.

One should take the process of purification of one's soul very earnestly, as the most important pursuit in one's life.

The believer should carry out the practices of the Seventh Arcanum regularly in the course of his entire life.

The Eighth Arcanum

## The Eighth Arcanum. Particular Judgement

The Eighth Arcanum states the following spiritual truth: man after the death of his physical body undergoes a particular judgement and no one can avoid it.

The symbolical representation of the Arcanum shows the white Angel of Justice whose eyes are blindfolded. He holds a sword in his right hand, and scales in his left hand. When the soul of the deceased arrives near the angel, all his sins are placed on the left plate of the scale, and on the right plate, all the good deeds done during his lifetime.

The good deeds are not only helping the poor and kindness towards one's neighbour, but most of all, his efforts in the spiritual warfare for the sake of achieving the Kingdom of Heaven.

There was a believer who pleaded the Lord incessantly to reveal to him his fate after death. He once had the following vision.

When his soul parted from the body, it came into the world behind the curtain, and the servants of death brought it to the place of waiting for the particular judgement. He saw a huge place, with sandy ground, which was surrounded by a fence several meters high. In the middle of this yard was a big round square, surrounded by one-storey wooden barracks of grey-yellowish colour, resembling the barracks of a concentration camp. Thousands of people were gathered on the square. The servants dropped his soul on the square and flew away hurriedly to fetch the next one.

The believer looked around and suddenly he noticed in the crowd many of his friends and acquaintances. They were discussing something. He approached them and he heard that they talked about the particular judgement that all people must undergo. One of the collocutors, a monk in a black cassock, pointed with his hand to the huge gates, which were opened and thousands of people were walking out of the camp. Like an enormous winding ribbon, the crowd walked on the road to the horizon, where the huge white figure of the Angel of Justice towered. His eyes were blindfolded. In his right hand he held a sword, and in his left hand he had scales. Each person, passing him by, stopped for a moment under the scales, and the plates of the scales came into motion. If the left plate was heavier, the angel lowered his sword, and if the right plate was heavier, the angel remained motionless.

'What does this all mean?' the believer asked the monk.

'What a surprise to see you here so soon!' said one of his acquaintances with amazement. 'We thought you would live on earth for quite a long while.'

'I also could not even imagine that I would meet all of you here,' answered the believer.

'The angel is blindfolded,' the monk answered his question, 'in order not to allow him to see whom exactly he judges. This makes the judgement just, as the personal inclinations of the angel do not have the chance to affect the scales. When the person walks under the scales, they weigh in a mysterious manner all the good and bad deeds that he did during his life. His good deeds are placed on the right plate, and his bad deeds are put on the left plate. If the left plate is heavier, the angel lowers his punishing sword, and the demons take this person to the lower worlds, where he must expiate all his sins through terrible suffering. Some say that when this happens, the angel sheds a few tears.

If the right plate turns out to be heavier, the sword remains motionless, and the angels take this soul to the Kingdom of Heaven, as the reward for a righteous life.

'What are the bad deeds precisely?' someone asked in a bass voice.

'The sins are well-known to everybody, and there are plenty of them. However there are the seven main, or deadly sins: pride, anger, gluttony, depression, avarice and fornication. If man indulges his passions during his life, he will gradually commit all the sins, even without noticing it.'

## The Eighth Arcanum

'What are the good deeds then?' someone, who stood behind the believer asked.

'The good deeds are the deeds which please God,' answered the monk. 'When man during his life tries to observe the Lord's commandments, attends church services, confesses and repents his sins before the priest, works at developing and strengthening his virtues and wages a spiritual war with his passions; when he strives to find God inside himself, carries out prayer and contemplation practices, tries to keep his heart, mind and body pure, in order after his death to enter the Kingdom of Heaven where Christ reigns.'

'Is it possible to confess one's sins here somewhere?' someone asked cautiously.

'If this were possible, I would be the first one standing in the row,' the monk answered sadly. 'The problem is that in this place there is neither church nor a priest who would have the right to forgive sins. There is no one to whom you can confess and repent your sins and it is useless to plead for mercy to the Angel of Justice. You should have confessed and repented your sins before the priest while living on earth, then you would have received absolution. For Christ said to the apostles, whose blessing was inherited by the priests: 'and whatsoever thou shalt bind on earth shall be bound in heaven: and whatsoever thou shalt loose on earth shall be loosed in heaven.' (Matt. 16:19)

'If I only had known when I lived on earth that the particular judgement really exists, I would have pleaded day and night for the forgiveness of my sins,' the believer said.

'It is too late to grieve here,' the monk said. 'Now we will atone for our sins by our suffering.'

When after this vision the believer returned into his physical body, he immediately went to church to repent his sins.

Perhaps everything that the believer saw in his vision was a symbolical description of the lot of the soul after death; however the existence of the particular judgement is unquestionable.

## Particular Judgement

There we become aware of the real weight of our sins. Woe us if we did not confess and repent our sins, and our soul remained stained, as we will carry the burden of our sins with us into the world behind the curtain. A bitter lot is awaiting those who did not repent, for there will be no alleviation in the judgement court for them. Bitter is the lot of those who sin and do not think of the day when their soul will part from their body and they will appear in the Lord's Court. Horror will strike the careless ones, who do not do anything to improve their future existence in the world behind the curtain. Repent before it is too late, before the time of life which is given to you, comes to its end, and you will be delivered to the court to answer for your deeds. The memory of the particular judgement is our best adviser on the Path to God.

Holy elders recommend: think every day about the particular judgement and then you will be able to stop committing the sins which burden your soul. If everyday you think that it's your last day, then passions will leave you alone, and you will be able to purify your mind, heart and body. Think that most probably you will die tomorrow and that your soul, burdened with sins, will have to appear at the particular judgement, and you did not repent your sins. Therefore you will be sentenced to the expiation of your sins, and when the demons will drag you into hell, you will just cry powerlessly and plead God for forgiveness. You will, seized by horror, gnash your teeth, but no one will be able to help you, because it is you yourself who has determined this verdict by your own deeds on earth. So repent before it is too late, and the Lord will forgive you your sins.

Think about the particular judgement and do not postpone the care for your soul to the last day. The time of your life flows unnoticeably and this day will come unexpectedly and you will find yourself on your deathbed. It will then be too late to call for Gods help and recall your sins, for it is impossible to repent all your sins at once. If you have been sinning your entire life then it is unreasonable to hope that you would be able to repent your sins just in one day. Repentance is a long lasting process which should take place during your entire life. If however, you realize the crucial necessity of repenting just at the end of your life then, in order to receive from God the forgiveness for your sins, you should repent them in church for at least three hours every day during one year.

And then the Lord will forgive you and you will experience an incredible illumination inside your soul, as if you had broken out of the thick darkness of a cellar and enjoy fresh air and warmth and the light of the sun.

The laws according to which the sinner is judged at the particular judgement, are known to us from the Old Testament: punishment for disobeying the commandments, rendering evil with evil, and other laws, are known and understandable for us. The king and prophet David says about the inevitable punishment for doing evil: 'God judgeth the righteous, and God is angry with the wicked every day.

If he turn not, he will whet his sword; he hath bent his bow, and made it ready.

He hath also prepared for him the instruments of death; he ordaineth his arrows against the persecutors.

 Behold, he travaileth with iniquity, and hath conceived mischief, and brought forth falsehood.

 He made a pit, and digged it, and is fallen into the ditch which he made.

 His mischief shall return upon his own head, and his violent dealing shall come down upon his own pate.' (Ps. 7:11-16)

'Upon the wicked he shall rain snares, fire and brimstone, and an horrible tempest: this shall be the portion of their cup.

For the righteous Lord loveth righteousness; his countenance doth behold the upright.' (Ps. 11:6-7)

Christ brought another notion of justice, which is not understandable for the followers of the Old Testament and He confirmed God's new commandment by His death on the cross. Saint Seraphim of Sarov quotes in his notes the following words of Saint Isaac the Syrian: 'Do not call God 'just', for your deeds do not give evidence of

His justice. It is true that David called Him 'just and righteous', but His Son had shown us that God is more likely kind and merciful. Where do you see His justice? We were sinners, and Christ died for us.' (Isaac the Syrian, Writings 90)

Jesus explains to the apostles what is the core of the justice of the New Testament, in His answer to the question of the apostle Peter. 'Then came Peter to him, and said, Lord, how oft shall my brother sin against me, and I forgive him? Untill seven times?

Jesus saith unto him, I say not unto thee, Until seven times: but, Until seventy times seven.' (Matt. 18:21-22)

Jesus explains to the apostles, why God considers this to be just: 'For if ye forgive men their trespasses, your heavenly Father will also forgive you.' (Matt.6:14)

From God's point of view, man acts justly not when he punishes the sinner but when he forgives the sinner. It is know that Great Prince Vladimir, the illuminator of Russia, after his conversion felt his duty as ruler to deal out justice, as a burden. He did not even want to sentence people whose crimes where obvious but he forgave them, in spite of the discontent of his retinue.

Jesus gives another example of the heavenly, New Testament justice, in the parable about the workers' wages. The owner of the vineyard hired workers to work there for a fixed price. When he saw in the course of the day that there were not enough workers, by the third hour he hired some more people. And so he went on until late in the evening, until eleven o'clock, and he paid everyone who worked in his vineyard exactly the same wage. The workers who had worked the whole day, grumbled at the owner 'Saying, These last have wrought but one hour, and thou hast made them equal unto us, which have borne the burden and heat of the day.' (Matt.20:12). The answer of the owner of the vineyard explains to us how the justice of the Kingdom of Heaven is:

'But he answered one of them, and said, Friend, I do thee no wrong: didst not thou agree with me for a penny?

## The Eighth Arcanum

Take that thine is, and go thy way: I will give unto this last, even as unto thee.
Is it not lawful for me to do what I will with mine own? Is thine eye evil, because I am good?' (Matt. 20:13-15)
When being reproached that because of his various duties, he was late for Vespers, Nahum, a monk of the Solovetski Monastery, would answer smiling: 'you will receive a recompense not much bigger than mine for the Lord rewards the last equally to the first.'
Jesus tells us further about the new commandment:
'Ye have heard that it hath been said, An eye for an eye, and a tooth for a tooth:
But I say unto you, That ye resist not evil: but whosoever shall smite thee on thy right cheek, turn to him the other also.
And if any man will sue thee at the law, and take away thy coat, let him have thy cloak also.
And whosoever shall compel thee to go a mile, go with him twain.
Give to him that asketh thee, and from him that would borrow of thee turn not thou away.
Ye have heard that it hath been said, Thou shalt love thy neighbour, and hate thine enemy.
But I say unto you, Love your enemies, bless them that curse you, do good to them that hate you, and pray for them which despitefully use you, and persecute you.'
His following words reveal the meaning and the purpose of the New Testament justice: to help the souls to revive their heavenly nature:
'That ye may be the children of your Father which is in heaven: for he maketh his sun to rise on the evil and on the good, and sendeth rain on the just and on the unjust.
For if ye love them which love you, what reward have ye? do not even the publicans the same?
And if ye salute your brethren only, what do ye more than others? do not even the publicans so?

Be ye therefore perfect, even as your Father which is in heaven is perfect.'

The believer, in order to receive the Lord's forgiveness and to purify his soul from sins should confess and repent his sins before a priest.

**On repentance**

One of the important tasks on the path to God is to learn to repent. Repentance is a complex inner work which includes a believer's weekly confession and repentance before the priest in church; the believer's repentance of his sins in his spirit before the Lord; pleading the Lord to help him not to forget his forgiven sins, in order not to commit them once more.

Another important task for the believer, is to free his or her soul of bonds with the people in their past, using the so-called prayer of forgiveness.

It is difficult for believers to conquer their passions, even after they have repented their sins. They lapse into temptation and commit the sin once again. A believer should oppose the cunning thought that the demons, our enemies, instil into us: there is no sense to confess and to repent for I cannot restrain myself from committing the same sin again and again. It is necessary to repent also again and again, after each fall, and in this way, gradually, the believer will conquer one or other passion.

In order to struggle with the passions successfully a believer should call for help to Jesus Christ and the Holy Theotokos, for passions are aroused by demons, whose purpose it is to cause the believer's fall and his abandonment of the spiritual Path.

Saint John Climacos writes the following: 'The believer who wishes to get rid of the burden of sins, should imitate the anchorites in the desert, who mourn over their sins incessantly, and to recite the Jesus Prayer until he finds the Lord in his heart. The Lord will remove the stone of bitterness from the soul and He will open the way to the Kingdom of Heaven.' (The spiritual Ladder)

## The Eighth Arcanum

Jesus said: 'I am the way, the truth, and the life: no man cometh unto the Father, but by me. Believest thou not that I am in the Father, and the Father in me? the words that I speak unto you I speak not of myself: but the Father that dwelleth in me, he doeth the works. Believe me that I am in the Father, and the Father in me: or else believe me for the very works' sake.' (John 14:6,10,11)

Therefore the one who calls upon the name of the Lord Jesus Christ, will be saved.

'If ye love me, keep my commandments. At that day ye shall know that I am in my Father, and ye in me, and I in you. He that hath my commandments, and keepeth them, he it is that loveth me: and he that loveth me shall be loved of my Father, and I will love him, and will manifest myself to him.'(John 14:15,20,21)

These words of Jesus make it clear that if the believer prays incessantly to the Lord, but doesn't observe the Lord's commandments, the Lord will not come to him and will not manifest Himself in the believer's heart.

Those believers who observe Christ's commandments, love Christ truly. Christ loves such believers, and if the believer calls upon Christ's name, Christ will come to him, according to His words: 'If a man love me, he will keep my words: and my Father will love him, and we will come unto him, and make our abode with him.' (John 14:23)

### The practice of repenting one's sins in church

Divide your life into periods of seven years. Write down in chronological order, starting from the day when you started this practice, all your sins according to the seven kinds:

1. The sins of anger, irritation, impatience, jealousy, envy
2. The sins of sadness, melancholy and depression
3. The sins of masturbation and fornication
4. The sins of gluttony and of drinking alcohol and using drugs
5. The sins of condemnation of your neighbour, slander and backbiting

## Particular Judgement

6. The sins of vanity, wanting the praise of other people, dependence on the opinion of others.

7. The sins of pride which also include arrogance and disdain of other people and their opinion; the feeling of being extolled above other people; feeling of being an exception to the rule, to whom the Lord will forgive things He would not forgive to others; all your actions which came forth from this kind of feelings.

In order for repentance to be fruitful, it is necessary to go to church every day or at least four days a week during many months. A sign that repentance was sincere is a feeling of purity and lightness which appears in the soul more and more often.

About confession: in order for the confession to be, not a formal one, but one that is effective and changes you to the better, confess and repent not more than three sins of each kind during one confession.

Confessing the sins in which other people were involved, tell the name of the place, where it happened, the time, and the name of the person, who was involved in your sinning.

Write down the sins which you can recall easily. When you have repented them, other, forgotten sins will come to light in your memory.

You will eventually have a long list of sins, which might take a hundred pages. This list however will become even longer when you will remember, after several confessions before the priest, your forgotten sins.

Doing this, the believer will realize that it is impossible to repent of all the sins at once. The repentance of the past sins is a long-lasting process, which might take several years of systematic work on oneself according to the above-described methods.

It is necessary to work in the line of the Eighth Arcanum regularly through one's entire life, for living on earth man cannot avoid sinning: 'there is no man alive who does not sin' (from the Burial Service). Therefore the believer should prepare himself for the posthumous trial until the very last moment of his life, placing his hope in the merciful promise of Christ: 'I will judge you according to what you were doing when I found you.'

The Ninth Arcanum

## The Ninth Arcanum. Spiritual Guidance

The ninth Arcanum states the following spiritual truth: the spiritual guidance of an experienced elder is indispensable for the believer when he or she wants to follow the Path to the Kingdom of Heaven. We see on the representation of the Arcanum an elder who accepts a believer as his disciple and will render him spiritual guidance on the Path. The believer humbly kneels, which symbolizes that he promises obedience to his mentor. Above them, we see the image of Christ, with Whom the elder is inseparably connected.

To a believer, spiritual guidance means that he becomes the elder' novice and learns from him spiritual warfare. Relying on his own limited strength and understanding, a believer wouldn't be able to find the Lord. The elder, who has accomplished the Path to a certain extent and therefore has experience in waging spiritual battles, receives spiritual guidance and strength from the Lord. Thus he can fill in the lack of strength and experience of his novice. There are on the path to spiritual growth, many invisible traps and obstacles, and the ascension along this path entails the constant risk of a fall. Saint Theophane the Anchorite wrote the following about the role of the elder, the spiritual mentor and guide: 'Just as a newly born baby cannot live without a mother who cares for him, pampers and nurses him, so one newly born in spirit and converted needs in the beginning indispensably a nurse and a nursery, a guide and guidance. Anyone who seeks his or her salvation should not start doing it just on his own, and according to his own understanding and wishes, but from the very beginning he must become someone's disciple. If one steps on a new and totally unknown path, let one then make use of true instructions, and not become fixed on his guesses only.' (The Path to Salvation, Saint Theophane the Anchorite)

## Spiritual Guidance

We find in the lore of the church many examples of the Divine help given to believers through the elders. In his youth Saint Seraphim wanted to become a monk of the Pechersky Monastery in Kiev. However one of the elders of the monastery, whose name was Dosipheus, recommended him to go to the Monastery of Sarov in Russia, as it is there that Prochor (this was the worldly name of St. Seraphim) would find his salvation.

A similar thing happened to the Solovetski anchorite Theophanes, who for many years was Dosipheus' disciple. When Dosipheus was on his deathbed, he said to his disciple that there was no place for him in the Pechersky Monastery and that he must go to the far North, to the Solovetski Monastery. Though it was Theophanes's dream to continue living in the Pechersky Monastery after his elder' death, and he made several attempts to do so, it did not work out and he had to obey the elder's command. Elder Dosipheus passed away at the age of 53, after 30 years of seclusion. It became known after his death that the anchorite Dosipheus was a woman, whose name was Darya Tyapina, a member of the gentry from Ryazan. In her childhood she lived from the age of two to nine in the cell of her grandmother Porphyria, who was a nun in the Ascension Convent in Moscow. When Porphyria received the schema, Darya was sent back to her parents. However her habits and aspirations had become that of a nun, and when she reached the age of fifteen she secretly left her home. Having disguised herself as a youth, which gave her much more freedom, she became novice in a monastery and she received the name Dosipheus.

During his many years of seclusion Dosipheus neither came out of his cell nor received visitors there. Those who wished to receive his blessing and instruction or advice, could talk to him through the small window of his cell. He had a special gift of eloquence and sagacity; he exposed secret transgressions and set the believer on the Christian path of repentance. He also could foresee the coming tribulations and temptations and he warned people about them.

## The Ninth Arcanum

When the last elder of the Monastery of Optina, Father Joseph, was young, he dreamt of the monasteries of Athos as the only place where he could come to know and carry out the Will of God. Before his departure, he went to visit his sister, who was a nun in a Convent, which was under the spiritual guidance of the Monastery of Optina. The wise Eldres Alipia, the spiritual mother of his sister, said to Joseph: 'lay off your Athos and go to the elders of Optina.' The young Ivan, the future Elder Joseph, listened to her and he was accepted as a novice in the Monastery of Optina. He even was appointed directly as a junior cell-monk of Elder Ambrose, the spiritual heir of the great elders of Optina. Ivan however felt disappointed, as life in Optina was different from what he imagined monastic life to be. Once, sitting at the table in the cell, he was grumbling in his thoughts that the monastery was not as is should be, according to what he read in books, visitors came and went constantly, the place was bustling, he had no time even to pray or to read a useful book. 'Wouldn't it be better to leave Optina and to go to Athos,' Ivan was reasoning in himself, 'there I will find genuine sanctity, prayers, the elders anchorites, while here in Optina everything is somehow confusing...' Suddenly he heard the voice of Elder Ambrose behind him, patting him on his shoulder, saying: 'Stay with us, brother Ivan, here it is better than on Athos!' Ivan was shocked by the wisdom of the elder and realized that his wish to leave Optina was just a temptation. From that moment on, he became the most faithful disciple of Elder Ambrose and eventually his spiritual heir.

Conversing with the Theotokos, praying in the presence of the Lord Jesus Christ and God the Father, the Creator of heaven and earth, everything that the believer wishes to achieve in spirit, is impossible without a special blessing of his elder. Most of all, a blessing to practice the Jesus Prayer is necessary, as this prayer is the basis of the inner work of the believer. After receiving such a blessing he should with all his strength and zeal pray in combination with the so-called 'spiritual breath' to Christ, the Theotokos and God the Father in order to acquire for himself a passage to heaven.

The believer should dedicate his life to the work of God, keeping at the same time his heart, mind and body pure. For this he should for at least 3-4 hours a day practice prayer and contemplation combined with the spiritual breath.

It is often difficult for a believer to find an experienced elder who will guide him on the spiritual path. Because of their humility elders do not always open themselves to the world, and not always willingly. Only a few monks, to whom God reveals it, know about them. It can be seen by the example of Saint Simeon the New Theologian: he was almost the only one to whom the superior spiritual achievements of his mentor, Simeon the Reverend, were revealed. Also Saint Silouan the Athonite, during his life was considered by his fellow-monks as a dull-witted, ignorant person.

Following the way of life, prescribed by the church, listening to the instructions of his confessor and struggling with his passions with the help of special physical exercises, fasting and prayer and contemplation practices, the believer gradually acquires the ability to communicate in prayer with the holy elders, who already left this temporary life. God has revealed their sanctity to the world by miracles and special signs, and everyone who wishes it, may ask them for help through prayer. Each holy elder, while accomplishing during his earthly life the mission that God laid on him, receives a special kind of blessing for solving particular problems in life and on the spiritual path.

Thus prayers to Saint Sergius of Radonezh and Saint Seraphim of Sarov help to acquire humility.

Reading the biographies of the saints and their spiritual instructions, makes for spiritual awakening and purification of the mind and the heart, for through their words we are put in touch with 'the well of water springing up into everlasting life', (John 4:14), that they have received from God.

We learn there what we should strive for, what we should and what we shouldn't ask of God, as it is told for example in the story about Saint Albertus Magnus.

One of the passions which can make a believer lose all his acquired virtues and fall, is vanity. A vain believer will never find God as he seeks the praise of his fellow-men and therefore he is not worthy of seeing God. Such a believer should learn the methods of struggling with the passion of vanity.

**About the diversity of vanity (Philokalia, abridged)**
1. Saint John Climacos says: vanity is the beginning of the believer's fall and pride is its end.
2. A vain believer seeks the praise of his fellow-men and not the praise of God.
3. When the number of a believer's virtues grows, the demon of vanity appears immediately and steals all the believer's merits.
4. The demon of vanity has a particular ability to stick to any virtue and steal it.
5. No matter how diligently a vain believer does inner work, torturing himself by fasting, night vigils, long-lasting prayers, abstinence, it doesn't bring him any fruit for he does it, not for the sake of finding God inside his heart but for the sake of the praise of his fellow-men.
6. Vanity is so perfidious that it makes proud believers look meek when they are with other people.
7. Praise extols the soul above fellow-men, stains and spoils it. When the soul feels extolled above all then the demon of pride visits it. Pride lifts up the soul falsely to the heavens and then it pushes the believer into the abyss.
Behind the passion of vanity there lurks a demon, which is fed by this passion and can manifest himself through it. Therefore the demon keeps the believer imprisoned by this passion.

**On the demon of vanity**
1. The demon of vanity compels believers to seek praise for their ascetic work, not from God, but from their fellow-men.

2. Vanity is a deadly passion; believers, do not allow the demon of vanity to stick to your virtues, otherwise he will lead you to a sinful death and he will ruin your contact with God.

3. Do not allow the demon of vanity to take possession of the fruits of the ascetic life and to avert your gaze from the Lord.

4. A vain believer wastes his efforts, trying to advance on the path to God, as it is the demon of vanity that reaps the fruits of his work.

5. As a cracked jug cannot hold wine, so a vain believer loses all his acquired virtues.

6. Do not boast before your fellow-men of the fruits of your prayer, in order to receive praise from them, because you will immediately lose God's grace.

7. As the stone which is thrown up in the air, will immediately fall down to earth, so the prayer of the vain believer will never reach God.

8. Do not expose your achievements and successes on the path to God, as the demon of vanity will steal your spiritual treasure.

9. The demons willingly cause slander and humiliation to come upon the wise and the humble so that they will become angry, as the Lord abandons those who are irate.

10. The lover of praise from his fellowmen is surrounded by the following demons: jealousy, envy, condemnation, slander, backbiting and hatred.

11. The most horrible wound for the vain and those who seek fame, is an insult, and they cannot restrain themselves from hatred towards the one who insulted them.

12. Hide the fragrance of your spiritual fruits under the seal of silence, for the demon of fame will steal them immediately. (Saint John Climacos, 'The Spiritual Ladder')

**The struggle with the passion of vanity**

1. In order to cure the believer from the passion of vanity, the Lord allows much disgrace to come onto him. By enduring it, his soul becomes purified.

2. Believer, do not become someone who pleases his fellow-men, do not strive to please many, but desire to please God.
3. Believer, resist with all your might earthly fame, for it will cause the pollution of your soul and your death. Seek not praise from your fellow-men but praise from God.
4. Seeking the praise of fellow-men leads the believer away from God. Therefore avoid it with all your might, and you will be saved.
5. Remember believer, that your code of honour is to act according to the Will of God and His commandments, while breaking this code is breaking the commandments and living according your will.
6. Do not care too much about being widely-read, but rather learn Christ's teaching from the experience of the elders.
7. Nothing should be done for show, one should act out of the purity of one's heart. For the Lord knows both the concealed and the manifested and you should strive only for His reward.
8. Do not hope to receive a reward from God if you have already received one from your fellow-men. (Saint John Climacos, 'The Spiritual Ladder')

**Prayer exercise for the struggle with the passion of vanity**
1. Make a list of the manifestations of this passion during your whole life, divided into periods of seven years. Recollect the persons to whom you have boasted and how exactly this passion became rooted in you.
2. Sit on a chair in solitude before your iconostasis, let your mind sink in your heart, and recite mentally for half an hour, the following prayer: 'Most Holy Theotokos, Virgin Mary, deliver me from the passion of vanity.'
Recite during another half hour the following prayer: 'Most Holy Theotokos, Virgin Mary, forgive me the sin of vanity', alternating it with the names of the people, to whom you boasted of your achievements.
Recite during another half hour the following prayer: 'Most Holy Theotokos, Virgin Mary, cleanse me of the sin of vanity.'

Remember to keep your mind focused on your heart.
Plead the Holy Theotokos for forgiveness of this sin until you feel light at heart.

**Prayer and contemplation exercise combined with the spiritual breath (See Enclosure) for pleading the Theotokos for support in the struggle with the passion of vanity.**
1. Recite for half an hour the following prayer, combined with the spiritual breath, addressing the Theotokos:
'Most holy Theotokos, deliver me from the sin of vanity.'
Moving life energy upwards along the spine channel while inhaling, pronounce: 'Most holy Theotokos'.
Moving energy downwards along the rear of the 'tube' of the spine, pronounce: 'Deliver me from the sin of vanity.'
2. In order to improve our sinful nature, pronounce for another half hour the following prayer:
'Most holy Theotokos and Virgin Mary, I repent my sin of vanity.'
Moving life energy upwards along the spine channel while inhaling, pronounce: 'Most holy Theotokos and Virgin Mary'.
Moving energy downwards along the rear of the 'tube' of the spine, pronounce: 'I repent my sin of vanity.'

**Prayers, combined with the spiritual breath to the Lord Jesus Christ, the Holy Spirit and God the Father**
Sit on a chair in solitude and recite mentally for half an hour, the following prayer, combining it with the spiritual breath: 'Lord Jesus Christ, forgive me the sin of vanity.' At the same time recall and pronounce the names of those whose praise you have been seeking and to whom you have boasted of your achievements on the spiritual path.
Pronounce during the next half hour the following prayer: 'Lord, Holy Spirit, the Comforter, forgive me the sin of vanity.' At the same time recall and pronounce the names of those whose praise you

## The Ninth Arcanum

have been seeking and to whom you have boasted of your achievements on the spiritual path.

Pronounce during the next half hour the following prayer:

'Oh God, our Heavenly Father, forgive me the sin of vanity.' At the same time recall and pronounce the names of those whose praise you have been seeking and to whom you have been boasting of your achievements on the spiritual path.

It is necessary to turn to the Ninth Arcanum regularly until the end of one's days.

The Tenth Arcanum

## The Tenth Arcanum

### The Tenth Arcanum. The Law of ascending to the Kingdom of Heaven and of the fall into the lower worlds

The Tenth Arcanum states the following spiritual truth: he, who does not strive to ascend to the Heavenly Kingdom during his earthly life, falls after the parting of his soul from his body, into the lower worlds of torture and suffering.

In the upper half of the picture of this Arcanum we see an elder who struggled his entire conscious life and won Christ's grace, and after his death Christ let him enter the Heavenly Kingdom.

Below there is a representation of a negligent monk who lived his life idly, without prayers and spiritual struggle. After his death he became the prey of the demons.

Ascension to the Heavenly Kingdom starts with converting oneself. In order to become a believer, pleasing God and serving Him, it is necessary to be engaged in the inner work or work on oneself during one's entire conscious life. The inner work is also called the 'spiritual Path' or the 'spiritual warfare'.

It includes in general the following:
-purification of one's body, mind and soul;
-developing the virtues of the soul;
-carrying out regular prayer and contemplation exercises for many hours, which lead to conversing with God.

The detailed meaning of these three pursuits is as follows:
1. Repentance of one's sins and elevation of the soul.
2. Serving God and struggling with oneself; spiritual struggle, struggle with the passions and striving for the Kingdom of Heaven.
3. Pious prayer and struggle with demons which bar the path of ascension to God.
4. Tracking down one's passions, tracking down the demons which lurk behind our passions and an unending struggle with them.

5. Regaining one's lost energy of the soul: prayer of forgiveness regarding each person that we have met in our life; daily practice of prayer and contemplation exercises, combined with the spiritual breath, which leads to conversing with God; struggle with one's scepticism, disbelief and disobeying the Lord.

6. Gaining God's love and grace and resigning before God.

7. Patient and peaceful endurance of criticism, mockery and persecution and of the hardships on the spiritual Path.

8. Persistent prayer and daily repentance of sins, acquiring merit of the Lord, so that He will pay attention to us, sinners, will forgive all our sins before Him and will open to us the path to the Kingdom of Heaven.

9. Struggle with one's pride, with contempt for others, with the temptation to feel an elect, who is allowed anything he wants and who will be forgiven all his transgressions. One should remember that everything is given and taken by the Lord: if we trust in Him, He gives us all we need; if we trust in ourselves only, forgetting about Him, then He also turns His face away from us.

10. Remembrance of the day of death when our soul will part from the body and will be taken to another world.

11. Remembrance of God's Last Judgement, of the necessity of repentance, remembering that if we work on ourselves, we will reach the Kingdom of Heaven, and if we just sin, then the demons will drag us away to hell with malicious joy.

12. Remembering that it is not permitted to break the Lord's commandments, because then our soul becomes burdened with sins.

13. Remembering that the soul can become light again through repentance.

14. Remembering that it is not permitted to love your fellow-men passionately, more than God, because this will lead to the flames of passions and the fall.

15. Remembering that no matter how high you have ascended on the path to the Kingdom of Heaven, you will fall back to the starting point or even lower, if you commit serious sins.

16. Remembering the rule that if you fall, then repent the sin you have committed and start ascending again from the point where you found yourself after the fall.

17. Remembering that the believer must not despair and grieve no matter how heavy his sins are, for there is no sin too heavy for God's mercy: repent before God and He will forgive you and will instruct you to do good deeds which pave the path to the Kingdom of Heaven.

18. Sadness and depression discourage the believer from following the path to God, they cause disbelief, scepticism and even denial of God. For if the believer's heart is depressed it is defenceless and the demons, the enemies of the human race, immediately seize it. They fill it with passionate, sinful designs, disbelief in God; they instil the idea to fall away from God and oppose Him. The demons make the believer open his soul to them, so that they may fill it with their dark attributes.

19. Remembering that once your earthly life will come to an end, and you will be taken to another world to reap the fruits of what you have sown during your earthly life. It doesn't matter whether you believe it or not, as this lot is awaiting everybody. Man cannot cancel the laws that he did not create, for these laws as well as man himself are created by God.

20. Disbelief in the personal judgment is a kind of blindfold which will be torn off the eyes at the moment of death.

21. Do not think that reading books about the spiritual Path and keeping a diary can replace inner work. Reading spiritual books purifies the conscience for a while, and inspires to follow the spiritual Path, but then you should really follow it, and that means carrying out the inner work. Keeping a diary helps to digest your daily impressions, but as a rule it doesn't go further than psychoanalysis.

22. If you want to find God inside you, you should re-arrange your life in such a way that you have enough time and a place for inner work. With other words, you should go against the current of nor-

mal life and make time to carry out the practices of purification and the prayer and contemplation exercises.

In order to reach the level where you will be able to converse with the Lord, you need to carry out these exercises daily for several hours your entire conscious life.

If one doesn't strive to reach the Kingdom of Heaven and does not engage in inner work, one's soul might gradually die.

**On the death of the soul**

Jesus said: 'He that is not with me is against me; and he that gathereth not with me scattereth abroad.' (Matth. 12:30)

If the believer carries out the inner work, he comes closer to God, if not, he grows estranged from Him.

If the believer doesn't care for his spiritual salvation, doesn't strive to find God, his or her soul gradually hardens and becomes insensitive to the spiritual impulse. It drowns in many sins and dies. It is often in despair and depression and is susceptible to the idea of suicide, the false replacement of hope, to stop suffering. Such a soul doesn't feel subtle inner states, it loses the sense of life and fear of God. The Philokalia says the following about unfeelingness:

'An unfeeling person might even consider himself a spiritual mentor, speak a lot about the spiritual Path, having at the same time a fallen, cold and unfeeling heart.

He might pray for deliverance from passions and at the same time be carried away by them. He can discourse about the last judgment, but he doesn't attempt to prepare for it. Such a person, being filled with a passion, repents, and then does anything to enjoy it again. He teaches meekness, being himself angry. He condemns himself in public for his vanity in order to be praised by people. He looks voluptuously at the faces in his audience, while talking about chastity.'

Thus if you want to prevent your fall into hell and ascend to the Kingdom of Heaven, you should accept the message of the Tenth Arcanum and start without postponement working on yourself daily for a minimum of two hours a day.

## On the passion of gluttony (Philokalia, abridged)

Holy elders teach believers not to indulge in the passion of gluttony and to train themselves to make do with a little amount of food. They say:

1. Believer, restrain yourself in drinking wine and do not eat meat, otherwise your mind will grow coarse and your daily concerns will be limitless.
2. Believer, restrain yourself as much as possible in eating, in order not to be rejected by God.
3. Believer, get used to be always slightly hungry, do not care for your belly, and your soul will feel at rest.
4. Believer, the more you eat the more your passions flame.
5. Believer, remember that the soul which is burdened with the bad habits of the body, that is: gluttony, drinking wine, much sleep, daily concerns, becomes spiritually fruitless.
6. Therefore the Saviour says: 'And take heed to yourselves, lest at any time your hearts be overcharged with surfeiting, and drunkenness, and cares of this life.' (Luke 21:34)
7. Believer, cherish no hope to be free from the attacks of your belly before your soul has parted from the body.
8. If the passion of eating much is in you, the belly cannot be satiated and demands food constantly.
9. At a table full of tasty food the passion of gluttony hurries to gulp it down all at once.
10. The more, believer, you indulge your body, the quicker grows its brutality.
11. Remember believer that when you restrain your belly in consuming food, then at the same time you tame the passions in your heart.
12. If you satiate your belly by food, then your heart becomes also overwhelmed by sinful thoughts.
13. Believer, you should know that the demon of gluttony often sticks to the stomach and does not let it feel satiated even though it should devour and drink up all that the eye sees.

14. If you have promised Christ to follow the narrow path, then restrain your belly. For broad is the way of gluttony leading to fornication, and narrow is the path leading to salvation. (Philokalia)

**The struggle with the passion of gluttony**
First of all, a believer who suffers from the passion of gluttony, should repent before the priest of this passion and ask his blessing to struggle against it. Holy elders state that it is possible to tame this passion by gradually diminishing the amount of food. This will cause the volume of the stomach to diminish and subsequently, the amount of food needed. One should learn to eat once in twenty-four hours, in the evening, and not to drink alcohol.

**Prayer practice for struggling against the passion of gluttony**
1. Make a list of the manifestations of this passion during your whole life, divided into periods of seven years.
2. Sit on a chair in solitude before your iconostasis, let your mind sink in your heart, and recite mentally for half an hour, the following prayer: 'Most Holy Theotokos, Virgin Mary, deliver me from the passion of gluttony.'
Recite during another half hour the following prayer: 'Most Holy Theotokos, Virgin Mary, forgive me the sin of gluttony'. Recollect during this prayer the moments when you indulged in gluttony.
Recite during another half hour the following prayer: 'Most Holy Theotokos, Virgin Mary, cleanse me from the sin of gluttony.'
Remember to keep your mind focused on your heart.
Pray to the Holy Theotokos until you feel light at heart.

**Prayer and contemplation exercise combined with the spiritual breath for pleading the Theotokos for support in the struggle with the passion of gluttony**
1. Recite for half an hour the following prayer, combined with the spiritual breath, addressing the Theotokos:
'Most holy Theotokos, deliver me from the sin of gluttony.'

Moving life energy upwards along the spine channel while inhaling, pronounce: 'Most holy Theotokos'.
Moving energy downwards along the rear of the 'tube' of the spine, pronounce: 'Deliver me from the sin of gluttony.'
2. In order to improve our sinful nature, pronounce for another half hour the following prayer:
'Most holy Theotokos and Virgin Mary, I repent my sin of gluttony.'
Moving life energy upwards along the spine channel while inhaling, pronounce: 'Most holy Theotokos and Virgin Mary'.
Moving energy downwards along the rear of the 'tube' of the spine, pronounce: 'I repent my sin of gluttony.' Recollect during this prayer the moments when you indulged in gluttony.
The more advanced level of this practice is to focus your mind on your heart by carrying out the above-mentioned.

**Prayers, combined with the spiritual breath to the Lord Jesus Christ, the Holy Spirit and God the Father**
Sit on a chair in solitude before your iconostasis and recite mentally for half an hour, the following prayer, combining it with the spiritual breath: 'Lord Jesus Christ, forgive me the sin of gluttony.' Pronounce during the next half hour the following prayer: 'Lord, Holy Spirit, the Comforter, forgive me the sin of gluttony.'
Pronounce for another half hour the following prayer:
'Oh God, our Heavenly Father, forgive me the sin of gluttony.' Recollect during the prayers the moments when you indulged in gluttony.

**On lies and joking**
Lies stain the heart and therefore the lying believer cannot converse with God. The holy elders state:
1. The believer, who is possessed by the passion of lying, ruins by this his love for God. Lie is the offspring of verbosity and joking.
2. A lie is not a minor sin as many think, for it kills the aspiration to the Spirit.

3. Joking kills the love of God and gives rise to abuse and condemnation.
4. Hypocrisy and cunning are given birth by lies, it is their shameless mother.
5. He who comes to fear God, will be afraid to lie, knowing that he will be punished for this. Conscience is the best judge of lies.

**Prayer practice for struggling with the passion of lying and joking**

First of all, a believer who suffers from the passion of lies and joking, should repent before the priest of this passion and ask his blessing to struggle against it.

1. Make a list of the manifestations of this passion during your whole life, divided into periods of seven years.
2. Sit on a chair in solitude before your iconostasis, let your mind sink in your heart, and recite mentally for half an hour, the following prayer: 'Most Holy Theotokos, Virgin Mary, deliver me from the passion of lies and joking.'

Recite during another half hour the following prayer: 'Most Holy Theotokos, Virgin Mary, forgive me the sin of lies and joking. Recollect during this prayer the persons to whom you lied and about whom you made sarcastic and sharp remarks.

Recite during another half hour the following prayer: 'Most Holy Theotokos, Virgin Mary, cleanse me from the sin of lies and joking.'
Remember to keep your mind focused on your heart.
Pray to the Holy Theotokos until you feel light at heart.

**Prayer and contemplation exercise combined with the spiritual breath for pleading the Theotokos for support in the struggle with the passion of lying and joking.**

1. Recite for half an hour the following prayer, combined with the spiritual breath, addressing the Theotokos:
'Most holy Theotokos, deliver me from the sin of lies and joking.'

Moving life energy upwards along the spine channel while inhaling, pronounce: 'Most holy Theotokos'.

Moving energy downwards along the rear of the 'tube' of the spine, pronounce: 'Deliver me from the sin of lies and joking.'

2. In order to improve our sinful nature, pronounce for another half hour the following prayer:

'Most holy Theotokos and Virgin, Mary, I repent my sin of lies and joking.'

Moving life energy upwards along the spine channel while inhaling, pronounce: 'Most holy Theotokos and Virgin, Mary'.

Moving energy downwards along the rear of the 'tube' of the spine, pronounce: 'I repent my sin of lies and joking.' Recollect during this prayer the persons to whom you lied and about whom you made sarcastic and sharp remarks.

The more advanced level of this practice is to focus your mind on your heart during the carrying out of the above-mentioned.

**Prayers, combined with the spiritual breath to the Lord Jesus Christ, the Holy Spirit and God the Father**

Sit on a chair in solitude before your iconostasis and recite mentally for half an hour, the following prayer, combining it with the spiritual breath: 'Lord Jesus Christ, forgive me the sin of lies and joking.'

Recite for another half hour the following prayer: 'Lord, Holy Spirit, the Comforter, forgive me the sin of lies and joking.'

Recite for the next half hour the following prayer:

'Oh God, our Heavenly Father, forgive me the sin of lies and joking.' Recollect during these prayers the persons to whom you lied and about whom you made sarcastic and sharp remarks.

It is necessary to work in the spirit of the message of the Tenth Arcanum during one's entire conscious life, otherwise one's chance to enter the Kingdom of Heaven is almost unreal.

The Eleventh Arcanum

## The Eleventh Arcanum. The Super-Effort

The Eleventh Arcanum states the following spiritual truth: if the believer won't make the super-effort in the work of purification of his body, mind and heart from sins, that is, if he will not wage spiritual warfare and carry out the prayer and contemplation practices doing his utmost best and even more than that, he will not be able to enter the Kingdom of Heaven.

The picture of the Arcanum represents a kneeling believer who, making a super-effort, prays daily for many hours to Christ and the Theotokos for the salvation of his soul. The demons below attempt to seduce him with the pleasures of life, so that if he would yield and fall, they could use it as a charge against him at the personal judgment, and drag him away to hell.

Jesus said: 'And from the days of John the Baptist until now the kingdom of heaven suffereth violence, and the violent take it by force.' (Matth. 11:12)
He explains further what kind of force, effort He means:
'And I say unto you, Ask, and it shall be given you; seek, and ye shall find; knock, and it shall be opened unto you.
For every one that asketh receiveth; and he that seeketh findeth; and to him that knocketh it shall be opened.
If a son shall ask bread of any of you that is a father, will he give him a stone? or if he ask a fish, will he for a fish give him a serpent?
Or if he shall ask an egg, will he offer him a scorpion?
If ye then, being evil, know how to give good gifts unto your children: how much more shall your heavenly Father give the Holy Spirit to them that ask him?' (Luke 11:9-13)
A believer needs to make efforts to make him knock daily at the door of the Heavenly Kingdom, that is to carry out the inner work. However, the transition to a new stage of inner work demands not just an effort, but a super-effort. As Saint Ignatius Brianchaninov

## The Super-Effort

says, 'carrying out Christ's commandments is done by the novices with such violence to themselves that it is called a 'crucifixion'.' The things that are extremely difficult for a novice, are simple and understandable for an experienced believer and he does them easily. Thus the meaning of the notion 'super-effort' changes correspondingly to the experience of the believer and the stage he has reached on the path to the Heavenly Kingdom.

1. To attend a church service would require a serious effort from an unbelieving, materialistic person, who is afraid of church. However, to be baptised, would require from such a person a super-effort that he would have to make himself. To take a further step, and to start regularly reading the morning and evening prayers would require from the newly converted a super-effort. However, when he becomes accustomed to this, he will gradually recognize how much support his soul receives from regular prayers and what a spiritual pleasure it is, and he will read prayers even when exhausted.

2. The next super-effort that the believer must make is to bring himself to say the prayer of forgiveness and to repent his sins inwardly during the church service, in order to rid himself from the burdening ties of the past on his path to the Kingdom of Heaven. He will find it a very tiresome and difficult task, as demons will obstruct him in all possible ways. But if he persists, he will then joyfully attend two services a day, doing at the same time the inner work of forgiveness and repentance, because he will realize that the heavy burden of passions from his past becomes lighter and lighter due to these practices.

3. A super-effort is necessary in order to overcome the next obstacle on the spiritual path and to arrive at the new level, while to function at the new level requires regular efforts. Now the meaning of the term 'super-effort' is clear: it is a sacrifice on the spiritual path. When the sacrifice is made, then it is possible to advance for a while doing just regular efforts. However as the firewood burns to ashes quickly, so the sacrifice allows us to advance only for a while, and

in order to climb further on the ladder leading to the Kingdom of Heaven, we have to make a sacrifice yet again.

4. The next super-effort for the believer will be to learn to watch his passions: how exactly the passions become active in him and how they seize his soul.

5. Next, the super-effort will be to struggle with these passions, which can last until the end of his days. It is the constant work of purifying the soul from angry, lecherous, envious, depressive and other sinful thoughts. But gradually we will become more and more skilful and it will require just regular efforts from us. The first super-effort in this, is learning the bodily methods of struggling with passions, like e.g. fasting and bowing. Another super-effort that we will need to make, is learning and carrying out prayer and contemplation practices. In the beginning we will hardly be able to spend a quarter of an hour a day at this, experiencing great difficulties. However if we persist and gradually increase the length of these exercises we will carry them out with joy for five - six hours a day.

6. In order to learn to pray the Jesus Prayer continuously, we will also need to make a super-effort. But when we become firmly established in this prayer, then we will recite it, feeling a great spiritual sweetness, for many hours a day. This prayer will keep our body, heart and mind pure and it will help us eventually to converse with God.

7. We need to apply a super-effort to ourselves when we wish to curb and to tame our passions. This is contrary to the dark ones, who want to conquer the Kingdom of Heavens by violence, hoping to find bliss in an illegal way. They think that the state of bliss is somewhere outside and that one can conquer or steal it, as they do not know that a blissful state can only come out of the inner purity of an open heart. The blissful state then comes when the spiritual sun of our Heavenly Father shines through the pure soul.

8. All the bliss of the world is in the Lord, it comes from the Father in Heaven and fills the entire creation with the spiritual radiance of crystal purity. It is uncreated, limitless happiness, which flows

from the open heart and overflows in us with love that is pure like a transparent morning sky.

9. We need a super-effort in order to be able to notice when the passions try to penetrate into our soul, and immediately to cut them off.

10. For the sake of this struggle with the passions the believer beseeches God to grant him the willpower to keep body, mind and heart pure.

11. Only with the help of God's power can he conquer his passions, defeat the demons and find the Lord in his heart.

12. We cannot find God, relying solely on our own capability, because there are on the path to Him many invisible obstacles, which the believer cannot overcome without His help.

13. On the other hand, inner work requires so many efforts that only a believer with well-developed willpower can carry them out.

14. As a novice doesn't have enough willpower and energy to make super-efforts, he needs to find an elder and to become his disciple. The elder will help him by his developed willpower to find God, for he has advanced much further on the path to God; he has found God's grace and he knows from experience how to wage the inner, spiritual warfare.

Having become the disciple of an elder, the novice learns how to carry out the inner work. In the first place he must purify his soul from the sins that he has committed in his worldly past. In a monastery it is done by means of obedience, prayer and repentance, which is in fact grieving before God about one's sins. This grieving, as the holy Fathers used to say, 'wipes off the list of sins'. The soul becomes purified and starts living in God as if it didn't have a past, but it has become like the soul of a child again. The Lord said: 'Verily, I say unto you, Except ye be converted, and become as little children, ye shall not enter into the kingdom of heaven.'

Believers who live a worldly life attempted to create methods of purification which suit their way of life.

One such believer, who lived a worldly life, became converted and turned to God; he suffered a lot because he felt his prayers to God were fruitless. He pleaded God zealously for forgiveness of his sins, but his soul was still heavy and dark. Once, after confession, the priest told him: 'Learn to forgive others and the Lord will forgive you.' Pleading the Theotokos for help in what seemed for him an impossible task, the believer received inspiration from Her and wrote a prayer of forgiveness. He discovered that after he prayed this prayer about persons he was close to in the past, his passions regarding these persons or their passions regarding him, felt less strong and overwhelming. His soul grew more and more clean and at a certain moment the Lord answered his prayers.

Another believer, when he was twelve years old, once felt deeply and intensely the love of Christ, and a desire to find God flamed up in him. His mentors however, were devoted to the eastern and western mystical and magical teachings, and he was striving to find God, carrying out exercises from the Kriya, Tao and Toltec traditions. After many years of systematic work in this manner, he understood that notwithstanding all sorts of interesting and gripping inner states, he reached nothing real and God was even further away from him than in his childhood. He realized that it is not the techniques and exercises of the old spiritual traditions, but following Christ and the Theotokos that lead man to the union with God. He improved the exercises and made them suitable for the Christian spiritual path. These exercises help to develop the willpower, purify and restore the energy of the soul and prepare believers for the struggle with the passions and sinful designs, for waging the spiritual warfare.

Learning how to observe correctly the laws of heaven and earth, the believer can find God inside himself. In the first instance the believer must learn to stand firmly on his own feet, but at the same time the most important pursuit for him must be the inner work on the path to God and to serving Him.

## The Super-Effort

The message of this Arcanum can be of help to you in case, having read the previous ten Arcane, you still did not do any of the exercises which are described there. Try to make a super-effort and do the following:

1. Start with reading the morning and evening prayers, which will take about forty minutes of your time per day. This is the practice of the fifth Arcanum. Do not worry whether you will be able to manage all your daily obligations or that you might miss answering a couple of telephone calls: for man, the most important is to follow the spiritual path.

2. When you manage to read prayers every day during a month, then make another super-effort and start carrying out the practice of the Sixth Arcanum, that is, the prayer of forgiveness. For this you should go to church and standing before the icon of Christ or the Theotokos, which is dear to your hart, pronounce this prayer for at least a hundred times about one or several persons from your past or your present life.

3. After some time, make another super-effort and start regaining the energy of the soul that you lost in your past. When you return home after having attended the church service, carry out the exercise of reconsideration regarding the people from your past, especially those about whom you have read the prayer of forgiveness that day. In this way you get back the energy of your soul which got stuck in them in the past.

4. Doing these exercises regularly for several years, you will restore the energy of your soul. Then you will need to make the next super-effort and start carrying out the prayer and contemplation exercises. Begin with doing the exercise for five minutes a day and make it gradually one hour a day. Then you can read a reduced number of the morning and evening prayers.

## On verbosity and prayerful silence (Philokalia, abridged)

The holy Fathers state that verbosity is a serious obstacle on the spiritual path, as verbosity gives rise to the sins of condemnation, vanity and backbiting. Therefore a believer who hasn't eliminated the passion of verbosity in himself, cannot ascend to the Kingdom of Heaven.

It leads to ridiculing one's neighbour and eventually to lies. Verbosity ruins the silence of the heart and destroys the fruits of prayer: the heart becomes polluted, and depression seizes the believer. He who talks much loses the wish to pray and wastes the energy of his soul.

Verbosity results from a bad and excessive life, committed sins and attempts to justify oneself.

Silence allows one to pray ceaselessly, guards from sinful designs and boldness.

The believers who have experienced God's grace, avoid verbosity and people who talk excessively, for where there is verbosity there is no grace.

Prayerful silence preserves spiritual warmth in the heart and directs the thoughts towards God. It brings to the soul peace and contentment.

Prayerful silence preserves divine fire in the heart, which was kindled by prayer, it helps to remember the last judgment and leads to inner silence.

## The struggle with the passion of verbosity

First of all, a believer, who suffers from the passion of verbosity, should repent before the priest of this passion and ask his blessing to struggle with it. In order to conquer the passion of verbosity he should acquire prayerful silence.

1. Make a list of the manifestations of this passion during your whole life, divided into periods of seven years.
2. Sit on a chair in solitude before your iconostasis, let your mind sink in your heart, and recite mentally for half an hour, the follo-

wing prayer: 'Most Holy Theotokos, Virgin Mary, deliver me from the passion of verbosity.'

Recite during another half hour the following prayer: 'Most Holy Theotokos, Virgin Mary, forgive me the sin of verbosity.' Recollect during this prayer the moments when you have been talking too much, with whom and about what.

Recite during another half hour the following prayer: 'Most Holy Theotokos, Virgin Mary, cleanse me from the sin of verbosity.'

Remember to keep your mind focused on your heart.

Pray to the Holy Theotokos until you feel light at heart.

**Prayer and contemplation exercise combined with the spiritual breath for pleading the Theotokos for support in the struggle with the passion of verbosity**

1. Recite for half an hour the following prayer, combined with the spiritual breath, addressing the Theotokos:

'Most holy Theotokos, deliver me from the sin of verbosity.'

Moving life energy upwards along the spine channel while inhaling, pronounce: 'Most holy Theotokos'.

Moving energy downwards along the rear of the 'tube' of the spine, pronounce: 'Deliver me from the sin of verbosity.'

2. In order to improve our sinful nature, pronounce for another half hour the following prayer:

'Most holy Theotokos and Virgin, Mary, I repent of my sin of verbosity.'

Moving life energy upwards along the spine channel while inhaling, pronounce: 'Most holy Theotokos and Virgin, Mary'.

Moving energy downwards along the rear of the 'tube' of the spine, pronounce: 'I repent my sin of verbosity.' Recollect during this prayer the moments when you indulged yourself in verbosity.

The more advanced level of this practice is to focus your mind on your heart during the carrying out of the above-mentioned.

**Prayers, combined with the spiritual breath to the Lord Jesus Christ, the Holy Spirit and God the Father**
Sit on a chair in solitude before your iconostasis and recite mentally for half an hour, the following prayer, combining it with the spiritual breath: 'Lord Jesus Christ, forgive me the sin of verbosity.' Pronounce during the next half hour the following prayer: 'Lord, Holy Spirit, the Comforter, forgive me the sin of verbosity.'
Pronounce during the next half hour the following prayer:
'Oh God, our Heavenly Father, forgive me the sin of verbosity.' Recollect during the prayers the moments when you indulged yourself in verbosity.

**On the sin of depression and sadness**
Depression and sadness are sins because they eliminate faith, hope and love in the heart of the believer, which are the three most important pillars of the spiritual path. When a believer lapses into this sin, he becomes overwhelmed with a strong wish to return to the secular life; a faint-hearted one might even give in to idleness and abandon the spiritual path.

**Struggle with the passion of depression and sadness**
First of all, a believer who suffers from the passion of depression and sadness, should repent before the priest of this passion and ask his blessing for the struggle with it. Behind the passion of depression there lurks a demon which casts utter sadness, grief and depression on the believer. The demon whispers diligently that 'there is no Creator of heaven and earth, and if there is One, then it is impossible to have contact with Him and the gates of Heaven will never open. There is no sense in wasting time on purifying the soul from sins and useless prayer and contemplation exercises. The best solution is to return to a worldly life and give in to all the passions: this is real life, according to him, while the spiritual warfare is just a boring illusion which causes grief and depression.'

## Prayer practice for struggling with the passion of depression and sadness

Holy elders say that the way to struggle with depression and sadness is prayerful vigil. It is necessary to learn to kindle the fire of prayer in the heart and receive help from the Lord through sincere prayer in the silence of the heart.

Holy elders say that depression and sadness seize man when his or her soul wallows in fornication, pride and vanity. Also when the soul has become strongly attached to the worldly life and cannot keep aloof from it.

## The prayers to the saints, the Most Holy Theotokos, the Lord Jesus Christ, the Holy Spirit and God the Father

Sit on a chair in solitude before your iconostasis, and carry out the spiritual breath in combination with the following prayers:

1. Saint Seraphim of Sarov, deliver me from the demon of depression and sadness.
2. Saint Nicolas the Miracle Worker, deliver me from the demon of depression and sadness.
3. Saint Sergius of Radonezh, deliver me from the demon of depression and sadness.
4. Most Holy Theotokos, Virgin Mary, deliver me from the demon of depression and sadness.
5. Lord Jesus Christ, deliver me from the demon of depression and sadness.
6. Lord Holy Spirit, the Comforter, deliver me from the demon of depression and sadness.
7. O God, our Father in Heaven, deliver me from the demon of depression and sadness.

It is necessary to turn regularly to the message of the Eleventh Arcanum during one's entire life.

The Twelfth Arcanum

THE TWELFTH ARCANUM. THE SACRIFICE

The Twelfth Arcanum states the following spiritual truth: in order to find God the believer should sacrifice the multitude of his passions.
The picture of the Arcanum represents a holy elder who abandoned the world and settled on a deserted isle. He dedicated his entire life to finding Christ inside himself. By means of fasting and prayers he earned contact with the Lord.

If a believer won't make a great sacrifice, he won't be honoured by conversation with Christ.
Jesus Christ, the Son of God, was sent by His Father in Heaven, to earth, in order to save the earth from the fall into the lower spheres. The Lord Jesus Christ sacrificed His abode in heaven at the right side of His Father and descended to earth as a man. He travelled from town to town in Judea and preached about the true God. Jesus brought people the new Message of the Father in Heaven so that people, following it, could return to Him. Christ brought on earth the divine love and He endowed his apostles and faithful with it. He sacrificed Himself by His voluntary death on the cross, in order to fulfil the Will of His Father in heaven.
'Jesus said unto him, Thou shalt love the Lord thy God with all thy heart, and with all thy soul, and with all thy mind. This is the first and great commandment. And the second is like unto it, Thou shalt love thy neighbour as thyself. On these two commandments hang all the law and the prophets.' (Matt. 22:36-40)
With the coming of Christ people came to know the true divine love. Christ brought back to people the love, with which Adam lived in paradise and which he lost when he lapsed into sin.
Man's love gives rise to passions and eventually causes great suffering. The divine love of Christ comes in the silence of the heart and it carries in itself the unspeakable, supreme divine grace. He who

## The Twelfth Arcanum

has felt His love even for a moment, will never be able to forget this incomparably elevated feeling.

Christ brought salvation to all people without exception, He suffered for us and He redeemed our sins. And now, and always, until the Last Judgement, Christ takes our sins upon Himself and suffers for us, giving us in this way consolation and forgiveness for our sins. Christ constantly sacrifices His grace for the sake of those who repent their sins before Him. He sacrifices Himself, suffering for our sins, because according to the law of justice someone should suffer for the committed sins. Christ carried out on earth the most elevated form of the law of sacrifice.

Many people on our planet suffer and are not able to put an end to their suffering. Only a great, light-bearing soul can do this, moved by compassion, by atoning for their sins through self-sacrifice. It was exactly this compassion which prompted the most spiritually mature souls, purified by the spirit, to undertake the great feat of self-sacrifice for the salvation of others. Such a great soul, illuminated by the Holy Spirit, is born on earth in order to teach people the ascension to the Kingdom of Heaven. It sacrifices its blessed state in the Kingdom of Heaven in order to guide those who are ready, and it gives them real hope that they can find God. This great soul calls upon people to build monasteries, to leave behind them their worldly life and take monastic vows for the sake of finding God, or, staying in the world, to aspire to God and strive to live according to His commandments.

The lot of these souls, chosen by God is to suffer immensely and to forgive many unjust things done to them. They take on themselves the duty to atone for the sins of many who break the Divine laws. They struggle with evil by the means of good and in this way they triumph over evil. Such great souls are for example Saint Sergius of Radonezh, Saint Seraphim of Sarov, Saint Bernard of Clairvaux. They brought many souls to the Kingdom of Heaven and nowadays, and always they help believers to ascend to the throne of God.

## The Sacrifice

In order for the believer to receive God's grace and find the Lord in his heart, that is, to find an imperishable, inner, heavenly richness, a believer should sacrifice his passions, also the passion of amassing money. At the same time and first of all, the believer should love the Lord more than anything else, more than his family and parents.

Jesus said: 'He that loveth father or mother more than me is not worthy of me: and he that loveth son or daughter more than me is not worthy of me.

And he that taketh not his cross, and followeth after me, is not worthy of me.' (Matt. 10:37,38)

'And, behold, one came and said unto him, Good Master, what good thing shall I do, that I may have eternal life?

And he said unto him, Why callest thou me good? there is none good but one, that is, God: but if thou wilt enter into life, keep the commandments.

He saith unto him, Which? Jesus said, Thou shalt do no murder, Thou shalt not commit adultery, Thou shalt not steal, Thou shalt not bear false witness,

Honour thy father and thy mother: and, Thou shalt love thy neighbour as thyself.

The young man saith unto him, All these things have I kept from my youth up: what lack I yet?

Jesus said unto him, If thou wilt be perfect, go and sell that thou hast, and give to the poor, and thou shalt have treasure in heaven: and come and follow me.

But when the young man heard that saying, he went away sorrowful: for he had great possessions.

Then said Jesus unto his disciples, Verily I say unto you, That a rich man shall hardly enter into the kingdom of heaven.

And again I say unto you, It is easier for a camel to go through the eye of a needle, than for a rich man to enter into the kingdom of God.' (Matt. 19:16-24)

If a believer wishes to find God inside his heart, he should sacrifice many of his habits and empty amusements. These are the habits of a worldly life, that is, money and status in society; attachments to bodily pleasures, that is, gluttony and drinking; and the soul-bodily pleasure, that is sex. A believer should sacrifice many of his harmful or useless habits, his desire to be amused, to watch TV, to leisure.

The amount of time which would come free when this is done, the believer should use for inner work: prayer and contemplation practices combined with the spiritual breath, regaining the lost energy of the soul, prayer of forgiveness, repentance and confession to the priest; ennobling of the instinctive energy and other exercises. Speaking generally, the earthly values should be sacrificed for the sake of the heavenly values, for the sake of conversation with God.

It seems to us sometimes that we could immediately change ourselves and the way we live if we just wished to do this. In reality however, man has many different 'selves'. One 'self' says: 'I want to pray.' Another 'self' prompts: 'First wash the dishes, then have a rest for five minutes, and then you may pray.' By the time the dishes are washed and the time to rest is almost over, another 'self' appears on our inner stage and demands to watch an interesting TV program for just five minutes, and 'then you may pray even for half an hour!' However if we give in to the pressure of our habits we are carried away and we forget about our initial wish to say the evening prayers. Only when we go to bed we will suddenly remember this, but then we are so sleepy that we can only make a solemn promise: 'I will try to get up early and then I will read both morning and evening prayers!' However when the alarm clock goes off we cannot make ourselves get up, and then we must rush to our work and we are busy for the whole day and in the evening we postpone reading the prayers to the next morning. Thus one and the same scheme of postponing the reading of the prayers repeats itself every day. The same scheme of postponing is valid for practising the spiritual and contemplation exercises.

Then we come to the understanding that in order to start inner work or the work on ourselves, we should first overcome the old desires and habits. We realize also that this is a daily psychological labour, which demands, like any labour, a certain amount of efforts. We also realize that the inner work is much more difficult than cooking and washing the dishes and cleaning the room. We become aware of a not obvious fact, that it is much easier to do a physical effort than a psychological effort. Gradually, we realize that inner work is much more difficult than going to the office every day, and that in order to change ourselves we should invest in this undertaking much more energy than would be needed, for example, for repairing our house. Then we might better understand why the attempt to change our old habits and ourselves is called 'inner work'. It can not only be compared with the work we do in order to earn our living, but it is immeasurably more difficult. It is not for nothing that holy elders point out that the path of ascension to the Kingdom of Heaven demands a very difficult inner work. Thus 'inner work' is a very capacious term, about which has been written in thousands and thousands books.

As each work requires a certain amount of time to be done, you will need to reconsider your daily routine and to allot at least one hour to inner work, the work which will change you and will open in you your spiritual origin. For this you should find which habits and which parts of your daily routine you can sacrifice for this.

Then you should increase your motivation to carry out the inner work. This is done by reading books on the spiritual path, the works of the holy fathers and hagiography, where you find explained, why man should do inner work and grow spiritually.

Man is divided inwardly in four parts: the intellectual centre, that is the mind; the emotional centre, that is the heart, the will centre and the motion-instinctive centre. These four centres are, in the majority of people, not interconnected: each centre functions on itself without considering the other centres. A manifestation of this disconnection is that man is often unable to put into practice decisions which are made on the level of the intellectual centre, because the same decision would have to be made in the emotional, will and motion-instinctive centres. Making a decision on the emotional

level means to conceive the wish to put into practice the decision which was made intellectually, to make your emotions flame, so to say. Then, making a decision on the level of the will and motion-instinctive centres means building a logically well grounded plan to reach your goal, that is, defining the concrete steps which should be made. You should make a detailed cost-benefit analysis and time-schedule, based on your estimation of your capacity. And if your goals will be deserved and your plan will be well-thought out, you will be able to fulfil your decision and it will bring you profit. The above-mentioned is to the same extent valid for the realization of finding God in your heart. For Jesus said: 'For which of you, intending to build a tower, sitteth not down first, and counteth the cost, whether he have sufficient to finish it?
Lest haply, after he hath laid the foundation, and is not able to finish it, all that behold it begin to mock him,
Saying, This man began to build, and was not able to finish.' (Luke 14:28-30)
 Besides, you should remember that the path to God requires sacrifices, and first of all the believer should sacrifice his inertia and usual comfort.
Eventually, the believer should sacrifice all his earthly attachments and renounce the worldly life, according to the word of the Lord:
'Or what king, going to make war against another king, sitteth not down first, and consulteth whether he be able with ten thousand to meet him that cometh against him with twenty thousand?
 Or else, while the other is yet a great way off, he sendeth an ambassage, and desireth conditions of peace.
So likewise, whosoever he be of you that forsaketh not all that he hath, he cannot be my disciple.' (Luke 14:31-33)
A believer should leave behind those who do not seek the Kingdom of Heaven and join those who seek God. It is useless to live with worldly people and seek the Kingdom of Heaven at the same time; it is useless to throw pearls before the ignoramus and those who do not wish to knock incessantly on the doors of the Kingdom of Hea-

ven, because they will turn against you. A believer should sacrifice his laziness and part of his worldly pleasures and amusements for the sake of the prayer and contemplation exercises, for the sake of finding God. A believer should sacrifice part of his worldly concerns for the sake of finding God and serving Him. A believer should sacrifice his peaceful life and his well-ordered life for the sake of finding God. A believer should rearrange his life in such a way that he will have part of his time dedicated to seeking God.

A believer should use his will-power in order to allot several hours a day to prayer and contemplation exercises and to carry out this inner work steadily. In order to find God a believer should sacrifice his or her career in society and build a saving ark, on which he can sail to the Kingdom of Heaven. A believer should restrain himself from eating much and lead a contemplative way of life. A believer should renounce amassing perishable valuables and should gather the imperishable, heavenly treasures, because it is these which will be the pledge of eternal bliss for him in the Kingdom of Heaven.

A believer should find an elder, a spiritual mentor, who has found God in himself, and follow the elder's instructions and admonitions. In order to be able to do so, a believer should sacrifice his pride, vanity and passion for amassing money. In order to be able to bring this sacrifice the believer should cultivate in himself the three principal virtues of the soul: faith in God; hope for salvation, that is finding God inside himself; love of God. However, a lazy and negligent believer will not reach the Kingdom of Heaven. only the believer who uses the time of his life for carrying out prayer and contemplation exercises may hope for salvation, as through them he can find God in himself. In order to follow the path to God, a believer should kindle in his heart the spiritual fire, and for this he should sacrifice the passion of anger. Then he will be able to preserve in his heart his subtle energy, spiritualized by prayers, which otherwise is wasted when he is angry with his neighbours. And in order not to be angry, a believer should sacrifice, as holy elders teach, his pride.

## The Twelfth Arcanum

If you would conquer your pride you would spare plenty of time, because we waste a lot of time just protecting our pride. Then you can use this time for your inner work.

Pride is the biggest obstacle on the Path as it cools the heart and makes it indifferent to the suffering of other people and insensitive to the light Message of Jesus Christ, but it invites Lucifer instead. Pride shuts off the heart to human as well as to God's love; it mortifies the soul and makes it insensitive to God's instructions. It is pride which suppresses the spiritual fire in your heart that you try to kindle through sacrifice, and it ruins all the good that you have gathered on the path to God. There lurks behind pride a cold and unfeeling demon, the enemy of the human race. Pride can throw down into the depth of hell even very high beings. The most endowed angel of God, Lucifer, fell because of his pride as he ascribed the light that was in him not to God, His creator, but to himself. At the very same moment when he thought this he fell and from angel of light he turned into angel of darkness, giving birth to lie and theft, which are the essence of pride. Thus pride is the most dangerous passion. The demon of pride is extremely cunning and he will always find a convincingly sounding justification of pride. His reasoning is logical, but this is the dark logic, without any light and compassion: it is anti-human logic. The demon of pride has a lot of power when he opposes the Christian idea of goodness and humility, as he draws his power from Lucifer himself.

Instead of protecting his pride before his fellow-men, a believer should plead God for salvation from this deep and hard to cure ulcer, and his heart will gradually become clean.

In order to kindle spiritual fire in his heart a believer should sacrifice the passion of vanity. Cease seeking praise for your good deeds from your fellow-men, but seek praise from God. You can merit praise from God by the work of virtue which is, in first instance, inner work and the tireless following of the path to God. Pray to God incessantly, recite aloud and inwardly the Jesus Prayer and once the

## The Sacrifice

Lord will hear you and He will respond to your prayers, for the Lord responds to the prayers of a pure heart.

And if you would sacrifice the passion of fornication for the sake of kindling spiritual fire in your heart, and would cease running after sexual pleasure, you would be completely amazed at how much time you spare! Again you can use this spare time for inner work and good deeds according to the Lord's commandments. An additional positive effect of this will be that you will preserve your spirituality due to your prayers' energy, which otherwise is consumed by lecherous pleasures. And when you have accumulated enough energy and your heart is purified, the Lord will appear in it in all His radiant glory.

If you sacrifice the passion of gluttony, you won't waste your time in excessive eating and then dozing cosily on a sofa or reading the newspaper and watching TV, sipping a glass of wine.

If instead of talking excessively and sharply about your neighbours, you recite the Jesus Prayer to yourself, you will certainly increase your chances of salvation.

If you would learn to be content with little and would sacrifice the passion of amassing money, you would spare a lot of time that can be used for working on yourself.

Do not yield to the attacks of the demon of sadness and despondency, and you will preserve the aspiration to God inside you and the hope for the salvation of your soul.

A believer should sacrifice his ego and learn to control his negative emotions and instincts. Blessed are the merciful and they who can sacrifice themselves for the sake of those who suffer.

Jesus calls upon us to give our possessions to the poor and to follow Him. He says also:

'He that hath my commandments, and keepeth them, he it is that loveth me: and he that loveth me shall be loved of my Father, and I will love him, and will manifest myself to him.

He that loveth me not keepeth not my sayings: and the word which ye hear is not mine, but the Father's which sent me.

But that the world may know that I love the Father; and as the Father gave me commandment, even so I do. Arise, let us go hence.' (John 14: 21,24,31)

Jesus speaks not His words, but the words of God the Father, Who sent Christ into the world to proclaim the Good News. Jesus loves the faithful who observe His commandments and God the Father will also love them and will open for them the gates of the Kingdom of Heaven.

Jesus said: 'It is easier for a camel to go through the eye of a needle, than for a rich man to enter into the kingdom of God.' (Matthew 19:24)

It means that he who hopes to enter the Kingdom of Heaven, should cease to amass material wealth and should accumulate spiritual goods, which will not disappear at the death of his body but will remain with him eternally.

**The demon of avarice (Philokalia, abridged)**
1. Wise elders say that the demon of avarice comes second after the demon of lechery with regards to the degree of danger for the believer.
2. Believers who yield to the demon of the avarice lose the true faith in God and replace it with the faith in money.
3. They reduce their work on themselves and their prayers, using illnesses as an excuse.
4. The lover of money becomes apostate and abuses the Gospels.
5. The believer who has defeated the demon of the avarice becomes forever free from the concerns about his body, but the one who is trapped by this demon, cannot pray purely.
6. The believer who loves money will never be able to get rid of two serious sins: anger and a longing for a worldly life.
7. The demon of the avarice is considered to be the root of all evil; it gives rise to hatred, vengeance, hostility, murders, cruelty of heart, discords, theft, treachery, rancour.

8. A believer can defeat the demon of the avarice by passionlessness only. Having become passionless, he will not be liable to the above-mentioned sorts of evil. (Philokalia)

**Prayer practice for struggling with the passion of the avarice**
First of all, a believer who suffers from the passion of avarice, should repent before the priest of this passion and ask his blessing to struggle with it.
1. Make a list of the manifestations of this passion during your whole life, divided into periods of seven years. Recall how exactly you sinned while trying to satisfy this passion and those whom you caused to suffer because of this.
2. Sit on a chair in solitude before your iconostasis, let your mind sink in your heart, and recite mentally for half an hour, the following prayer: 'Most Holy Theotokos, Virgin Mary, deliver me from the passion of avarice.'
Recite during another half hour the following prayer: 'Most Holy Theotokos, Virgin Mary, forgive me the sin of avarice.' Recollect during this prayer the persons whom you refused to help materially and caused to suffer because of this passion.
Recite during another half hour the following prayer: 'Most Holy Theotokos, Virgin Mary, cleanse me from the sin of avarice.'
Remember to keep your mind focused on your heart.
Pray to the Holy Theotokos until you feel light at heart.

**Prayer and contemplation exercise combined with the spiritual breath for pleading the Theotokos for support in the struggle with the passion of avarice.**
1. Recite for half an hour the following prayer, combined with the spiritual breath, addressing the Theotokos:
'Most holy Theotokos, deliver me from the sin of avarice.'
Moving life energy upwards along the spine channel while inhaling, pronounce: 'Most holy Theotokos'.

Moving energy downwards along the rear of the 'tube' of the spine, pronounce: 'Deliver me from the sin of avarice.'
2. In order to improve our sinful nature, pronounce for another half hour the following prayer:
'Most holy Theotokos and Virgin, Mary, I repent my sin of avarice.'
Moving life energy upwards along the spine channel while inhaling, pronounce: 'Most holy Theotokos and Virgin, Mary'.
Moving energy downwards along the rear of the 'tube' of the spine while exhaling, pronounce: 'I repent my sin of avarice.' Recollect during this prayer the persons whom you refused to help materially and caused to suffer because of this passion.

The more advanced level of this practice is to focus your mind on your heart during the carrying out of the above-mentioned.

**Prayers, combined with the spiritual breath to the Lord Jesus Christ, the Holy Spirit and God the Father**
Sit on a chair in solitude before your iconostasis and recite mentally for half an hour, the following prayer, combining it with the spiritual breath: 'Lord Jesus Christ, forgive me the sin of avarice.' Recollect during this prayer the persons whom you refused to help materially and caused to suffer because of this passion.
Pronounce during the next half hour the following prayer: 'Lord, Holy Spirit, the Comforter, forgive me the sin of avarice.' Recollect during this prayer the persons whom you refused to help materially and caused to suffer because of this passion.
Pronounce during the next half hour the following prayer:
'Oh God, our Heavenly Father, forgive me the sin of avarice.' Recollect during this prayer the persons whom you refused to help materially and caused to suffer because of this passion.

It is necessary to turn to the message of the Twelfth Arcanum regularly during your entire conscious life, for as soon as you cease sacrificing your passions, your spiritual growth also stops.

The Thirteenth Arcanum

## The Thirteenth Arcanum. Death

The Thirteenth Arcanum states the following spiritual truth: constantly remembering death helps the believer not to recklessly waste the time of his life in searching comfort and pleasures, but to use it to find God and reach the Kingdom of Heaven.
Therefore the believer should constantly keep in mind the day when his soul will part from his body.
The picture of the Thirteenth Arcanum represents an angel carrying the soul of an elder to heaven, as the elder, due to his righteous life, observing the commandments of Christ and praying merited the Kingdom of Heaven. Below, a devil appears from the abyss, regretting that he could not get the elder's soul.

The faithful, who follow Christ, who observe His commandments, wage the spiritual warfare, carry out the inner work, that is, who do the prayer and contemplation exercises for several hours a day, will find God in their heart. Such a person is not afraid of death, for his soul will have eternal life in the Kingdom of Heaven.
The holy Fathers instruct that the believer should constantly remember death, which comes unexpectedly for us. Many of the ascetics who became saints, had made coffins for themselves and put them somewhere near their cells as a reminder of death. Saint Seraphim of Sarov made such a coffin for himself and placed it in the small entrance-hall of his hermitage.
However, the remembrance of death does not mean for the believer cherishing sentimental thoughts about how his funeral will be and what people will say at his graveside, and whether they will be sad or indifferent, but he should direct his mind to the possible lot of his soul.
Remembering death helps the believer to guard the purity of his heart; it guards him from temptation and lapsing into sin. Remembering death inspires the believer to seek God inside himself, to

wage spiritual warfare, to carry out the prayer and contemplation exercises in combination with the spiritual breath for several hours a day. Forgetting about one's own death causes recklessness, carelessness and wasting time. And then the time will come and one will regret it, because there will be no one who can help him. Believers, do not waste the time of your life, do not give in to temptations and do not try to find the means of satisfying sinful passions, but dedicate your lives to seeking God and serving Him. Do not waste time in empty concerns and pleasures, for when the hour of death will strike, your entire life will be reviewed before your inner eyes, and you will see all that you have done, the good and the bad, and when you'll see your sins, your grief will be great, but it will be too late and woe unto those who did not repent during their life.

So let the remembrance of death turn you away from the stinking fumes of hell, and seek the Kingdom of Heaven.

Remember death and try to find God inside you before you reach the end of your life. Use your lifetime as assiduous husbandmen for seeking the Kingdom of Heaven, work hard while you are here, in order to abide eternally in the magnificence of the Kingdom of Heaven. If on the contrary, you live carelessly, then you will suffer in hell and regret the fruitless days and lost chances of salvation.

One of the things which help one to remember one's own death are the stories of the Christian ascetics and saints who after their death, visited their fellow-ascetics in order to help them to become firmly established on the spiritual path. There is a well-known story in Christian tradition, by the monk Gregory, the disciple of St. Basil the New, who lived in Constantinople in the first half of the 10th century. Elder Basil had a female disciple, whose name was Theodora. When Theodora died, old of age, Gregory wanted very much to know where she was taken: with the righteous or to hell, and he asked Elder Basil to help him. Due to the elder's prayer he received a conscious dream in which blessed Theodora told him about the ordeals that she had been going through after her death, before she was finally taken to the bright dwelling of Elder Basil in the Kingdom of Heaven that he had merited by serving God.

Generally speaking, there are seven so called dark toll-houses which the soul comes to after parting from the body, when the angel carries it to the Throne of God. The aerial demons, the dark 'publicans' try to get their 'tax', that is to capture the soul and to take it to hell because of its sinful deeds during its life in the body. Blessed Theodora describes twenty toll-houses, but, generally speaking, there are the seven principal toll-houses, corresponding to the seven deadly sins. Each toll-house bars the way along which the soul ascends at a certain height. If the soul, carried by an angel, passes successfully through the first toll-house, after a while the demons of the second toll-house bar its way, and so long and so forth. In each of the toll-houses the demons present to the soul the list of charges, that is the list of the soul's transgressions of one of the seven sorts of sins which these demons have noted watching the soul during its earthly life. Demons add to this list at will, because of their wicked nature, even transgressions that the soul didn't commit, in order to make the charge more weighty. The angel which carries the soul, protects it from the demon's accusations for they do anything at all in order to draw the soul into hell. It may look approximately as follows:

The angel carries the soul to the Kingdom of Heaven and suddenly a dark, howling pack of demons bars the way. These are the demons of the toll-house of lechery and fornication. 'Halt!' they yell. 'This soul belongs to us: it fornicated during its entire life and now we are entitled to do violence to it.'

'Show me the list of charges,' the angel says.

The chief demon gets a long script and reads it.

'He repented all these sins and the priest gave him absolution,' the angel says, 'therefore you do not have power over him.'

Howling demons attack the soul: 'He belongs to us anyway,' they shout, 'he repented many times, and then he fornicated yet again!' The Angel, holding the soul firmly, breaks through the lines of de-

mons and carries the soul further on. After a while they meet another horde of demons which occupy the toll-house of anger. 'Halt!' they shout angrily. 'It is our soul, it was angry so often that its place is with us in hell only!'
'No,' the angel objects, 'read the list of its transgressions first.'
'We are not going to read it, we do not have time to look into each sinner!'
'No, read out,' the angel insists.
The chief demon comes forth and reads a huge list.
The angel, who knows all the good deeds of the soul like repentance, prayers, fasting, helping its neighbours and so on, says that as this soul repented all its sins in church and received absolution from the priest, the demons of anger do not have power over it. The demons howl from anger, because they do not want to let go the soul. The Angel embraces the soul and carries it further upwards.
'The next toll-house will get you!' the demons yell fiercely.
After a while the toll-house of the love of money bars the way. The demons crowd like a wall, in order not to let the soul reach the Kingdom of Heaven. 'This soul belongs to us as it amassed money until the end of its days on earth!'
'First present the list of indictments,' the angel says.
Demons get long scripts and read out the long lists of greed and avarice.
'Most of these sins were absolved,' the angel comments.
'But not all of them!' howl the demons. 'Now this soul belongs to us for sure!'
'No!' the angel exclaims. 'Here is my list! This person accomplished many good deeds during his life which outweigh the sins of greed.'
The demons howl furiously from vexation that they didn't get the soul.
The angel embraces the soul and carries it further on, protecting it with his list of good deeds in the other toll-houses. In the toll-house of pride however the demons rejoice as the soul had committed

more sins of pride than good deeds, and howling joyfully, they draw the soul to hell.

The Lord God Jesus Christ reigns in the Kingdom of Heaven, illuminating it and the worlds which lie below with the fiery radiance of the Holy Spirit, which comes from His Father in heaven. This spiritual light which is also fire, brings to the pure soul or to the soul which repented its sins, the supreme grace and unspeakable bliss. A pure soul, nourished by God's grace, grows and becomes more and more elevated; and spiritual light shines brightly through it. Gradually it becomes prepared to see the Lord and it will rejoice in meeting Him.

On the contrary, the soul which did not repent its sins cannot bear spiritual light, as when the light comes into the unclean soul it meets a big resistance which man feels as a burning fire inside. Jesus said: 'For every one that doeth evil hateth the light, neither cometh to the light, lest his deeds should be reproved.' (John 3:20)

We can understand from these words that an unclean, sinful soul, cannot live in the Kingdom of Heaven, without undergoing first special purification, for it will be unbearably painful for such a soul to feel the pure radiance of the spiritual light. Therefore, it is not only the guarding angels who do not allow the soul to enter the Kingdom of Heaven, but the soul itself doesn't want to go there in order not to feel this pain.

After the death of the physical body, such a soul will be imprisoned by the demons of one or several toll-houses, according to the sins that this soul has committed, and it will have to spend a certain period of time with them in their dwelling, that is in hell.

The lower the soul descends in hell, the more darkened becomes its conscience, the colder becomes its heart and the more and more dark it becomes. Moving in the space around it, becomes unbearably heavy and slow; an enormous feeling of heaviness, which is impossible to throw off, seizes the soul.

Hell is the place where human beings are tortured so that they atone for the sins they have committed, according to the law of cosmic justice, in order to make them not commit these sins. Hell resembles a system of concentration camps in the other world. There are parts of hell where human beings are chained to the walls of stinking caves; there are places where persons are completely frozen in the ice of the lake because of the sins they have committed and they lose their reason. They forget completely who they are, how their life on earth was, who they were and what they have done.

Sinners who have fornicated a lot are in the part of hell where the demons, animals and huge insects rape them.

There are in hell huge lakes of fire where the sinners feel that they are burning, but they cannot be burnt to ashes, but just feel the pain. This was what the scull of a pagan priest once told Saint Macarius the Great.

There are the shallow lakes of eternal anguish and despair, where the sinners stand with only their heads above the water, in the dark, smothering fog. There is neither a shaft of light nor fresh air, but only gloom, darkness and stuffy heat in the soul, and no hope of salvation.

There are places of sadness where the twilight, cold and limitless despondency seize man's soul and it suffers because of the absence of any light.

There are places where the demons mock and torture the souls, humiliating and outraging them.

In order not to be sentenced to these horrible places in the world behind the curtain, man should turn to God and call for His mercy incessantly. Conversion to God is a long and gradual process, by means of prayers and contemplation exercises in combination with the spiritual breath.

Meditate on the fragment of the 16th chapter of the Gospel by St John, where Jesus predicts to the apostles that He will be soon crucified, and that He will resurrect and appear to the apostles, and they will realize that He is the true Son of the Father in heaven, Who came to save the world.

## The Thirteenth Arcanum

'These things have I spoken unto you, that ye should not be offended.

They shall put you out of the synagogues: yea, the time cometh, that whosoever killeth you will think that he doeth God service.

And these things will they do unto you, because they have not known the Father, nor me.

But these things have I told you, that when the time shall come, ye may remember that I told you of them. And these things I said not unto you at the beginning, because I was with you.

But now I go my way to him that sent me; and none of you asketh me, Whither goest thou?

But because I have said these things unto you, sorrow hath filled your heart.

Nevertheless I tell you the truth; It is expedient for you that I go away: for if I go not away, the Comforter will not come unto you; but if I depart, I will send him unto you.

And when he is come, he will reprove the world of sin, and of righteousness, and of judgment:

Of sin, because they believe not on me;

Of righteousness, because I go to my Father, and ye see me no more;

Of judgment, because the prince of this world is judged.

I have yet many things to say unto you, but ye cannot bear them now.

Howbeit when he, the Spirit of truth, is come, he will guide you into all truth: for he shall not speak of himself; but whatsoever he shall hear, that shall he speak: and he will shew you things to come.

He shall glorify me: for he shall receive of mine, and shall shew it unto you.

All things that the Father hath are mine: therefore said I, that he shall take of mine, and shall shew it unto you.

A little while, and ye shall not see me: and again, a little while, and ye shall see me, because I go to the Father.

Then said some of his disciples among themselves, What is this that he saith unto us, A little while, and ye shall not see me: and again, a little while, and ye shall see me: and, Because I go to the Father? They said therefore, What is this that he saith, A little while? we cannot tell what he saith.
Now Jesus knew that they were desirous to ask him, and said unto them, Do ye enquire among yourselves of that I said, A little while, and ye shall not see me: and again, a little while, and ye shall see me?
Verily, verily, I say unto you, That ye shall weep and lament, but the world shall rejoice: and ye shall be sorrowful, but your sorrow shall be turned into joy.
A woman when she is in travail hath sorrow, because her hour is come: but as soon as she is delivered of the child, she remembereth no more the anguish, for joy that a man is born into the world.
And ye now therefore have sorrow: but I will see you again, and your heart shall rejoice, and your joy no man taketh from you.
And in that day ye shall ask me nothing. Verily, verily, I say unto you, Whatsoever ye shall ask the Father in my name, he will give it you.
Hitherto have ye asked nothing in my name: ask, and ye shall receive, that your joy may be full.' (John 16:1-24)
It is difficult for believers to follow steadily the spiritual path and to struggle with their passions, and therefore they should plead God for help in the spiritual warfare.
Plead the Father in Heaven in the Name of Christ to spread Christianity and He will help you;
Plead with God in the Name of Christ for help in taming your passions and God will help you;
Plead with God in the Name of Christ for help in observing the commandments and God will help you;
Plead with God in the Name of Christ for protection from demons and God will help you;
Plead with God in the Name of Christ for help on the spiritual Path and God will help you.

Jesus said: 'These things have I spoken unto you in proverbs: but the time cometh, when I shall no more speak unto you in proverbs, but I shall shew you plainly of the Father.
At that day ye shall ask in my name: and I say not unto you, that I will pray the Father for you:
For the Father himself loveth you, because ye have loved me, and have believed that I came out from God.
I came forth from the Father, and am come into the world: again, I leave the world, and go to the Father.' (John16:25-28)
'Behold, the hour cometh, yea, is now come, that ye shall be scattered, every man to his own, and shall leave me alone: and yet I am not alone, because the Father is with me.
These things I have spoken unto you, that in me ye might have peace. In the world ye shall have tribulation: but be of good cheer; I have overcome the world.' (John16:32-33)
One of the big obstacles on the path of finding God inside you are blaspheming thoughts.

**About blaspheming thoughts (Philokalia, abridged)**
1. Blaspheming thoughts are thoughts which insult and abuse the Lord.
2. Blaspheming thoughts come from a demon which penetrates into the believer's soul and insults the Lord, for the demons hate God and slander His Name.
3. Sometimes it is drink which allows a demon-slanderer to settle in the believer's soul, but the main cause of being possessed by such demons is great pride.
4. Usually the blaspheming thoughts intrude in the believer when he wants to pray; the demon tries to prevent him from repenting and asking God for help.
5. The demons not only blaspheme God, but they also instil in the believer who prays the most loathsome swear-words aiming at driving the believer into despair so that he stops praying.

6. This kind of demon appears all of a sudden, pronounces swearwords using the believer's tongue, and disappears instantaneously. Therefore it is extremely difficult to fight them.
7. Other kinds of demons enter the believer slowly, which gives him time to ward off the attack.
8. The cause and the root of blaspheming thoughts is pride and condemnation of one's neighbour. If we stop condemning our neighbour, blaspheming thoughts will have no power over us.
9. Those who despise the demons of blasphemy get rid of them, but those who attempt to struggle with them by words, lose the battle.
10. The best means to fight these demons is to call upon the Name of the Lord, that is to recite the Jesus Prayer.

**The prayer practice for the struggle with blaspheming thoughts**
Sit down before your home iconostasis and recite the following prayers, each for half an hour, combining them with the spiritual breath:

'Most Holy Theotokos, deliver me from the demon of blasphemy and foul language.'
'Lord Jesus Christ, deliver me from the demon of blasphemy and foul language.'
'Lord, Holy Spirit, deliver me from the demon of blasphemy and foul language.'
'O God, our Father in Heaven, deliver me from the demon of blasphemy and foul language.'

**Prayer practice of the Thirteenth Arcanum**
Sit down before your home iconostasis and recite the following prayers, in combination with the spiritual breath:

Introductory prayer for five minutes: 'Most holy Theotokos, I promise to carry out the prayer and contemplation practices with the spiritual breath for three hours a day.'

Main prayer: 'Most holy Theotokos, delay the day of my death so that I can find the Lord inside myself.'
Moving life energy upwards along the spine channel while inhaling, pronounce: 'Most holy Theotokos, delay the day of my death'.
Moving energy downwards along the rear of the 'tube' of the spine while exhaling, pronounce: 'so that I can find the Lord inside myself.'

Introductory prayer for five minutes: 'Lord Jesus Christ, I promise to carry out the prayer and contemplation practices and the spiritual breath for three hours a day.'
Main prayer: 'Lord Jesus Christ, delay the day of my death so that I can reach the Kingdom of Heaven.'
Moving life energy upwards along the spine channel while inhaling, pronounce: 'Lord Jesus Christ, delay the day of my death'.
Moving energy downwards along the rear of the 'tube' of the spine while exhaling, pronounce: 'so that I can reach the Kingdom of Heaven.'

Introductory prayer for five minutes: 'Lord, Holy Spirit, the Comforter, I promise to carry out the prayer and contemplation practices and the spiritual breath for three hours a day.'
Main prayer: 'Lord, Holy Spirit, the Comforter, delay the day of my death so that I can merge with You.'
Moving life energy upwards along the spine channel while inhaling, pronounce: 'Lord, Holy Spirit, the Comforter, delay the day of my death'.
Moving energy downwards along the rear of the 'tube' of the spine while exhaling, pronounce: 'so that I can merge with you.'

Introductory prayer for five minutes: 'O God, our Father in Heaven, I promise to carry out the prayer and contemplation practices and the spiritual breath for three hours a day.'

Main prayer: 'God, our Father in Heaven, delay the day of my death so that I can merge with You.'
Moving life energy upwards along the spine channel while inhaling, pronounce: 'God, Our Father in Heaven, delay the day of my death'. Moving energy downwards along the rear of the 'tube' of the spine while exhaling, pronounce: 'so that I can merge with you.'

In order to find God in one's heart it is necessary to turn regularly to the message of the Thirteenth Arcanum during one's entire conscious life.

The Fourteenth Arcanum

## The Fourteenth Arcanum. Serenity of the Heart

The Fourteenth Arcanum states the following spiritual truth: the serenity of the heart is acquired by humility.

In order to find God inside one's heart one should immerse in inner silence, which is impossible without acquiring inner balance. Inner balance comes through meekness, lack of anger and humility. The picture of the Arcanum represents two ascetics living on top of pillars. They acquired the state of inner silence and serenity; they renounced the world and converse with God. The novice who bows before the elder symbolizes meekness, lack of anger and humility.

When we have acquired inner serenity, our prayers reach the Lord quicker, and He then opens our heart and converses with us.

At such a moment we realize that our nature is light-bearing, for we are created by the Lord in His image. The deeper we immerse ourselves in His innermost purity, the better is our awareness of our higher nature. When we identify ourselves with our body, we immediately forget the necessity to re-unite with our Creator. Being carried away by our feelings, we forget our most important duty to the Lord: to become aware of our spiritual nature and to find the Lord inside us.

Our desires bind us to the world around us, which makes us forget our Creator and our supreme goal. Wise elders know that it is impossible to satisfy our desires, for they are endlessly various. In this sense our desires and wishes are our enemies. On the other hand, it is our own lower nature which gives rise to these wishes, and therefore it is very difficult to eliminate them. However, it is possible to use their energy to seek God. And when we have found inner serenity, the Lord will allow us to come to know His infinite beauty and creativity. He will reveal to us such incredible bliss of the higher worlds that the external world will fade in comparison with their eternal glory. However, in order to be worthy of this revelation, a believer should cultivate such qualities as lack of anger, meekness and humility.

Irritability is caused by an unconscious desire of the believer to 're-make' the world according to his idea of how 'this all should be'. Anger is the next stage, and it is a wish to do evil to the one who opposes you. As fire can burn a wooden house to ashes, so anger can burn inside the believer's soul everything which was obtained by his persistent work on himself. A believer's lack of anger means the ability to endure humiliation, ridicule and insults from one's fellowmen. A believer should be indifferent to all this.

The best means of curing anger is humility. One of the practical ways to teach an irritable and irate believer humility, is to put him in a situation where he will have to communicate with people like himself. Rough and irate people will not tolerate his anger and they will respond with the same or even greater anger. Thus the believer will have a choice: either to learn to restrain his anger and improve his character or to become aware of his inveterate weakness. In any case the believer should observe the following rule: when someone treats him roughly, he should restrain his anger and not let it manifest itself. Thus he will learn humility.

Anger is caused by a certain kind of demons which settled in our soul. If the believer allows the feeling of anger to be expressed by word or action, the demon of anger grows and becomes stronger. If there is no spiritual mentor or other believers to correct him and the demon realizes that there is no one at the moment to punish him, he will drive the believer to manifest himself more and more recklessly. And when the demon of anger gains a firm hold in the believer's soul it will be very difficult to drive him away. Therefore, he should fight his, which is in fact the demon's, anger without any pity for himself and should never react angrily to insults and ridicule no matter who does this to him.

It seems to be relatively easy to endure even severe criticism or mockery from an older and more experienced believer, or a layman. But when a young and inexperienced novice laughs at a joke which your spiritual mentor has made about you, in your presence, then restraining the anger becomes a very difficult task.

Anger is actually the consequence of demons of anger seizing the believer, and he needs all his willpower to get his soul out of their dreadful embrace. Anger burns the finest and gentlest sprouts of the virtues, obtained by means of prayer inside the soul and it eliminates the aspiration to God. The Lord does not accept irate believers and their labour in the field of piety and prayer practices is in vain.

Therefore the believer should develop the quality of not being angry at those who criticise him, especially unjustly, or ridicule him. He shouldn't lose control over the demons of anger even for a moment, because in a couple of minutes they can ruin everything that he has been building for many days, months, years and drive him into deepest hell. A believer should be especially alert when someone is angry at him, because someone's anger feeds 'his' demons of anger and they become even stronger.

Next to humility, meekness is the powerful weapon against anger. The believer should cultivate the quality of meekness and arm himself with it. Meekness however, like a small plant, needs great care and it grows when the believer vigilantly guards the purity of his heart, not allowing angry and malicious spirits that entrenched themselves in the depth of his soul, to penetrate there. Therefore humility and meekness are not to be found in fainthearted and weak believers, but only in those who have enough willpower to keep themselves under control.

A sign of supreme meekness can be that a believer preserves peace and love in his soul for someone who insults and jeers at him. A sign of extreme irascibility is that even when alone, a believer continues to quarrel with his insulters by means of words and gestures. The Holy Spirit brings light, peace and joy to the believer's soul, while anger brings darkness, irritation and gloomy thoughts. Therefore, as long as there is anger in the believer's heart, the Holy Spirit cannot enter.

The believer shows his humility if he is not angry at his neighbours criticism; if he doesn't respond with roughness when someone is rough with him; if he is not irritated with someone who is irritated with him. If someone slanders him, he accepts this without anger, because he sees it as God's ordeal: God investigates the degree of his humility and checks whether the believer has become proud of himself. The believer thinks that it is the Lord Who lets people abuse him so that he will be able to atone for them through the patient endurance of their anger. The believer is humble if he is not angry when things around him don't go the way he wants; when something he has created is spoiled or destroyed. Therefore he should control his passions and be able not to allow them to seize him.

In order to be humble, a believer should indispensably read the morning and evening prayers, repent his sins at least once a week in church and try not to increase their number and seriousness and regularly read the prayer of forgiveness for all his neighbours and people around him. This is one of the generally known forms of humility, but there is another, less known form of humility: not to grumble against one's spiritual mentor, but to fulfil his demands and requests and to accept humbly his admonitions, corrections and remarks. It is the most difficult task, as the words of an elder hit the very core of the passion and of the sinful acts of the believer. Being meek means never to respond rudely to the sharp remarks of his spiritual mentor, which can cause an intense inner pain, but to humbly endure the suffering of his soul, knowing that it purifies him from sinful passions and brings him great spiritual profit. A believer should learn meekness and humbleness of heart from the Theotokos.

**Exercises which help to cultivate humility**
Jesus said: 'But I say unto you, That ye resist not evil: but whosoever shall smite thee on thy right cheek, turn to him the other also.
And if any man will sue thee at the law, and take away thy coat, let him have thy cloak also.' (Matthew 5:39-40)

1. Try during the moments when you are unjustly accused, ridiculed, humiliated or abused, not to answer this with anger, but to accept the accusations, jeers and anger humbly. Say to the one who slanders you: 'I accept it.' If you should feel your anger rising, inhale and exhale slowly and deeply several times, it will help to diminish the anger and to curb it.

Attend church services and say not less than forty prayers of forgiveness for the person who accused you unjustly or insulted, or jeered at you and humiliated you.

2. Humility means not only acceptance of mockery and ridicule of fellow-men, but also to accept humbly the illnesses that the Lord allows to come on you so that you can atone for your sins in this way. If this happens and you become ill, then your practice will be to thank God in your prayers that He allowed this illness so that it may tame your raging passions, and you may think of your inevitable death; you will then do the prayer and contemplation exercises, combined with the spiritual breath, and no longer postpone it day by day.

3. If misfortune or grief has struck you, then your practice will be to thank God in your prayers that He allowed you to become aware of the fact that you have become too identified with e.g. your beloved and you have forgotten the spiritual path. Thank God that He reminded you of the first commandment: to love God more than anything in the world for Jesus said: 'He that loveth father or mother more than me is not worthy of me: and he that loveth son or daughter more than me is not worthy of me.' (Matthew 10:37)

The above-mentioned exercises seem to be simple but putting them into practice is incredibly difficult.

He who has acquired true humility never condemns his neighbours, never backbites or slanders.

One's condemnation of one's neighbours is a serious obstacle on the path to God, for such a believer, instead of saying the Jesus Prayer, tracks down the shortcomings of his neighbours and voluptuously criticises them.

### About the demon of condemnation (Philokalia, abridged)

Jesus said: 'He that is without sin among you, let him first cast a stone at her.' (John 8:7)

1. When the demon of condemnation takes possession of the believer, then he forgets his own sins and remembers the sins of his neighbours.
2. Condemnation stains the soul and moves it away from God.
3. The Lord is merciful, He forgives the sinners who repent and He waits patiently and mercifully for the repentance of those who haven't yet repented.
4. The demon of condemnation instils constantly into one's mind malicious thoughts about the sins of one's fellow-men. It is true that 'there is no man who lives without sinning', as it is said in the burial service, but Christ said: let the one who doesn't have sins cast the first stone at the unfaithful woman.'
5. The demon of condemnation leads the believer away from repenting his own sins.
6. The believer who is trapped in the web of the demon of condemnation doesn't see the log in his own eye but notices even a speck of dust in the eye of his neighbour.
7. Condemnation turns easily into backbiting and slander of one's neighbour.
8. It is a big sin to condemn spiritual mentors and priests, for the spiritual mentors and priests lead the believers to God, this is their sacred duty. They have the church which supports them, while their critics have nothing but backbiting and the desire to lead people astray from the path to God.

The passion of condemnation is cured by humility and remembrance of one's own sins.

Backbiting and slander are enormous barriers on the path to the Kingdom of Heaven. A believer who is captured by these passions, instead of loving his neighbours, being compassionate with them and helping them to ascend to the Lord, slanders and criticizes them. By doing this he closes his heart and then becomes more and more embittered. Christ will never appear in an evil heart, for it is against His teaching.

## About the passion of backbiting and slander (Philokalia, abridged)

1. Virtues elevate the believer to the Kingdom of Heaven, while passions drag him down, like iron chains, into the depth of hell.

2. Malice and hatred give rise to backbiting and slander, they are like a concealed disease which defiles the soul.

3. Backbiting and slander eradicate the love of God, defile and eliminate the purity of heart.

4. If you recall that Judas was among Christ's disciples, and the robber was among murderers, but then Judas betrayed Christ, while the robber was forgiven by Christ and was taken to heaven, you will stop backbiting and condemning those who sin.

5. Let the one who wants to defeat the demon of backbiting and slander, ascribe the guilt not to the one who sins but to the demon which seduces him to commit sins.

6. If you hear your neighbour backbiting and condemning, stop him and tell him that each of us has many sins and it is better to condemn ourselves than our neighbour. 'Judge not, that ye be not judged.' (Matthew 7:1)

7. It is he who did not repent his own sins who condemns his neighbours, backbites and slanders them. Do not condemn sinners for God's judgment is not known to men. It happens sometimes that those whose sins are known, have repented in secret, while those who have been condemning them did not repent their sins. Sometimes great sinners have accomplished in secret, as atonement, even more good deeds, while those who laughed at them, remained as they were, without repenting their own sins.

8. It happens often that those who backbite, slander and condemn their neighbours fall into the trap of the same sins.

## The Fourteenth Arcanum

9. If a believer should see his sins as clearly as the Lord sees them, he would not have time for backbiting, slander and condemnation, for day and night he would plead God for forgiveness.
10. He who slanders, backbites and condemns his neighbours, condemns his own soul to perish soon.
11. Backbiting is the result of hatred and rancour. Backbiting is a serious disease which kills love and gives rise to hypocrisy.
12. Backbiting defiles and burdens the believer's heart, ruins its purity and throws him in the abyss of darkness.
13. In order to eradicate backbiting, it is necessary to blame not the one who sinned but the demon that seduced the believer.

**Prayer practice for struggling with the passion of condemnation, backbiting and slander**
First of all a believer, who has the passion of condemnation, backbiting and slander, should repent before the priest of this passion and ask his blessing to struggle with it.
1. Make a list of the manifestations of this passion during your whole life, divided into periods of seven years. Recall how exactly you have condemned, about whom you have been backbiting and whom you slandered.
2. Sit on a stool in solitude before your iconostasis, let your mind sink in your heart, and recite mentally for half an hour, the following prayer: 'Most Holy Theotokos, Virgin Mary, deliver me from the passion of condemnation, backbiting and slander.'
Recite for another half hour the following prayer: 'Most Holy Theotokos, Virgin Mary, forgive me the sin of condemnation, backbiting and slander.' Recollect during this prayer the persons whom you have condemned, about whom you have been backbiting and whom you slandered.
Recite for another half hour the following prayer: 'Most Holy Theotokos, Virgin Mary, cleanse me from the sin of condemnation, backbiting and slander.'
Remember to keep your mind focused on your heart.

Pray to the Holy Theotokos until you feel light at heart.

**Prayer and contemplation exercise combined with the spiritual breath for pleading the Theotokos for support in the struggle with the passion of condemnation, backbiting and slander.**

1. Recite for half an hour the following prayer, combined with the spiritual breath, addressing the Theotokos:
'Most holy Theotokos, deliver me from the sin of condemnation, backbiting and slander.'
Moving life energy upwards along the spine channel while inhaling, pronounce: 'Most holy Theotokos'.
Moving energy downwards along the rear of the 'tube' of the spine, pronounce: 'Deliver me from the sin of condemnation, backbiting and slander.'
2. In order to improve our sinful nature, pronounce for another half hour the following prayer:
'Most holy Theotokos and Virgin, Mary, I repent my sin of condemnation, backbiting and slander.'
Moving life energy upwards along the spine channel while inhaling, pronounce: 'Most holy Theotokos and Virgin, Mary'.
Moving energy downwards along the rear of the 'tube' of the spine while exhaling, pronounce: 'I repent my sin of condemnation, backbiting and slander.' Recollect during this prayer the persons whom you have condemned, about whom you have been backbiting and whom you slandered.
The more advanced level of this practice is to focus your mind on your heart during the carrying out of the above-mentioned.

**Prayers, combined with the spiritual breath to the Lord Jesus Christ, the Holy Spirit and God the Father**

Sit on a chair in solitude before your iconostasis and recite mentally for half an hour, the following prayer, combining it with the spiritual breath: 'Lord Jesus Christ, forgive me the sin of condemnation,

## The Fourteenth Arcanum

backbiting and slander.' Mention at the same time the names of the persons whom you have condemned, about whom you have been backbiting and whom you slandered.

Pronounce for another half hour the following prayer: 'Lord, Holy Spirit, the Comforter, forgive me the sin of condemnation, backbiting and slander.' Mention at the same time the names of the persons whom you have condemned, about whom you have been backbiting and whom you slandered.

Pronounce for another half hour the following prayer:
'Oh God, our Heavenly Father, forgive me the sin of condemnation, backbiting and slander.' Mention at the same time the names of the persons whom you have condemned, about whom you have been backbiting and whom you slandered.

It is necessary to carry out the exercises of the Fourteenth Arcanum until you have eliminated inside you the passion of condemnation, backbiting and slander and have obtained inner balance through humility, lack of anger and meekness.

The Fifteenth Arcanum

## The Fifteenth Arcanum. Overcoming Lucifer's Temptation

The Fifteenth Arcanum states the following spiritual truth: on the path to God the believer clashes with Lucifer, the Evil One.

The picture of the Arcanum represents the path to the Kingdom of Heaven which is barred by the devil. He tempts or frightens the believer in all possible ways in order to make him fall away from God and then to throw him in hell.

The devil is also that very force which perverts and turns into evil the sexual relationship between man and woman, distorts the commandment that God gave to people: 'Be fruitful and increase in number; fill the earth and subdue it.' (Gen. 1:28). Lucifer, the Evil One swore an oath that he wouldn't allow humanity to ascend to the Kingdom of Heaven. Therefore he bars the way to those who want to find the Lord. Many do not believe this as they consider it an old myth or a fairy tale. However, those who aspire to reach heaven meet insurmountable obstacles inside and outside themselves. For example, the people most close and dear to your heart suddenly condemn your striving and consider you a madman. There grows suddenly in you apathy and a feeling of senselessness in striving to find God, and a little voice inside you, pretending to be the most intimate to your soul, constantly whispers about the senselessness of your purpose to live according the God's commandments and find God inside. The little voice inside you whispers that you should live a normal life and then all will be all right, and you become overwhelmed with sadness and despondency. You notice that no matter how hard you try to begin a new life, filled with prayers, repentance of your sins and fasting, something makes you 'postpone it for the day after tomorrow', then for another day and so long and so forth. Then you discover that you have no time at all for the prayer and contemplation exercises and for works of virtue. Then a thought comes that the Lord will admit you to the Kingdom of Heaven anyway, because of His mercy, and you need not do anything, just wait for this. This kind of thought will come until the end of your days just to prevent you from starting the spiritual warfare.

Immediately when you decide to pray, something will try to distract you, under any pretext, significant or less significant, and there will be no end to it.

Then you will discover that you have sinned a lot, which will fill your soul with heaviness, so that whenever you try to do the prayer and contemplation exercises, you will fall asleep and the only thing you can do is to fall on your bed from a feeling of exhaustion. This, however, happens not because of a lack of energy on your side, but because the dark power of the Evil One and of the army of his innumerable servants, the demons, will try to hinder in all possible ways your attempt to follow the path of spiritual warfare which will lead you to finding God inside yourself.

The Evil One tries to turn away the believers from God and directs them to cultivating and satisfying their passions, for any passion can deter you from waging the spiritual warfare for a long time, at least until you become aware of it, and oppose it by repentance and willpower. And behind each and every passion there lurks a demon which gives rise to the passion inside you. The difference between the passion and a natural wish, is that the passion is insatiable and no matter how often you satisfy it, it grows more and more until it ruins you completely. If a passion has got a hold on you, it means that you allowed the demon of the passion to settle in your soul and he immediately starts to torture you and eventually he will destroy you.

These are the passions that destroy your soul and turn you away from God:

1. The passion of avarice, when you think that money is the most important thing in life. In this case, earning money takes the biggest part of your time and energy and you have nothing left for the quest for God.

## The Fifteenth Arcanum

2. The passion of fornication and the addiction to the bodily pleasure, when it seems that the principal meaning of life is enjoying a sexual relationship. Giving in to this passion, the believer pollutes to a large extent his soul and his body, and, because of this, bars his path to God, and opens instead the path to the lower worlds of malice and suffering.

3. The passion of gluttony, when man eats, as the saying goes, not in order to live, but lives in order to eat, and this passion bars his way to the Kingdom of Heaven.

4. The passion of condemnation of one's neighbour, backbiting and slander. Giving in to this passion a believer, instead of cultivating pious prayers to God in his soul, allows pride, irritability to grow, darkens and shuts off his heart which is predestined to love God.

5. The passion of verbosity prevents you from immersing yourself in prayer and surrounds you with worldly bustle.

6. The passion of irritability and anger fills your heart with malice and makes you similar to the demons, who hate the Lord.

7. The passion of vanity – the insatiable love of fame – leads you astray from the spiritual path and makes you seek the encouragement and praise of your fellow-men, whom you bring in this way to the passion of flattering and lying.

8. The passion of pride cools your heart quickly and carries you away into the worlds of Lucifer which are at enmity with the Lord and mankind.

9. The passion of despondency and sadness kills your faith in God. You cease the spiritual warfare and fall in the power of mocking demons.

God created the world out of His love and goodness. He granted all the spiritual beings that He created after His image, the capacity to grow towards Him and to become more and more like Him. The first angel He created was Lucifer – the bearer of God's light, who was given the task of governing the Universe. However it seemed to Lucifer that the light which was in him, was not the light of God, but his own light and he conceived the wish to govern the Universe on his own, without God. He immediately lost touch with God, and the spiritual light which God had given him, disappeared from his heart. Lucifer fell into the cold and darkness and became the father of slander and malice, receiving the name 'Satan'.

But the archangel who was second after Lucifer by his talents, had expressed his love of God in the following words: 'There is no one like God'. These words in Aramaic are 'Michael' and this is exactly the meaning of the name of the archangel who became the Supreme Commander of God's hosts. Together with the majority of the angels who remained faithful to God he banished the Satan and the angels who followed him from God's world and they fell to earth and then even deeper. Their dwelling is exactly the hell.

Lucifer wanted to ascend to the worlds of light by force, but God did not allow him to. Then Lucifer decided to take vengeance on God and he seduced our forefather Adam. Adam broke God's commandment and fell, and together with him the entire human race fell from the spiritual heights and lost the connection with God and forgot Him.

Jesus Christ, God the Son was incarnated as man and He accomplished His mission: to re-unite the fallen spirit and soul of man with God. To live with God and in God is the true salvation of the soul. Therefore Jesus said: 'All that ever came before me are thieves and robbers: but the sheep did not hear them' (John 10:8)

Lucifer and his servants, the demons, the fallen angels, continue to hinder in all possible ways the reuniting of man with God, by arousing passions, but most of all they hate those who attempt following Christ. Therefore the demons attack most intensely the Christian believers and ascetics, trying to seduce and trap them in all possible sinful designs, feelings and acts.

Read the passages from the Gospel of Luke and understand the difference between Christ, Who guides us to reunite us with God through faith, hope and love, and the cunning Lucifer-Satan, who deceitfully lures us because of his malice into the inferno, in order to condemn us to eternal suffering.

## The Fifteenth Arcanum

'And Jesus being full of the Holy Ghost returned from Jordan, and was led by the Spirit into the wilderness, being forty days tempted of the devil. And in those days he did eat nothing: and when they were ended, he afterward hungered.
And the devil said unto him, If thou be the Son of God, command this stone that it be made bread. And Jesus answered him, saying, It is written, That man shall not live by bread alone, but by every word of God.'
The body is fed by bread, but the soul is attracted to God and is nourished by God's Word, the spiritual nourishment: divine light, spiritual joy, love and divine, spiritual purity.

Jesus said: 'No man putteth a piece of a new garment upon an old; if otherwise, then both the new maketh a rent, and the piece that was taken out of the new agreeth not with the old. And no man putteth new wine into old bottles; else the new wine will burst the bottles, and be spilled, and the bottles shall perish. But new wine must be put into new bottles; and both are preserved. No man also having drunk old wine straightway desireth new: for he saith, The old is better.' (Luke 5:36-39)
People of the old faith will never accept a new faith, because the old faith will remain for them more understandable, dear and close. Therefore the Jewish clergy and the majority of the believers did not believe in Christ.

'For whosoever shall be ashamed of me and of my words, of him shall the Son of man be ashamed, when he shall come in his own glory, and in his Father's, and of the holy angels.' (Luke 9:26)
When the soul of the believer, who was ashamed of his faith in Christ before his fellow-men and fell away from Him each time it suited him, will stand at the last judgment before God, Christ will also turn His face away from him.

Jesus said: 'All things are delivered to me of my Father: and no man knoweth who the Son is, but the Father; and who the Father is, but the Son, and he to whom the Son will reveal him.' (Luke 10:22)
No one but the Father in Heaven knows the true divine aspect of Jesus Christ, and no one but Christ knows the Father in Heaven. Only they can come to know it, to whom Christ will reveal this great mystery.

Jesus said: 'And I say unto you, Ask, and it shall be given you; seek, and ye shall find; knock, and it shall be opened unto you.
 For every one that asketh receiveth; and he that seeketh findeth; and to him that knocketh it shall be opened.' (Luke 11:9-10)
'If ye then, being evil, know how to give good gifts unto your children: how much more shall your heavenly Father give the Holy Spirit to them that ask him?' (Luke 11:13)
Ask the Lord for help, and He will give it to you according to your faith; seek God and you will find Him; knock at the gate of the Kingdom of Heaven and they will open, and God's grace will be given to you in proportion to the purity of your soul.

Jesus said to the apostles: 'No man, when he hath lighted a candle, covereth it with a vessel, or putteth it under a bed; but setteth it on a candlestick, that they which enter in may see the light.' (Luke 8:16)
Those who received from the Lord the Holy Spirit, shouldn't isolate themselves but they should proclaim that Christ has come, and proclaim His teaching.

Jesus said: 'The light of the body is the eye: therefore when thine eye is single, thy whole body also is full of light; but when thine eye is evil, thy body also is full of darkness.'
The spiritual eye is like a lamp for the body. If the spiritual eye witnesses the Holy Spirit, then it will be clean and the body will become clean also. If the spiritual eye is darkened then the radiance

of the Holy Spirit won't come into the soul and it will not shine; the body then also will be dark.

Jesus said: 'I am come to send fire on the earth; and what will I, if it be already kindled?'

Jesus Christ brought the spiritual fire of His Father in Heaven on earth and His great wish was that this fire should flame in the hearts of the people who believed in Him.
Jesus said: 'Suppose ye that I am come to give peace on earth? I tell you, Nay; but rather division:
For from henceforth there shall be five in one house divided, three against two, and two against three.
The father shall be divided against the son, and the son against the father; the mother against the daughter, and the daughter against the mother; the mother in law against her daughter in law, and the daughter in law against her mother in law.' (Luke 12:51-53)
Those who believe in Christ will separate from those who do not believe in Him and they will have nothing in common.

Pharisees asked Jesus when the Kingdom of God will come? Jesus answered them: 'The kingdom of God cometh not with observation: Neither shall they say, Lo here! or, lo there! for, behold, the kingdom of God is within you.' (Luke 17:20-21)
The answer of Jesus contains the definition of the spiritual path: the believer should seek the Kingdom of God and the Lord Jesus Christ inside his clean soul. The soul is clean when the body, the heart and the mind are clean. In order to keep them clean it is necessary to live according to God's commandments and not according to one's passions, as passions stain the soul. And if the believer could not prevent lapsing in sin, then he should repent so that his soul becomes clean again.

**On the insanity of pride (Philokalia, abridged)**
1. As elders say, pride is the stronghold of the demons; the believer who falls in the trap of pride loses his achievements on the path to God.
2. The biggest pride is to reject God.
3. Pride is the main cause of anger, as the proud don't take into consideration the opinion of others. The proud man considers himself always right.
4. A believer who fell in the sin of pride becomes a hypocrite in order to justify himself. Pride becomes the reason of his fall.
5. Pride is the biggest depository of man's sins, it is the enemy of God and the basis of unmerciful condemnation.
6. A believer who is possessed by the demon of pride doesn't feel compassion for his neighbour, he might torture people and be their most inhuman judge.
7. A proud believer is not able to become a novice; he considers himself to be a spiritual mentor, without any reason.
8. If the believer has defeated all his passions, but not the passion of pride, then his victory is in vain, as the power of pride is equal to the power of all the other passions together.
9. In order to help the believer defeat the demon of pride, the Lord lets the believer be disgraced.
10. In order to get hold of the believer the demon of pride appears to him as an angel of light or a martyr, and he reveals to him the knowledge of demons under the disguise of God's gifts. Gradually the demon deprives those believers of their reason, and makes them insane.
11. A proud believer doesn't remember his sins and therefore he thinks that he has nothing to repent.
12. A proud believer has no virtues and in his heart sinful designs are born instead of prayer.
13. Many believers have acquired a cold heart and they become insensitive: their soul has grown numb and they feel nothing. They take this deathly state of the soul for impartiality. However, when

their soul parts from the body they become aware of the depth of their fall. (Philokalia)

### The methods of opposing the demon of pride
Holy elders teach that the believer, in order to oppose the demon of pride, should act as follows:
1. Humbly accept the admonitions and instructions of his spiritual mentor.
2. Endure humbly the mockery and insults of laymen with regard to the believer's faith in God.
3. Endure patiently and without anger unjust accusations and insults and pray for the offenders.
4. Pray God for the salvation of the souls of his enemies.

As the believer is not able to defeat the demon of pride on his own, he should plead God for help. For this he should recite for several hours a day the following prayers:
'Lord Jesus Christ, deliver me from the demon of pride.'
'Most Holy Theotokos, deliver me from the demon of pride.'
'Lord, Holy Spirit, deliver me from the demon of pride.'
'O God, our Father in Heaven, deliver me from the demon of pride.'

To make the prayers even more effective it is necessary to combine them with the spiritual breath.

Moving life energy upwards along the spine channel while inhaling, recite one of the prayers two or three times.

Having moved energy around the spiritual eye and moving energy downwards along the rear of the 'tube' of the spine, recite again that prayer two or three times.

Doing this, you can hit the root of the sinful passion and with God's help, protect yourself from it.

If you experience reciting these prayers as very arduous, it means that purifying yourself from the passion, this is, struggling with the passion, is going successfully. You will feel that the heaviness and dirt, which are the essence of pride, and which darkened your soul, will disappear. Each prayer should be recited for not less than half an hour.

These prayers should be recited daily until the passion of pride is eliminated in you. However, elders instruct us that the believer should vigilantly guard his purity of heart, mind and body, otherwise the passion of pride will assault him again.

**On the demon of fornication (Philokalia, abridged)**
Holy elders say that if the believer does not defeat the demon of fornication, he will not be able to ascend to the Kingdom of Heaven

1. The demon of fornication is one of the strongest and most perfidious demons and if he conquers a believer, then the believer will inevitably fall and move away from God. He will have to do a lot of inner work, praying, repenting and bodily work, such as fasting, in order to purify his soul and to step again on the ladder which leads to heaven.
2. It is impossible to stop the demon of fornication just by reasoning about how dangerous he is for those who strive to find God.
3. The demon of fornication pretends to be chaste when he approaches the object of his lust. Therefore never trust your body until you will be standing before God.
4. As elders say, satiation of the belly is the mother of fornication.
5. Fornication defiles the soul by lascivious dreams, and it defiles the body by pollutions.
6. The Lord is pleased when believers preserve the purity of their body and restrain from fornicating, and the demons are pleased when believers fall into the pit of fornication. Fornication is the demons' favourite sin.
7. Some believers admire and praise a beautiful woman, while other believers praise even more the Creator, Who created her.
8. To avoid nightly pollutions it is necessary to recite the Jesus Prayer at night.

The holy elders instruct us that the passion of fornication is killed by eating little and fasting, never being idle but always working, and by praying for help to Jesus Christ with the lips and with the heart. Also by not gazing at attractive women and men, and by not accepting the thought of fornication when it seizes us. (Abridged from the Philokalia)

**Prayer practice for struggling with the passion of fornication**
First of all, a believer who suffers from the passion of fornication, should repent of this passion to the priest and ask his blessing to struggle with it.
The believer can oppose the passion of fornication in himself in the following way.
Sit on a stool in solitude before your iconostasis and recite mentally the following prayer, carrying out at the same time the spiritual breath:
'Most Holy Theotokos, Virgin Mary, give me strength to resist the passion of fornication.'
'Lord Jesus Christ, help me to eliminate the passion of fornication.'
'Lord, Holy Spirit, help me to cut off the design to fornicate.'
'O God, our Father in Heaven, help me to drive off the passion of fornication.'
You should recite each prayer for not less than half an hour. You will feel while saying the prayer and carrying out the spiritual breath, that the passion of fornication is expelled from you and hangs around you like a grey cloud, which will be scattered by prayers.

The believer should consider the message of the Fifteenth Arcanum regularly in the course of his life and oppose the temptations praying God for help.

The Sixteenth Arcanum

THE SIXTEENTH ARCANUM. THE RULES FOR ASCENDING TO THE KINGDOM OF HEAVEN

The Sixteenth Arcanum states the following spiritual truth: a believer who attempts to enter the Kingdom of Heaven should observe the rules for ascending.

The picture of the Arcanum represents the symbolical ladder along which the monks and the believers climb to the Kingdom of Heaven in order to find Christ, while demons try to seduce them and to drag them into hell.

1. The Christian way which leads to the Kingdom of Heaven demands acquiring and preserving the crystal-clear purity of the soul, daily prayer and contemplation practice and faithfulness to the Lord Jesus Christ.

The believer should realize that the Lord doesn't accept anyone with an unclean soul. For him who conceived the wish to ascend to the Kingdom of Heaven, the stage of cleaning body, mind and heart is unavoidable.

2. The believer should read every day a little in the Holy Script and the works of the holy Fathers, in order to deepen his notion of the spiritual path and of how to follow it.

3. The believer should constantly keep in mind that ascending to the Kingdom of Heaven is his most important work and that it demands a very serious attitude, otherwise he might fall at the very first difficulties on the spiritual path.

4. A believer won't be able to reach the kingdom of Heaven without the help of someone who knows the way of ascending to the Kingdom of Heaven, for there are many hardships and hidden obstacles on the path which he won't be able to overcome on his own.

5. A believer should remember that if he wants to ascend to the heavens, where the Lord abides, he should curb his pride. Pride doesn't allow him to listen to the wise instructions of his spiritual mentor,

## The rules for ascending to the Kingdom of Heaven

so that he makes a lot of mistakes which slacken his climb on the ladder to heaven.

6. The word 'passion' signifies any sinful, insatiable desire. When it takes possession of the believer it doesn't allow him to pray, nor to think of God, nor to work on himself, but it consumes all his energy if he yields to this desire and tries to satisfy it.

7. The passion of self-will hampers the believer from listening to the advice of his spiritual mentor. Therefore he makes many mistakes which can lead him astray from the spiritual path. The manifestations of self-will are e.g. when the believer –novice carries out his spiritual exercises in his own, mistaken way or if he does something against the will of his mentor.

8. The passion of gluttony makes a believer to be constantly occupied with a stock of food instead of being concerned about the salvation of his soul.

9. The passion of condemnation makes a believer criticize his fellow-believers and laymen who are weaker and more liable to the impact of passions than him, instead of opposing the temptations which lead him astray from the spiritual path.

10. The passion of fornication doesn't allow the believer to think about God and to pray the Jesus Prayer, but instead it makes him elaborate plans to chase the objects of his passion and then to realize these designs, satisfying his passion under the disguise of romantic love. The passion of fornication pollutes body, mind and heart, while its actual satisfaction, no matter whether it is mental or physical, deprives the believer of the sublimed energy of the soul, spiritualized by his prayers. After sexual intercourse his soul becomes blind, deaf and mute for a long period of time, up to several weeks. Laziness takes hold of it and the believer loses the aspiration to the Kingdom of Heaven; his soul grows dull and is deprived of subtle, elevated feelings. Most of the time however, the believer is not aware of his fall and roughness after fornicating.

11. The passion of avarice, the amassing of riches doesn't allow the believer to amass the eternal, imperishable riches. Instead, he

amasses money that he will have to leave behind anyway when his soul leaves the physical body. This passion also doesn't allow a believer to use his money for good deeds, for helping his neighbours and for alms to the poor.

12. The passion of despondency and sadness doesn't allow the believer to work on himself, prompts him to be lazy, to stay in bed for days wallowing in an enormous self-pity, arouses many fears and apprehensions with regard to his wretched life and suppresses his aspiration to the Kingdom of Heaven.

13. The passion of anger doesn't allow the believer to accept humbly God's will and prompts him to cherish his pride, protecting it from the corrections of his spiritual mentor and his neighbours: anger instils in him the idea that he is always right. Anger ties the believer with the depth of hell.

14. The passion of vanity doesn't allow the believer to merit God's praise as it makes him seek the praise of his fellow-men. He plays the hypocrite to himself and his fellow-men. Vanity makes him replace work on himself by work for the sake of fame.

15. The passion of verbosity doesn't allow the believer to keep silence reciting the Jesus Prayer in his heart and warding off sinful thoughts, but instead makes him dump his psychological waste on the heads of his neighbours.

16. The passion of backbiting and condemning one's fellow-men doesn't allow the believer to come closer to God, as it stains his soul intensely. God cannot abide in an unclean soul.

17. The believer should remember his death and live each day as if this were his last day. This gives him strength to follow the spiritual path, and then he won't have time to satisfy his sinful passions, he will only have time to work on himself.

18. The believer should remember the last judgment and the fact that if he will not work on himself, for his sins he will be sent to hell and will be tortured there for a long time.

19. A believer should repent his sins regularly in church and not wait with repentance until his last day when his soul will part from the body.

20. Every evening a believer should note in his diary the results of self-observation: which sinful designs came to him, which of them he could oppose and overcome and which of them took possession of his soul and caused its fall.

21. When the believer does physical work he should recite the Jesus Prayer in his heart.

22. A believer should remember God constantly notwithstanding his current pursuits.

23. If a believer lapsed into a sin he should repent it in church; if he offended his neighbour he should ask his neighbour's forgiveness.

24. A believer shouldn't treat his fellow-men the way he wouldn't wish to be treated himself.

25. A believer should carry out daily the following exercises: one hour of meditation; half an hour of transformation of sexual energy and one hour of the spiritual breath.

26. A believer should daily read the morning and evening prayers, eventually in an abridged version.

27. A believer mustn't forget that the most important pursuit in life is to find God inside himself.

28. There is no so called 'spiritual growth' and 'spiritual path' without the Lord. The spiritual warfare in the name of Jesus Christ in combination with the contemplation and prayer exercises, which lead to the union with God *is* what is called 'spiritual path' and 'spiritual growth'.

29. Where there is no God, there is no spiritual Path, but only self-deception and waste of time.

30. He who doesn't carry out the prayer and contemplation exercises will never find God.

31. It is necessary to live in such a way as if you were constantly in the presence of God, then your conscience will not allow you to sin.

32. A believer should plead the Theotokos for acquiring the fear of God. Having acquired fear of God, the believer will always remember that for any of his sins which remained unseen and unpunished, after his death he will have to atone for through suffering.
33. Watch how passions penetrate your soul and seduce it.
34. Cut off sinful designs when they are just about to appear.
35. 'Remember oneself' means not to forget the necessity to work on oneself, that is, to recite in the heart the Jesus Prayer, to carry out the prayer and contemplation exercises and to keep the heart pure, for it is the door to the Kingdom of Heaven.
36. If you do not carry out daily for at least two hours a day the exercises for purification and prayer, and the contemplation exercises in combination with the spiritual breath, then do not think that you will grow spiritually.

**The fruits of the correct spiritual practice**
The fruits of the correct spiritual practice are as follows: the cold in the heart begins to thaw under the influence of the spiritual warmth; awakening of compassion towards one's neighbour, inner silence and warm prayer without distracting thoughts. At a later stage, the heart opens and the believer finds in it the Lord Jesus Christ. Christ teaches him what is divine love, mercy and humility, for Jesus Christ Himself *is* divine love, mercy and humility.

When your heart opens you will feel the emanations of graceful warmth and purity which come from the Holy Theotokos and you will come to know Her mercy and love, Her divine protection and support. Her most significant help is that She warms the believer's cold heart and fills his soul with divine grace. Do not lapse into 'spiritual materialism' thinking that the Theotokos' help expresses itself in healing physical illnesses only. The illnesses might have come on you in order to stop the growth of your passions and the aggravation of your sins; in order to remind you of death and the last judgment and that you should not waste your time in satisfying your passions, but start pondering on the path to the Kingdom of Heaven.

In the beginning your heart will open for just a couple of minutes, and then it will close again, returning to the usual cold and fuss of the passions. Then your heart might open and become alive for longer periods of time, until you will be able to communicate with the Lord and the Theotokos for several hours a day in the silence of your cleansed heart.

With time the left part of your body, which is responsible for the perception of the world behind the curtain, will become purified, and you will realize that you begin to perceive the higher, divine world. It will reveal its beauty to you and you will understand that there exist light worlds full of divine beauty and justice. However, do not forget that to a lazy and sinful man there will be revealed nothing more than the gates of hell, which is the only place where one can get without the necessity of making any efforts!

**On rancour (Philokalia, abridged)**

Rancour and anger are very serious offences against the laws of spiritual growth. This is what John Climacos says about the dreadful influence of the passion of rancour and backbiting which was sown in our soul by the devil, the enemy of God and the human race.

1. Holy elders state that rancour is the worthless mother of anger, it gives rise to it and feeds it. Rancour is one of the darkest sides of the soul, and should be kept under the most strict control.

2. He who is stricken by rancour, hates the truth, ruins his virtues, cannot love God, wallows in sin, is always discontent with his neighbour, irritated and angry.

3. Rancour is an insatiable passion which doesn't know mercy and forgiveness. Rancour eliminates the fruits of prayer and drags down to hell. Rancour is an obsession by demons.

4. The rancorous constantly condemn their neighbours in their thoughts.

5. Condemnation feeds rancour, the poisonous weed, like water.

6. A believer who is possessed by rancour cannot repent truly, for the sign of true repentance is goodness and kindness.

**On the passion of anger**
These are the passions which give rise to the passion of anger: pride, disobedience to the spiritual mentor, a false assumption 'only I know how to live in a proper way.' Anger is fed and strengthened by envy, revengefulness and vanity. Anger is born from the desire to govern fellow-men and also from the desire for the praise of fellow-men instead of the praise of God; from the desire of making people satisfy one's whims and passions; from the passion of love of money and outer and inner comfort, and then the anger comes down upon someone who disturbs the feeling of comfort, even if it has a just cause. Anger is raised by deception and hypocrisy when fellow-men unmask the deception and hypocrisy. The passion of fornication intensifies anger very much. There lurks a demon behind the passion of anger, which arouses and feeds it. If man would give in to the passion of anger and give it a free hand, it might result in obsession by the demon of anger. Such a person becomes addicted to the demonic enjoyment of feeling power over his fellow-men and to violence, even up to murder, for he thinks, being stupefied by the demon, that all means are allowed and he doesn't need to observe the laws of God and men. Anger is raised from one's habit not to take in consideration the opinion of others and to build one's comfort by encroaching on the comfort of others.

**Prayer practice for struggling with the passion of anger and rancour**
First of all a believer, who suffers from the passion of anger and rancour, should repent before the priest of this passion and ask his blessing to struggle with it. It is necessary, in order to conquer the passion of anger and rancour, to learn to accept meekly people's mockery and criticism, even if malicious.

## The rules for ascending to the Kingdom of Heaven

1. Make the list of the manifestations of this passion in you during your whole life, divided into periods of seven years. Recall how exactly you have condemned, about whom you have been backbiting and who you have slandered.

2. Sit on a stool in solitude before your iconostasis, focus your mind on your heart, and recite mentally for half an hour, the following prayer: 'Most Holy Theotokos, Virgin Mary, deliver me from the passion of anger and rancour.'

Recite for another half hour the following prayer: 'Most Holy Theotokos, Virgin Mary, forgive me the sin of anger and rancour.' Recollect during this prayer the persons with whom you were angry and on whom you have taken vengeance.

Recite for another half hour the following prayer: 'Most Holy Theotokos, Virgin Mary, purify me from the sin of anger and rancour.'

Remember to keep your mind focused on your heart.

Pray to the Holy Theotokos until you feel light at heart.

**Prayer and contemplation exercise combined with the spiritual breath for pleading the Theotokos for support in the struggle with the passion of anger and rancour.**

1. Focus on your physical heart, that is, let your mind 'sink' in your heart and carrying out the spiritual breath, recite for half an hour the following prayer, addressing the Theotokos:

'Most holy Theotokos, deliver me from the sin of anger and rancour.' Pronounce this prayer fully moving your life energy upwards during inhalation along the channel of the spine, and during exhalation, moving energy downwards along the rear of the 'tube' of the spine.

2. In order to improve your sinful nature, pronounce for another half hour the following formula of repentance, combined with the spiritual breath:

'Most holy Theotokos and Virgin, Mary, I repent my sin of anger and rancour.'

## The Sixteenth Arcanum

Pronounce this formula fully during inhaling and exhaling. Recollect during this prayer the persons with whom you were angry and on whom you have taken vengeance.

The more advanced level of this practice is to focus your mind on your heart during the carrying out of the above-mentioned.

**Prayers, combined with the spiritual breath to the Lord Jesus Christ, the Holy Spirit and God the Father**

Sit on a chair in solitude before your iconostasis and recite mentally for a half an hour, the following prayer, combining it with the spiritual breath: 'Lord Jesus Christ, forgive me the sin of anger and rancour.'

Pronounce during the next half hour the following prayer: 'Lord Holy Spirit, the Comforter, forgive me the sin of anger and rancour.'

Pronounce during the next half hour the following prayer:

'O God, our Heavenly Father, forgive me the sin of anger and rancour.' Recollect during these prayers the persons with whom you were angry or still are angry.

It is necessary to turn to the message of the Sixteenth Arcanum regularly during one's entire conscious life.

The Seventeenth Arcanum

## The Seventeenth Arcanum. Meeting the Theotokos in one's heart

The Seventeenth Arcanum states the following spiritual truth: a believer can find the Theotokos in his heart through the solitary way of life, fasting and unceasing prayer to Her.

The picture of the Arcanum represents a holy elder, who lived his whole life in the monastery and due to his inner work and prayers he found in his heart the Theotokos, who abides there, invisible to others.

After her death the Holy Theotokos was taken by Jesus Christ with her body to the Kingdom of Heaven. This event has been testified by the disciples of Christ. Her physical body was transformed into the radiant light in which she appears to many Christians.

But sometimes she can appear in her subtle body to those who are worthy of this meeting with her. Sometimes she visits people chosen by her, in their dream, asking them to fulfil some important task or other.

For two thousand years already the Holy Theotokos helps Christ to spread the Christian faith over the earth. In her body of spiritual light she appeared to many saints, helping them to find God. The Holy Theotokos works tirelessly on earth, protecting and supporting Christian cloisters and helping the believers in many wondrous ways, so that faith in the Lord Jesus Christ is preserved and grows deeper and wider. Many think that the Theotokos is a kind of mythic character, but these thoughts are sown into people's minds by the Evil One. The Theotokos really exists, she is amongst us, but only the pure in heart can see her.

The Theotokos is the evidence of the reality of the Kingdom of Heaven, where Christ is the ruler. Christians pray to her for intercession because they know that God fulfils her requests to Him and the miracles that she works testify of Gods omnipotence in our prosaic

21st century, which is full of scepticism and denial of God's manifestations. Many go to India or Tibet or Mexico in search of miracles, because they do not know that the greatest miracle happened in Russia: the Theotokos has chosen Russia as the field to carry out her mission and it is enough to purify one's heart in order to feel her presence and to receive her support.

1. The Holy Theotokos carries in her the divine light of Jesus Christ. The prayer to her in combination with the spiritual breath will gradually fill the soul with an unspeakably graceful light which will be like a mysterious tower of light for the believer. It will illuminate your path and it will show you the right direction. If the light fades away it means that you strayed from the spiritual path and went in a wrong direction.

2. A believer who merits to converse with the Mother of God, can become a temple, in which she will abide.

3. Trying to preserve this blissful state, the believer will understand, sooner or later, that he should observe the commandments of Christ, for by breaking them the light in his soul will fade away.

4. Anger, fornication, pride, vanity, love of money, condemnation of others, despondency darken the soul and the divine light fades away.

5. Regaining the purity of the soul demands a lot of effort and inner work. In order to understand it in the depth of our imperfect soul, we should repent yet again the seductive sins which are very difficult to resist and in which we lapse repeatedly.

6. Repentance is that very method which helps us gradually to become indifferent to the temptations of life, which now delude us with the promise of endless enjoyment.

7. The Theotokos calls us to aspire to the Lord with all the might of our soul and to observe His commandments, for otherwise the soul gets stained. Cleansing the soul means repenting, and then the heart will shine again with divine light.

8. The Holy Theotokos gives the world the light of Jesus Christ, the light which comes from our Father in Heaven.

## The Seventeenth Arcanum

9. Praying regularly 'Most holy Theotokos, cleanse me by thy light' in combination with the spiritual breath, a believer can acquire the state of inner silence in which he can merit to converse with the Mother of God.

10. The heavenly light comes down in the believer's heart and brings pure joy with it. God's grace and joy comfort and soften his heart.

11. The heavenly warmth of the Virgin Mary nourishes the suffering soul; the believer doesn't feel lonely, because the Queen of Heaven is with him during his prayer.

12. The believer should preserve and guard this blissful fruit of his prayer and God's grace.

13. If his heart becomes angry or irritated with somebody, the heavenly countenance will immediately disappear from his heart.

14. If the believer condemns someone, the light in his heart will fade at once.

15. If he forgets the Queen of Heaven, the heavenly radiance will not illuminate his soul.

16. If the believer is carried away by the passion of verbosity, he will immediately lose touch with the Holy Theotokos.

17. If he is too much involved with earthly concerns and forgets the Divine Virgin Mary, the light in his soul will fade away.

18. When the believer transgresses the sacred commandments, the light of the divine world immediately becomes imperceptible for him.

19. Therefore the believer, after he has acquired the favour of the Mother of God, should watchfully guard the clarity of his soul, which becomes darker with each new transgression.

20. The soul is darkened by blasphemous thoughts; it is darkened by worldly concerns; it is darkened when the believer forgets God; it is darkened when the believer falls in love and dedicates his heart to someone else, to another creature of God, and not to God.

21. The believer's heart should belong only to God, according to His commandments.

22. When the believer feels the Theotokos' light in himself, he will be inspired by her presence.
23. There is nothing more elevated in the world than finding God. The believer should not expect praise of his fellowmen for his spiritual practices and achievements. Most probably he will be mocked, for laymen know nothing about the Kingdom of Heaven.
24. The believer ought to desire the praise only of God to Whom he should strive tirelessly.
25. He is not allowed to be proud of his contact with the Theotokos, otherwise he will immediately lose it. It is not advisable for the believer to tell laymen about his contact with the Theotokos, because then she might hide herself from him.
26. It is better for him to be silent in his heart, meek and humble in order not to waste the Theotokos' grace.

**On chastity**
In order to merit the honour of conversing with the Mother of God, it is necessary to become firmly established in chastity.
The body becomes polluted because of the attraction of bodily pleasures, like food and caresses, which results in fornication and gluttony.
The mind and the heart become stained because of unclean thoughts and feelings: envy, perfidy, lies, hypocrisy, lust, greed, condemnation, pride, despondency, sadness, anger, vindictiveness, love and amassing of money, vanity and wanting praise of our fellow men, alcohol and drugs, frequent communication with worldly people.
Chastity means keeping clean body, mind and heart.
The fruit of chastity is purity. Purity is the cherished goal of believers, for the Lord can only abide in a pure heart.
The highest measure of chastity are the works of virtue: daily prayers, regular repentance of sins, the Eucharist, giving alms to the poor, helping our fellow men on the path to the Lord, faith in God, firm hope of salvation and of reaching the Kingdom of Heaven, wisdom and humility, meekness, lack of malice.

## The Seventeenth Arcanum

Remembrance of death and anticipation of the last judgment is also a virtue, which protects from sins and sinful thoughts.
Fear of God and awareness of His omnipotence is a virtue.
To love God more than his creation is a virtue.
Preserving one's hope of finding God in one's heart is a virtue.
Fasting, night vigil and being satisfied with little food is a virtue.
Daily inner work and carrying out of the prayer and contemplation practices which lead to conversing with God is a virtue.

### On prayerful vigil (From the Philokalia, abridged)

1. Holy elders say that the believer should sleep not more than 6 hours a day and pray as much as possible: wake up early in the morning and read the morning prayers; in the evening, even being tired, a believer should overcome his doziness and read the evening prayers; in the middle of the night he should wake up and read the prayers of the night vigil.
2. Elders say that much sleep hardens a believer's soul, while prayer purifies his mind and his heart.
3. A dozy believer is often visited by the demon of fornication, while prayerful vigil stifles lascivious thoughts, softens the heart, keeps the mind clean and helps to digest.
4. The believer who sleeps excessively long forgets God quickly, while the believer who prays often, remembers God with joy.
5. The believer is rich not with gold but with his morning, evening and night prayers, when he stands before God.
6. Those believers who are in prayer the whole day receive as a reward the continuation of the blissful prayers in their dream.
7. Having acquired passionlessness by means of prayerful vigils, the believer can keep his heart, mind and body clean; with the help of the prayer and contemplation exercises he can find inner silence when he can converse with the Theotokos.
8. Holy elders say that prayer is the queen of all the virtues. Prayer unites man with God and if God accepts the prayer, it brings peace and consolation.

9. The prayer of repentance gives us the possibility to receive forgiveness for our sins and reconciles us with God.
10. Prayer protects our soul from suffering; it is a bridge over the troubled water of temptations.
11. Prayer is an inexhaustible source of virtues. Prayer gives us the hope of salvation; it gives us divine love.
12. Prayer is the saving ladder along which believers climb to the Kingdom of Heaven.
13. The prayer of the believer who did not get rid of rancour will not bear fruit.
14. Holy fathers say that prayer should be as follows: first the believer should thank God, then confess his sins and express his repentance, and only then he may ask God something.
15. During his prayer to God a believer should stand as if in court and plead for pardon.
16. Prayers should be simple and understandable, without sophisticated expressions.
17. Even though the believer should acquire the highest degree of purity and virtues, he still should pray for the forgiveness of his sins, for the purity of the Father in Heaven is immeasurably greater than the purity of man.
18. The mind during prayer is usually distracted, therefore the believer should return again and again to the meaning of the words of the prayer.
19. Prayers are defiled if the believer while praying gives in to thoughts about sinful designs.
20. His prayer is worthless if the believer, during prayer, is busy with material concerns.
21. The prayer is stolen and becomes fruitless if the believer during prayer is distracted by memories.
22. Many believers who wallowed in passions, have become passionless through prayer.
23. A believer's love of God is shown during his prayer.
24. Do not stop praying until you feel that its fire has cleansed you.

25. A prayer can be defiled even by a word and then it will not bring forth the expected fruit.
26. When you confess to the Lord your carnal sins do not go into the details of fornication, otherwise you might slander yourself.
27. The demons are burnt by prayers as by fire and they run away.
28. Believer, pray ceaselessly, until God becomes your Teacher in prayer.

**Prayers to the Theotokos in combination with the spiritual breath, meant for the struggle with passions**
As man is weak and he cannot conquer one or other of his passions, he should ask the Mother of God for help and intercession:
'Holy Theotokos, protect me from the passion of gluttony.'
'Holy Theotokos, protect me from the passion of despondency and sadness.'
'Holy Theotokos and Virgin, Mary, protect me from the passion of love of money.'
'Holy Theotokos and Virgin, Mary, protect me from the passion of malice and envy.'
'Holy Theotokos and Virgin, Mary, protect me from the passion of pride.'
'Holy Theotokos and Virgin, Mary, protect me from the passion of vanity.'
'Holy Theotokos and Virgin, Mary, protect me from the passion of resentment.'
'Holy Theotokos and Virgin, Mary, protect me from the passion of backbiting and condemnation.'
'Holy Theotokos and Virgin, Mary, protect me from the passion of fornication.'
'Holy Theotokos and Virgin, Mary, protect me from the passion of verbosity.'
Using this formula the believer can ask the Theotokos for protection from any passion.

**Prayer of repentance to the Theotokos in combination with the spiritual breath**

When the believer becomes fully aware of his sins and their terrible consequences, he will immediately start cleansing himself from these passions and sins. The following prayer can be used for this purpose:

'Most holy Theotokos and Virgin, Mary, I repent my sin of fornication.' Recollect during this prayer the persons with whom you have fornicated and pronounce their names.

'Most holy Theotokos and Virgin, Mary, I repent my sin of anger and rancour.' Recollect during this prayer the persons with whom you have been angry and whose offences you didn't forgive and pronounce their names.

'Most holy Theotokos and Virgin, Mary, I repent my sin of sadness and despondency.' Recollect during this prayer the periods of your life when you felt sad and depressed.

'Most holy Theotokos and Virgin, Mary, I repent my sin of love of money.' Recollect during this prayer the persons you refused to help materially and pronounce their names.

'Most holy Theotokos and Virgin, Mary, I repent my sin of verbosity.' Recollect during this prayer the persons with whom you talked excessively and pronounce their names.

'Most holy Theotokos and Virgin, Mary, I repent my sin of condemnation.' Recollect during this prayer the persons you have condemned and pronounce their names.

'Most holy Theotokos and Virgin, Mary, I repent my sin of envy.' Recollect during this prayer the persons you have envied and pronounce their names.

'Most holy Theotokos and Virgin, Mary, I repent my sin of jealousy and vengeance.' Recollect during this prayer the persons of whom you have been jealous and on whom you have been taking vengeance.

## The Seventeenth Arcanum

'Most holy Theotokos and Virgin, Mary, I repent my sin of resentment.' Recollect during this prayer the persons who made you feel resentment and whom you didn't forgive for this.

Thus you can plead the Holy Theotokos for the forgiveness of all the sins that you have committed. However, you should first repent these sins, which polluted your soul, to the priest during confession. And if after receiving the absolution sinful designs continue torturing you and you still feel the heaviness of the committed sins inside your soul, make use of the abovementioned prayers in combination with the spiritual breath.

After the repentance prayers you can plead the Theotokos for help, using the following prayers in combination with the spiritual breath:

'Most holy Theotokos and Virgin, Mary, save me, sinner.'
'Most holy Theotokos and Virgin, Mary, cleanse me, sinner.'
'Most holy Theotokos and Virgin, Mary, have mercy on me, sinner.'

Pray to the Theotokos until you feel that the heaviness of the sin is gone and your soul feels light again. With time you will feel when the Theotokos forgives you your sins, you will be in contact with her and feel that she takes responsibility for you. However if you want results, these exercises should be done for several hours a day. Pronounce this formula fully during inhaling and exhaling.

**On the love of God**

The Holy Theotokos loves God with the most elevated and tender love and her heart emanates heavenly grace. As she has this love for the Lord, she doesn't need anything else.

The Holy Theotokos guards the purity of the faith in her Son, Jesus Christ, and protects it from heresy and schism.

A believer can move the Virgin Mary by entreaties to teach him to love God. This love is beyond what is known in this world, it is crystal clear and pure, unsullied and full of grace. Such love lets the soul receive God's grace and the most pure radiance of the divine light.

This love liberates the soul, it is altruistic, it shines like a lamp in the darkness, illuminating the way to the divine purity and simplicity of the soul. This love gives and helps; it is innocent like a small child and it shines like a ray of sun in the sky. This love elevates the heart and brings it closer to God and leads to the Kingdom of Heaven.

## Prayers in combination with the spiritual breath for kindling the divine love

In order for the believer to kindle in his heart the divine love, it is necessary to let his mind sink in his heart and to say mentally the following prayers, in combination with the spiritual breath:

'Most holy Theotokos and Virgin, Mary, fill my heart with love for the Lord.'

'Most holy Theotokos and Virgin, Mary, fill my heart with divine love.'

'Most holy Theotokos and Virgin, Mary, fill my heart with spiritual love.'

If the believer is able to recite these prayers during three or four hours, he will find himself in a state of spiritual contemplation and he will feel the motherly, spiritual love of the Mother of God for the believers, which is full of the spiritual fire. However the length of this exercise should be increased gradually, beginning with half an hour, as the soul should be prepared gradually for the higher energies of spiritual love.

Love of the Mother of God should be spiritual, without impure thoughts, otherwise the believer will receive a punishment instead of a blessing.

The believer should consider the message of the Seventeenth Arcanum daily until the end of his life, when his soul will part from the body and ascend to the Kingdom of Heaven.

The Eighteenth Arcanum

## The Eighteenth Arcanum. Finding the Lord Jesus Christ in one's heart

The Eighteenth Arcanum states the following spiritual truth: by leading a solitary life, fasting, praying and observing the commandments of Jesus Christ, a believer can merit the grace to converse with the Lord and find Him in his heart.

The picture of this Arcanum represents a holy elder, who by God's mercy has successfully waged spiritual warfare and found Christ in his heart. From that moment on Christ is always with him, invisibly.

Jesus Christ, the Son of God, was sent onto the earth by the Father in Heaven in order to bring people the new Message of the Father. Jesus Christ is God, Who was incarnated fully as man, in order to save the earth from falling into the infernal abyss. Christ did not abandon the earth after His ascension, He is always with us. He built the Kingdom of Heaven for us, not far from the earth, where He rules. There, in the Kingdom of Heaven, the Mother of God, all the Christian saints and those Christians who merited by their righteous life to live after their physical death abide, illuminated by the light of our Lord Jesus Christ.

Christ is always with us, for He is God, He can appear in the heart of the righteous, and thus they will be awarded to converse with the Lord. As Christ is with us, we can repent our sins before Him in Church, and He will forgive us our sins and He will help us to ascend to the next level of spiritual perfection. And though we continue committing sins, He commanded to forgive our sins as many times as we repent them. Who could possibly know better than God, our Creator, that the spiritual growth of man and the curing of his sinful nature goes very slowly.

If Christ would abandon our earth, there would be no one to whom we could repent our sins and receive forgiveness and absolution, because the priests receive this power from the Lord.

## On humble wisdom (Philokalia. abridged)

Only those who are humble of heart will find the Lord there.

1. If we obtain humble wisdom it means that we have climbed another rung on the ladder to heaven.

2. Humble wisdom is a beneficial quality of the soul, which can be obtained through experience only and which is unspeakably precious.

3. The true humble wisdom can be learned from the Lord Jesus Christ only. When the Lord Himself will come into our heart, we will learn from Him true meekness, humility of heart and of thought. Then we will be able to find true peace in our soul, eliminating with the help of humble wisdom our numerous passions, as we will become insensitive and scornful of the sinful designs which try to seduce us.

4. When true humble wisdom ripens in us, we will hate the praise of our fellow-men and fame, and we will avoid them as a fire which could destroy our virtues.

5. If we are wise and humble, then we will consider none of our deeds as a true work of virtue. He who is truly humble, is not susceptible to the temptations of the demons, the enemies of the human race.

6. Humility and wisdom are the most reliable vault for the spiritual treasures, in which the demons cannot penetrate.

7. Humble wisdom is born from sincere repentance when that very part of the soul that has sinned, repents. Then the Lord gives His humility to the soul, which has become purified from defilement, and the soul rejoices, feeling bliss.

8. The first sign of humility is when the believer feels no anger and irritation at his neighbours.

9. The second sign of humility is when the believer accepts gladly insults and humiliation from his neighbours, considering them as a 'bitter medicine' for curing the vices of his soul.

10. The third sign of the believer's humility is that he does not believe in his own virtues and strives constantly to do the work of virtues more perfectly.
11. Humble wisdom might dry up in the believer like water in the desert if he is praised and extolled by his fellow-men.
12. As elders say, 'repentance cleanses a fallen believer and humble wisdom opens the gates of the Kingdom of Heaven for him.'
13. Holy elders say that love of God raises the believer to heaven, and it is humble wisdom which prevents him from falling from there.
14. Humble wisdom is the spiritual teaching of Jesus Christ. It brings the believer from the abyss of sin back to earth and then it raises him to heaven.
15. Sacred humility is a gift of God; it allows all believers to climb on the first rungs of the ladder to the Kingdom of Heaven.
16. Only courageous believers can climb, by means of chastity, to the middle rungs of the ladder.
17. Only with the help of impassiveness can the upper rungs of the ladder be reached.
18. Many believers can endure insults from strangers, but only they who have great humility, can endure insults from their fellow-believers. No one has found salvation without humility.
19. He who asks God less than he deserves, will receive more than he is worth. (Philokalia)

Read the fragments of the Gospels of Matthew and John for a deeper understanding of the Good Tidings of the Father in Heaven that Jesus Christ, Son of God, brought to earth.

Jesus said: 'The disciple is not above his master, nor the servant above his lord.
It is enough for the disciple that he be as his master, and the servant as his lord. If they have called the master of the house Beelzebub, how much more shall they call them of his household?

## The Eighteenth Arcanum

Fear them not therefore: for there is nothing covered, that shall not be revealed; and hid, that shall not be known.
What I tell you in darkness, that speak ye in light: and what ye hear in the ear, that preach ye upon the housetops.' (Matthew 10:24-27)

What Jesus says to the apostles in darkness, that is, in secret from those who persecute Him, about the Message of God, the apostles are commanded to preach openly, to all the people, so that they can receive the Message of the Father in Heaven.

Jesus said: 'And fear not them which kill the body, but are not able to kill the soul: but rather fear him which is able to destroy both soul and body in hell.' (Matthew 10:28)

Do not fear those enemies who can kill your body, but who cannot kill your soul and make you fall away from God. Fear your true enemies, who can make your body and your soul fall away from God's commandments, ruin your faith and make you a disbeliever and throw you into hell for a long-lasting torture.

Jesus said: 'Whosoever therefore shall confess me before men, him will I confess also before my Father which is in heaven. But whosoever shall deny me before men, him will I also deny before my Father which is in heaven.' (Matthew 10:32-33)

He who will acknowledge before people his faith in Christ, without fear of punishment or mockery, the Lord in His turn will acknowledge and defend before His Father in Heaven. He who renounced his faith in Christ before people, Christ will renounce before the Father in Heaven, after his soul has parted from his body.

Jesus said: 'Think not that I am come to send peace on earth: I came not to send peace, but a sword.

For I am come to set a man at variance against his father, and the daughter against her mother, and the daughter in law against her mother in law.
And a man's foes shall be they of his own household.' (Matthew, 10:34-36)

If children came to believe in Christ, and their parents would forbid them this, then the parents would become the enemies of their children, but the truth would be on the side of the children.

Jesus said: 'He that loveth father or mother more than me is not worthy of me: and he that loveth son or daughter more than me is not worthy of me.
And he that taketh not his cross, and followeth after me, is not worthy of me.' (Matthew 10: 37-38)
In order to follow Christ, that is, to follow His teaching, a believer should crucify his passions and his attachments to the worldly life on the cross of sacrifice, gather his courage and leave the worldly life behind and observe the commandments of Christ. Jesus Christ is God and He preaches the Message of His Father, Who has sent Him. God is love, and the first commandment says that a believer should love Christ most of all; and if the believer loves his children, husband and wife more than Christ, he is not worthy of God's love and will not come to know it.
He who came to believe in Christ but who does nothing in order to observe Christ's commandments, who doesn't struggle with his passions, who doesn't aspire to the Kingdom of Heaven where Christ rules, who doesn't carry out the prayer and contemplation exercises, doesn't take up his cross and doesn't follow Christ on the way to the Father in Heaven, and he is not worthy of Christ's love.

Jesus said: 'He that findeth his life shall lose it: and he that loseth his life for my sake shall find it.' (Matthew 10:39)

## The Eighteenth Arcanum

He who cares for his earthly life more than for his eternal life, will not obtain the eternal life. He who ceased caring for his earthly life and follows Christ's teaching and observes the Lord's commandments, will find eternal life.

Jesus said: 'He that receiveth you receiveth me, and he that receiveth me receiveth him that sent me.'
Those who accept the teaching of Christ, brought by the apostles, accept Christ Himself. Those who accept Christ accept His Father in Heaven, Who sent Christ on earth.

Jesus said: 'For what is a man profited, if he shall gain the whole world, and lose his own soul? or what shall a man give in exchange for his soul?
For the Son of man shall come in the glory of his Father with his angels; and then he shall reward every man according to his works.' (Matthew 16:26-27)
While gaining earthly riches man will sink in sin so deeply that his soul will darken and it will cease radiating light. It will become heavy, gloomy and dark and this indicates that the death of this soul is near.

'And after six days Jesus taketh Peter, James, and John his brother, and bringeth them up into an high mountain apart,
 And was transfigured before them: and his face did shine as the sun, and his raiment was white as the light.' (Matthew 17:1-2)
Jesus appeared to the apostles in His divine aspect: His face was shining with spiritual light like a sun as Jesus manifested His unity with God the Father. The apostles witnessed it and they told those who believed in Christ that after Christ's transfiguration, it is possible also for all human beings to find unity with God, to open the divine aspect of the soul.

## Finding the Lord Jesus Christ in one's heart

'While he yet spake, behold, a bright cloud overshadowed them: and behold a voice out of the cloud, which said, This is my beloved Son, in whom I am well pleased; hear ye him.' (Matthew 17:5)
In order for the apostles to become firmly established in their faith in Christ and to bring Christ's Message to the people God the Father Himself came to them and He confirmed that all Christ's words were true.

Jesus said: 'Verily I say unto you, except ye be converted, and become as little children, ye shall not enter into the kingdom of heaven. (Matthew 18:3)
If the believer will not follow Christ's teaching and will not become pure of mind, heart and body as children are, he will not be able to enter the Kingdom of Heaven.

Jesus said: 'Woe unto the world because of offences! for it must needs be that offences come; but woe to that man by whom the offence cometh!' (Matthew 18:7)
Woe unto the world because of temptations and passions that the Evil One sends onto the earth, in order to tear people away from God and throw them into great suffering. People who will give in to temptations will turn away from God and fall into the outer darkness. However those through whom these temptations come will be punished even more severely.

Jesus said: 'For where two or three are gathered together in my name, there am I in the midst of them.
Then came Peter to him, and said, Lord, how oft shall my brother sin against me, and I forgive him? till seven times?
Jesus saith unto him, I say not unto thee, until seven times: but, until seventy times seven.' (Matthew 18:20-22)

Jesus said that one should forgive one's neighbour his sins as many times as he will repent them. Man is weak and often gives in

## The Eighteenth Arcanum

to temptations and lapses into sin, and the only way to overcome temptations is to pronounce the Lord's Name. Therefore no matter how often man sinned: if he repents, it is necessary to forgive him.

Jesus said: 'But if thou wilt enter into life, keep the commandments. He saith unto him, which? Jesus said, Thou shalt do no murder, Thou shalt not commit adultery, Thou shalt not steal, Thou shalt not bear false witness,
Honour thy father and thy mother: and, Thou shalt love thy neighbour as thyself.
If thou wilt be perfect, go and sell that thou hast, and give to the poor, and thou shalt have treasure in heaven: and come and follow me.
But when the young man heard that saying, he went away sorrowful: for he had great possessions.
Then said Jesus unto his disciples, Verily I say unto you, That a rich man shall hardly enter into the kingdom of heaven.
And again I say unto you, It is easier for a camel to go through the eye of a needle, than for a rich man to enter into the kingdom of God.
And every one that hath forsaken houses, or brethren, or sisters, or father, or mother, or wife, or children, or lands, for my name's sake, shall receive an hundredfold, and shall inherit everlasting life. (Matthew 19: 18,19,21- 24,29)
Jesus said that man should honour his father and mother and love his neighbour like himself. However He also said that he who wants to follow Him, should give his possessions to the poor, love God more than anyone else including himself, and follow Him. And he, who will follow Christ's teaching and will leave behind, for the sake of finding God in himself, his house, family, parents and children, will receive hundred times more in heaven, much more that he had left behind on earth. If he will find Christ inside his heart, he will receive eternal comfort in the Kingdom of Heaven, as the Kingdom of Heaven is inside us, inside our heart when it is cleansed.

## Finding the Lord Jesus Christ in one's heart

'Then one of them, which was a lawyer, asked him a question, tempting him, and saying,
Master, which is the great commandment in the law?
Jesus said unto him, Thou shalt love the Lord thy God with all thy heart, and with all thy soul, and with all thy mind.
This is the first and great commandment.
And the second is like unto it, Thou shalt love thy neighbour as thyself.
On these two commandments hang all the law and the prophets.' (Matthew 22:35-40)
If a believer follows these two commandments, then he will find the Lord Jesus Christ in his heart and he will avoid gatherings and crowds as they scatter the fire of God's love.

Jesus said: 'Jesus saith unto him, I am the way, the truth, and the life: no man cometh unto the Father, but by me.
Believest thou not that I am in the Father, and the Father in me? the words that I speak unto you I speak not of myself: but the Father that dwelleth in me, he doeth the works.' (John 14:6,10)
Therefore the believer, who ceaselessly calls upon the Name of the Lord Jesus Christ will be saved.

Jesus said: 'If ye love me, keep my commandments.
Yet a little while, and the world seeth me no more; but ye see me: because I live, ye shall live also.
At that day ye shall know that I am in my Father, and ye in me, and I in you.
He that hath my commandments, and keepeth them, he it is that loveth me: and he that loveth me shall be loved of my Father, and I will love him, and will manifest myself to him.' (Matthew 14:15,19-21)
It can be understood from Christ's words that if a believer calls upon His Name, but he doesn't observe the Lord's commandments,

the Lord will not come to him and will not reveal Himself in his heart.

In order to come to love Christ, a believer should sacrifice his passions, that is, not commit the seven mortal sins and observe the commandments. Then Christ will love such a believer and if the believer calls upon Christ's Name, He will come to him.

Jesus said: 'If a man love me, he will keep my words: and my Father will love him, and we will come unto him, and make our abode with him.

He that loveth me not keepeth not my sayings: and the word which ye hear is not mine, but the Father's which sent me.

But that the world may know that I love the Father; and as the Father gave me commandment, even so I do.' (John 14:23-24,31)

Jesus speaks not out of Himself but He transmits the words of God the Father, Who sent Him in the world to proclaim the Good News. Christ loves the believers who observe His commandments and the Father in Heaven will love them too and will open the gates of the Kingdom of Heaven to them.

Christ abides in the eternal shining light of the Father in Heaven and is one with Him. Also, the Father in Heaven eternally abides in Christ's heart. Therefore he who believes in Christ, believes in the Father, Who sent Him. Christ is the door through which believers come to the Father in Heaven.

**The Jesus Prayer in combination with the spiritual breath for keeping the heart clean**

The main stages of cleansing the heart:
- the believer confesses and repents of all his sins before the priest;
- the believer is reconciled with all the people from his past with the help of the prayer of forgiveness, which is said in church before the icon of the Theotokos, for every person in his past;

# Finding the Lord Jesus Christ in One's Heart

- the believer tracks down his passions, making a detailed list of them and cutting off the passions with the help of inner prayer and an effort of the will.

When this stage is completed, to a certain extent, it is necessary to keep the heart clean so that it can converse with God. The heart becomes clean and is kept clean through reciting the Jesus Prayer in the heart: 'Lord Jesus Christ, Son of God, have mercy on me, sinner', in combination with the spiritual breath. The prayer must be said fully during inhalation and exhalation.

The detailed description of this exercise is to be found in the previous Arcana. While doing this exercise you might feel a growing inner tension, because the demons will oppose this prayer: you may feel bad, dizzy, depressed and sad and you will wish to stop praying. However, if you don't give in to the demons' harassment you will feel inner peace after a while and also that you have become cleaner inside. If you continue praying, then Christ will reveal Himself in the silence of your heart. Do not attempt to imagine, to think up Christ' countenance, otherwise you might lapse into a delusion and the demons will come to you under the guise of angels of light.

## Prayers to the Lord Jesus Christ in combination with the spiritual breath, meant for the struggle with passions

As man is weak and he cannot defeat the demon of one or other passion, he should ask God for help:

'Lord Jesus Christ, protect me from the passion of gluttony.'
'Lord Jesus Christ, protect me from the passion of despondency and sadness.'
'Lord Jesus Christ, protect me from the passion of love of money.'
'Lord Jesus Christ, protect me from the passion of malice and envy.'
'Lord Jesus Christ, protect me from the passion of pride.'
'Lord Jesus Christ, protect me from the passion of vanity.'
'Lord Jesus Christ, protect me from the passion of resentment.'
'Lord Jesus Christ, protect me from the passion of backbiting and condemnation.'

## The Eighteenth Arcanum

'Lord Jesus Christ, protect me from the passion of fornication.'
'Lord Jesus Christ, protect me from the passion of verbosity.'
Using this formula the believer can ask the Lord Jesus Christ for protection from any passion.

### Prayer of repentance to Jesus Christ in combination with the spiritual breath

When the believer becomes fully aware of his sins and their terrible consequences, he will immediately start cleansing himself from these passions and sins. The following prayer can be used for this purpose:

'Lord Jesus Christ, I repent my sin of fornication.' Recollect during this prayer the persons with whom you have fornicated and pronounce their names.

'Lord Jesus Christ, I repent my sin of anger and rancour.' Recollect during this prayer the persons with whom you have been angry and whose offences you didn't forgive and pronounce their names.

'Lord Jesus Christ, I repent my sin of sadness and despondency.' Recollect during this prayer the periods of your life when you were sad and depressed.

'Lord Jesus Christ, I repent my sin of love of money.' Recollect during this prayer the persons whom you refused to help materially and pronounce their names.

'Lord Jesus Christ, I repent my sin of verbosity.' Recollect during this prayer the persons with whom you talked excessively and pronounce their names.

'Lord Jesus Christ, I repent my sin of condemnation.' Recollect during this prayer the persons whom you have been condemning and pronounce their names.

'Lord Jesus Christ, I repent my sin of envy.' Recollect during this prayer the persons whom you envied and pronounce their names.

'Lord Jesus Christ, I repent my sin of jealousy and vengeance.' Recollect during this prayer the persons of whom you were jealous and on whom you took revenge.

## Finding the Lord Jesus Christ in one's heart

'Lord Jesus Christ, I repent my sin of resentment.' Recollect during this prayer the persons who made you feel resentment and whom you didn't forgive for this.

Thus you can plead the Lord for the forgiveness of all the sins that you have committed. However, first you should repent these sins, which polluted your soul, before the priest, during confession. And if after receiving absolution, the sinful designs continue torturing you and you still feel the heaviness of the committed sins inside your soul, make use of the abovementioned prayers in combination with the spiritual breath.

After the prayers of repentance you can plead the Lord for help, using the following prayer in combination with the spiritual breath:
'Lord Jesus Christ, cleanse me, sinner.'

Plead with Christ for the forgiveness of your sins until you feel that the heaviness of the sin is gone and your soul feels light again. With time you will feel when the Lord forgives you your sins; you will feel contact with Him and His responsibility for you. In this way you will gradually learn to converse with Christ. These prayers should be recited in combination with the spiritual breath for several hours a day.

### Prayer for finding the Lord Jesus Christ inside the heart

Recite in your heart the abridged Jesus Prayer 'Lord Jesus Christ, have mercy on me' in combination with the spiritual breath. Pronounce this prayer fully during inhaling and exhaling. The path of energy differs slightly in this exercise: when during inhaling the energy reaches the spiritual eye, move it one metre further along the horizontal line projected forward from the spiritual eye. By exhaling bring energy back along this line and then along the rear of the 'tube' of the spine back to the coccyx.

When this prayer has borne fruit you can alternate it with the following prayers:
'Lord Jesus Christ, come into my heart.'
'Lord Jesus Christ, illuminate me by Thy light.'

## The Eighteenth Arcanum

'Lord Jesus Christ, let me enter the Kingdom of Heaven.'
The basis of these prayers is in the Gospel. Jesus said: 'Verily, verily, I say unto you, Whatsoever ye shall ask the Father in my name, he will give it you.

Hitherto have ye asked nothing in my name: ask, and ye shall receive, that your joy may be full.' (John 16:23-24)
'Ask, and it shall be given you; seek, and ye shall find; knock, and it shall be opened unto you:
For every one that asketh receiveth; and he that seeketh findeth; and to him that knocketh it shall be opened.' (Matthew 7:7-8)
Therefore if the believer will observe Christ's commandments and will keep his mind, body and heart clean, the Lord will make his prayers come true. Jesus Christ, the Son of the Father in Heaven, has an immeasurable power, given to Him by His Father, to forgive sins and to fulfil prayers.

The Kingdom of Heaven is not of this world, while we are in this world only temporarily and we shouldn't forget these facts. This remembrance helps us not to identify with our temporary shelter and to work for the sake of our eventual goal: reaching the Kingdom of Heaven.
We now live in such a way as if we would stay on this earth for ever, as if our soul will never part from our body. All our concerns are about our body and not about our soul. Isn't this being kept imprisoned by the great delusion? Rise from the ashes, believer, and use your energy which is still left for the salvation of your soul and to find the Lord in your heart. Do not forget the Kingdom of Heaven and Christ Who awaits us there.
'If ye abide in me, and my words abide in you, ye shall ask what ye will, and it shall be done unto you.' (John 15:7)
If you learn to make your prayer and contemplation practices fruitful, you will find the Lord Jesus Christ in your heart and you will be able to converse with Him. Then you may ask Christ for something

and He will fulfil your request. But this is so only for the believers who learned to keep their body, mind and heart clean.

A believer should turn to the message of the Eighteenth Arcanum every day of his life.

The Nineteenth Arcanum

## The Nineteenth Arcanum. Receiving the Holy Spirit

The Nineteenth Arcanum states the following spiritual truth: a believer is able to receive the Holy Spirit through a righteous life and prayerful work and contemplation.

The picture of this Arcanum represents a holy elder, who through his great ascetic feats and works of virtue has received the Holy Spirit from the Lord.

The Holy Spirit is the Third Hypostasis of the Holy Trinity. He is also called 'the Comforter' for He comforts the souls of the believers, who have become exhausted waging spiritual warfare and who beg for help and rest on the narrow and arduous path to the Kingdom of Heaven. 'Seek first of all the Holy Spirit,' says Saint Seraphim of Sarov.

When the fire of the Holy Spirit comes onto a believer, he feels that his soul is carried away to the highest spiritual spheres while his body remains on earth. He feels an endless joy and happiness as he leaves behind the material life with all its problems. He abides in a state of bliss as he has become one with the Divine eternal light and time doesn't have power over him. He realizes that his spirit soars beyond time and space, and that it abides in the world where there is no grief and loss, but where there is peace, love and eternal bliss, which are the qualities of the Holy Spirit. The believer finds the happiness there that he sought vainly on earth, as it is impossible to find this happiness in the manifested world.

Holy elders know that earthly happiness is followed by suffering and therefore they seek the true happiness and joy, which come from contact with the Holy Spirit. God the Father sent God the Holy Spirit to support and to comfort the believers who seek Him. The Holy Spirit is the beginning and the end of all and of everything, He abides invisibly in all things but unbelievers cannot perceive Him, for He reveals Himself only to the pure of heart.

## The Nineteenth Arcanum

Worldly desires pollute the heart and it cannot perceive the unspeakably clear light of the Holy Spirit. Unbelievers however are not aware of this and they still rotate in the circle of cause-and-effect ties, trying to find their happiness in the manifested world, but there is no happiness for them, neither in the physical world nor in the world behind the curtain. They cannot grasp that there is no greater happiness than communication with the Holy Spirit and it is only through the Holy Spirit that people can have true unity with each other.

Those believers, who truly came to know the Holy Spirit, sacrificed their attachment to the fruits of their earthly works to Him. By the sword of wisdom they cut off their doubts about the existence of the Holy Spirit and they found the ultimate liberation. And though they constantly lived in the manifested world, they were not liable to its law of cause and effect.

The ignorance of believers with regard to their spiritual nature is the reason why they are reluctant to start the quest for the Holy Spirit. If they only would believe that their nature is of the spirit, they would boldly throw off all the doubts which have their seat in our hearts and step on the path of spiritual growth.

In order to merit receiving the Holy Spirit and conversing with Him, it is necessary to acquire inner silence.

**On silence**

The Holy Spirit, full of mercy, descends onto him who has acquired silence.

1. Holy elders say that a believer should first acquire silence of the body, and then silence of the soul.

2. Silence of the body is acquired when it is curbed and doesn't have passions, is content with little food and short sleep; doesn't have voluptuous and lecherous desires neither during the day nor at night, doesn't feel attracted to physical pleasures.

3. Silence of the soul is a state in which the soul doesn't cherish passionate designs; doesn't feel attracted to pleasures of the flesh,

is not irritated or angry; is not proud and doesn't seek praise of fellow-men; accepts quietly mocking and insults; is not envious and doesn't fall into depression, boredom and sadness; is not infected by the love of money; is not burdened by excessive concern of earthly well-being; doesn't fear, but has a pure faith in God, loves Him and has a firm hope of salvation.

4. The believer who has taken the vow of silence keeps in mind a strict and manly intention to receive the Holy Spirit, which vigilantly guards his heart, cutting off all the passionate designs and earthly concerns. He doesn't allow thoughts which are not about God, to settle in his heart.

5. The silent person prays incessantly in his mind and his heart; through prayer he converses with the Holy Spirit. He walks before God and he continues praying even while his body sleeps. All his works are open to God and he sees how the Lord watches him.

6. The ear of the silent hears a marvellous revelation of the Holy Spirit when he obtains the blissful sweetness of contact with God. In order not to lose this reward for his inner work he avoids people, without being a misanthrope.

7. The believer who has reached the heaven of silence praises and sings the Holy Spirit the Comforter; he is full of blissful love for God and secretly converses with Him.

8. He who has not yet come to know God, is not able to take the vow of silence and if he attempts to live as a hermit in an uninhabited place, he will find many troubles and will be attacked by demons.

9. Only delightful communication with the Holy Spirit saves the silent from misfortune and demons' attacks.

10. He who took the vow of silence must constantly serve the Holy Spirit and be focused on Him.

11. If the silent person stops praying he might immediately fall, like a novice who relies on his own will. (From the Philokalia, abridged) When the believer receives the Holy Spirit, his heart feels divine joy and peace.

## The Nineteenth Arcanum

Jesus said: 'And whatsoever ye shall ask in my name, that will I do, that the Father may be glorified in the Son.
If ye shall ask any thing in my name, I will do it.
If ye love me, keep my commandments.
And I will pray the Father, and he shall give you another Comforter, that he may abide with you for ever;
Even the Spirit of truth; whom the world cannot receive, because it seeth him not, neither knoweth him: but ye know him; for he dwelleth with you, and shall be in you.' (John 14:13-17)

Therefore the believer should plead with Jesus Christ, so that He will ask our Father in Heaven to send Him the Holy Spirit.

Jesus said: 'If ye then, being evil, know how to give good gifts unto your children: how much more shall your heavenly Father give the Holy Spirit to them that ask him?'
If the believer can converse in the silence of his heart with the Lord Jesus Christ, he can move the Lord by entreaties to send him the Holy Spirit, the Comforter. For this he should learn to make his prayer and contemplation exercises and the Jesus Prayer in his heart fruitful. Only when his prayer will be heard and accepted by the Lord, may he hope that his wish to receive the Holy Spirit will be fulfilled, for it is impossible to receive the Holy Spirit without the benevolence of Jesus Christ.
As the holy Fathers teach, the believer learns to converse with God through prayer. This learning process is an arduous work, which can only be accomplished by a constant super-effort of the believer.

Read the following fragments of the Gospel of John which tell about Christ's Message.

Jesus said: 'Believest thou not that I am in the Father, and the Father in me? the words that I speak unto you I speak not of myself: but the Father that dwelleth in me, he doeth the works.

Believe me that I am in the Father, and the Father in me: or else believe me for the very works' sake.

Verily, verily, I say unto you, He that believeth on me, the works that I do shall he do also; and greater works than these shall he do; because I go unto my Father.

And whatsoever ye shall ask in my name, that will I do, that the Father may be glorified in the Son.

If ye shall ask any thing in my name, I will do it.

If ye love me, keep my commandments.

And I will pray the Father, and he shall give you another Comforter, that he may abide with you for ever;

Even the Spirit of truth; whom the world cannot receive, because it seeth him not, neither knoweth him: but ye know him; for he dwelleth with you, and shall be in you.

I will not leave you comfortless: I will come to you.

Yet a little while, and the world seeth me no more; but ye see me: because I live, ye shall live also.

At that day ye shall know that I am in my Father, and ye in me, and I in you.' (John 14:10-20)

Jesus said these words to His apostles. He soon would be betrayed and crucified. But then Christ resurrected and appeared before the apostles full of the glory of His Father, and the apostles saw that Jesus Christ is the true God and that He abides in His Father in Heaven, and the Father in Heaven abides in Him.

Jesus said: 'He that loveth me not keepeth not my sayings: and the word which ye hear is not mine, but the Father's which sent me.' (John 14:24)

Passions are sacrificed for the sake of Christ's love. Otherwise Christ will not come in the heart. However the love for Christ should be confirmed by deeds, that is by observing His commandments.

Jesus said: 'These things have I spoken unto you, being yet present with you.

But the Comforter, which is the Holy Ghost, whom the Father will send in my name, he shall teach you all things, and bring all things to your remembrance, whatsoever I have said unto you.

Peace I leave with you, my peace I give unto you: not as the world giveth, give I unto you. Let not your heart be troubled, neither let it be afraid.

Ye have heard how I said unto you, I go away, and come again unto you. If ye loved me, ye would rejoice, because I said, I go unto the Father: for my Father is greater than I.

And now I have told you before it come to pass, that, when it is come to pass, ye might believe.

Hereafter I will not talk much with you: for the prince of this world cometh, and hath nothing in me.

But that the world may know that I love the Father; and as the Father gave me commandment, even so I do.' (John 14:25-31)

Jesus will be crucified and will resurrect on the third day in the Name of His Father, and will appear to the apostles so that they see that Jesus Christ is the true God. Jesus has little time to be with the apostles because the devil wants his death and he seduced the priests of the Jews for this evil deed. The devil wants Jesus' death, because Jesus was sent by God to save people from their imprisonment by the devil, who rules in the fallen world and is constantly seducing people to sin and to fall away from God, so that he can torture them eternally in hell.

Jesus said: 'He that hateth me hateth my Father also.

If I had not done among them the works which none other man did, they had not had sin: but now have they both seen and hated both me and my Father.

But this cometh to pass, that the word might be fulfilled that is written in their law, They hated me without a cause.

But when the Comforter is come, whom I will send unto you from the Father, even the Spirit of truth, which proceedeth from the Father, he shall testify of me:

And ye also shall bear witness, because ye have been with me from the beginning.'

**Prayer to Jesus Christ for calling upon the Holy Spirit**
The prayer 'Lord Jesus Christ, Son of God, send me the Holy Spirit, the Comforter' should be recited in combination with the spiritual breath, concentrating at the same time on the heart. While inhaling pronounce in your heart 'Lord Jesus Christ, Son of God' and move energy from the coccyx to the 'spiritual eye' and then move it one metre further along the horizontal line projected forward from the spiritual eye. By exhaling pronounce 'Send to me the Holy Spirit, the Comforter', bringing at the same time the energy back along this line and then along the rear of the 'tube' of the spine back to the coccyx.

**Prayers to the Holy Spirit**
Recite the prayer 'Lord Holy Spirit, the Comforter, come and dwell in us, and cleanse us of all impurity and save our souls, o Good One,' in combination with the spiritual breath.
While inhaling pronounce in your heart 'Lord Holy Spirit, the Comforter, come and dwell in us' and move energy from the coccyx to the 'spiritual eye' and then move it one metre further along the horizontal line projected forward from the spiritual eye. By exhaling pronounce 'and cleanse us of all impurity and save our souls, o Good One.', bringing at the same time the energy back along this line and then along the rear of the 'tube' of the spine back to the coccyx. If this exercise becomes fruitful for you, you may use the shorter prayers:
'Lord Holy Spirit, cleanse me, sinner'
'Lord Holy Spirit, forgive me, sinner.'

## Prayers to the Holy Spirit in combination with the spiritual breath, meant for the struggle with passions

The following prayers are used for protection from the demon of one or other passion:

'Lord Holy Spirit, the Comforter, protect me from the passion of gluttony.'

'Lord Holy Spirit, the Comforter, protect me from the passion of despondency and sadness.'

'Lord Holy Spirit, the Comforter, protect me from the passion of love of money.'

'Lord Holy Spirit, the Comforter, protect me from the passion of malice and envy.'

'Lord Holy Spirit, the Comforter, protect me from the passion of pride.'

'Lord Holy Spirit, the Comforter, protect me from the passion of vanity.'

'Lord Holy Spirit, the Comforter, protect me from the passion of resentment.'

'Lord Holy Spirit, the Comforter, protect me from the passion of backbiting and condemnation.'

'Lord Holy Spirit, the Comforter, protect me from the passion of fornication.'

'Lord Holy Spirit, the Comforter, protect me from the passion of verbosity.'

Another two prayers to the Holy Spirit:

'Lord Holy Spirit, cleanse me by God's fire.'

'Lord Holy Spirit, save me'

The believer should turn to the message of the Nineteenth Arcanum constantly, every day of his life.

The Twentieth Arcanum

## The Twentieth Arcanum. Finding God the Father in one's heart

The Twentieth Arcanum states the following spiritual truth: through leading a solitary life, hour-long prayer and contemplation exercises under the spiritual guidance of a holy elder, fasting, observing the commandments of Jesus Christ and working for Him, a believer can merit the grace to find God the Father inside his heart. The picture of this Arcanum represents a holy elder, who found God the Father in his heart; and God the Father gave him inner peace beyond any thought. Now the elder labours for God the Father, carrying out His will.

The holy elder has climbed the ladder which leads to the higher worlds, to our Father in Heaven, having completed the entire route of ascending. Like a prodigal son he returned into the spiritual world of the Father in Heaven who has been awaiting him an innumerable amount of time and he can contemplate the Creator of the Universe who has been pouring out His love for His creation.

The heaven is emanating spiritual fire, resembling the flaming sun, which doesn't burn the body but which could burn the soul. When the elder aspired to the invisible sun his soul was immersed in the centre of the spiritual fire which gives life to the entire creation.

The flaming sun of the Father in Heaven penetrates the entire universe with its spiritual radiance which brings life and joy to all beings in the Universe. If the elder, at a time of ordeal forgets about the Creator, his soul can fade away instantaneously and sink in the darkness of ignorance. However, if he remembers again the eternal Source of life behind the dazzling spiritual sun, the darkness pulls back, and joy illuminates his sad heart.

**On the Creator's love for His creation**
When the believer has elevated his consciousness by means of prayer and spiritual contemplation, he becomes aware of the fact that the Father in Heaven is inseparably with people, but people cannot perceive Him because their body, mind and heart are polluted. God always cares for people, His creation. When man is a baby, He manifests His most tender love for him through the love of his parents, and supports his growth. Later God manifests His love for man through the romantic feelings of people who are in love with each other. He gives us what we need through our close and loyal friends. He takes care of our spiritual growth through the prophets and our spiritual mentors, He let His Son be crucified on the cross for the sake of our salvation, He is always with us, but we cannot meet Him because of our imperfection.

However the believer can realize this only when God Himself reveals Himself in his heart and helps him to understand this: 'Behold, thou desirest truth in the inward parts: and in the hidden part thou shalt make me to know wisdom.' (Ps. 51:6) A believer will be amazed and stunned that before, he couldn't even guess it and he sought God everywhere while He lived in his heart and was always near, and only now he can realize this due to fervent prayer. And more to it, the believer can easily lose this understanding if he does not cherish it.

It is God Who gives us, through those who love us, His burning love, but we do not even have the slightest suspicion of it. Instead of thanking the Creator for the love he granted us, we attempt to possess our beloved, through whom God sends us elevated feelings. Therefore we are always on the loosing side, as when we possess our beloved we become attached to them and we cannot understand that the joy of love comes from the all-merciful Creator of the Universe. However even though we would obtain this understanding we won't be able to keep it if we won't immerse regularly in fervent prayer, for the elevated manifestations of the Creator disappear from this world because it is rough and cold.

## The Twentieth Arcanum

O God the Father! How intimate is Thy love for Thy creatures, how tenderly dost Thee care for them, manifesting Thy love through those who love us as long as they are ready to receive Thy immeasurable love. But if they deny Thee, they become frozen for a long time in the cold opposition, not being able to return to the marvellous land of eternal bliss. But when they ask Thee for help and repent their dark deeds, Thou, O Great Creator of the Universe, will always receive them in Thy radiant heart, and their eyes will open and their hearts will be cleansed. Having repented they will rise on the wings of piety to the Lord God and will enter His radiant palace filled with the spiritual light. The eternally radiating Father in Heaven penetrates the entire universe by His light, filled with eternal bliss and there are few who can perceive the pure light and contemplate its primordial beauty; only a few could meet the Creator without being burnt in His dazzling light.

The Creator of the Universe abides eternally in absolute bliss and His countenance never becomes darkened. To those who can see the dazzling purity of the Lord of Hosts He gives His love and care through our beloved ones who are close to us in spirit. O beloved Creator of the Universe, Thy love is immeasurably great and pure! Thou abidest always with us and Thou carest for us through those who love us. And when our soul and spirit are purified Thou revealest to us Thy radiant beauty, Thy unspoken mystery, which is concealed behind the seven seals, and the key to this mystery is the crystal purity of man's heart and aspiration to Thee.

The love for God the Father cannot darken our heart, it can only quieten and revive it.

All the love in the world is in the Father in Heaven and He is the One Who gave birth to it. The love that we feel for each other is a vague reflection of God's love which flames with its spiritual purity. It is full of spiritual fire which doesn't burn the souls that are ready, but it can scorch and burn the unclean hearts. Divine love leaves the hearts which are full of negativity and depression. The fire of God's love flows ceaselessly from the spiritual, inextinguishable sun in heaven and fills the pure souls which are faithful to God. These souls abide in constant bliss. Gods' beauty, filled with spiritual warmth, reaches us, His children, whom He loves so immeasurably, and His entire Creation. And there is no strength greater than God's strength, and there is no one who could oppose Him; there is also no one who could doubt this for a long time. In vain those whose heart is impure lament that God abandoned them, for they did not deserve His grace: for too long they were in doubt and in confrontation with His laws. And now they want to enjoy the light of the spiritual sun of the Creator of the Universe, without undergoing purification and suffering ...

All the love which was scattered over the earth and came into the hearts of people, is the manifestation of His ultimate mercy, given for the blossoming of the hearts of His sons and daughters, thrown into the fallen Universe. It is impossible for a rough, uncultivated heart or a heart overfull with worldly concerns and worldly suffering to feel this love. You will feel the highest love, God's love, if you, in your turn, devote your earthly heart to Him, Who created us, abiding in love in eternal bliss. Of course we can choose an illusory freedom: to love whom our heart wishes. We easily exchange God's love for us for an earthly love. We repeat this mistake until we have become aware of it and then we will direct all the ardour of our love to God, from Whom this love is poured into our straying hearts.

But then we cannot find the balance in our heart between love for God and love for a beloved person because of the impurity of our hearts. An impure heart cannot perceive the fiery love of the Holy Spirit, it feels love only for a man or a woman.

The heart however which doesn't love anybody, and is cold and indifferent cannot receive the life-giving love of God.

An envious and greedy heart cannot see the light of the highest love. The heart which is burdened by suffering through earthly love cannot feel the purity of the heavenly love too.

A jealous heart can never come closer to God because it always feels a 'just anger'.

A cold heart won't be warmed by spiritual fire because it is insensitive and rejects God's help beforehand.

A proud and vain heart will not be illuminated by God's love, it is like a dried up lake.

A cunning and perfidious heart is also too far from God and cannot perceive His most pure love which flows from an infinitely faraway world, where the beautiful Creator of the Universe abides.

In order to merit the mercy of conversing with God the Father, is necessary to obtain the state of passionlessness.

**On lack of passion**

1. Holy elders say: he who obtained passionlessness by holy prayers, comes closer to God for he can flow together with the highest spiritual light and will not be burned in the rays of the divine love.

2. A passionless believer sends his prayers to God day and night as he doesn't wish to think of anything else.

3. A passionless believer stands before God and converses with Him. He is not distracted by any thought which is not about God. His mind is as if chained to the Lord by the endless adoration of His eternal beauty.

4. There is no life for the passionless believer without the Lord and His highest love. The only sense of life for the believer is uniting with God the Father and receiving the highest, indescribable grace of God.

5. Elders defined several degrees of passionlessness.

The first degree is obtained when the believer, being seized by a bodily passion, doesn't give in to it and cuts it off.

The second degree of passionlesness is obtained when the believer cuts off all the passionate designs which penetrate into his heart.

The third degree is obtained when the believer has put an end to all his passionate, material day-dreams and wishes only to be one with God.

The fourth degree is obtained when the believer has become firmly established in his love for the Lord and doesn't allow the thoughts which are not of God to come into him. He prays constantly, day and night, awake and asleep. He abides constantly in unity with God, feeding his heart by God's sweetest grace. (from the Philokalia, abridged)

God the Father manifests Himself through the immaterial, un-created, spiritual light which can appear as a bright shining sun in the soul of an elder who has found salvation. The elder has become passionless and chaste, with a crystal clear mind, heart and body, like an innocent child.

**The necessary conditions for making the prayer to God the Father fruitful**

The believer should always remember God.

Every night, before going to sleep, the believer should note in his diary, how many times he recalled God that day.

It is possible for a believer to remember God constantly if he learns to divide his attention: one part of his consciousness can be directed to the worldly concerns and contacts with other people, while another part of him should remember God constantly, being focused on prayer, which he should recite incessantly in his heart: 'Our Father in Heaven, have mercy on me.'

If the earthly concerns demand more attention, it is possible to recite in the heart an abridged prayer: 'Lord, have mercy.' This prayer can be said wherever the believer is at that moment: at his work, travelling, talking to others and so on. When the believer has learned to say incessantly the abridged prayer he can start saying the full formula : 'Our Father in Heaven, have mercy on me, sinner.' It is a full formula in the sense that the believer acknowledges and confesses to God the transgressions of his sinful nature. Our enemies, the demons, try to create various obstacles for the believer, making praying difficult in all possible ways. However if the believer will not be frightened by these difficulties and will continue praying with the full formula of the prayer, then by the mercy of the Father in Heaven he will be gradually cleansed from his passions.

In the beginning the prayer can be recited for half an hour a day. Then he can gradually increase the duration of praying to five or six hours a day.

And if the believer makes a super-effort he can recite this prayer in his heart for the whole day without stopping his daily pursuits. In such a case the prayers can continue even in his dreams.

**Prayers to the Father in Heaven in combination with the spiritual breath, meant for the struggle with passions**

The following prayers are used for protection from the demon of one or other passion:

'Lord God, our Father in Heaven, protect me from the passion of gluttony.'

'Lord God, our Father in Heaven, protect me from the passion of despondency and sadness.'

'Lord God, our Father in Heaven, protect me from the passion of love of money.'

'Lord God, our Father in Heaven, protect me from the passion of malice and envy.'

'Lord God, our Father in Heaven, protect me from the passion of pride.'

'Lord God, our Father in Heaven, protect me from the passion of vanity.'

'Lord God, our Father in Heaven, protect me from the passion of resentment.'

'Lord God, our Father in Heaven, protect me from the passion of backbiting and condemnation.'

'Lord God, our Father in Heaven, protect me from the passion of fornication.'

'Lord God, our Father in Heaven, protect me from the passion of verbosity.'

Another two prayers to God the Father:

'Lord God, our Father in Heaven, Creator of all the worlds, cleanse me by Thy fire.'

'Lord God, our Father in Heaven, Creator of all the worlds, save me'

**Prayer and contemplation practice in combination with the spiritual breath for learning to converse with our Father in Heaven**

In order to learn to converse with the Father in Heaven it is necessary to recite inside the heart the following prayer: 'Lord God, our Father in Heaven, have mercy on me', performing at the same time the spiritual breath.

Pronounce this prayer fully during inhaling and exhaling. When during inhaling the energy reaches the spiritual eye, move it one metre further along the horizontal line projected forward from the spiritual eye. By exhaling bring energy back along this line and then along the rear of the 'tube' of the spine back to the coccyx.

When you have learned to say this prayer for at least one hour, you can recite another prayer: 'Our Father in Heaven, Creator of all the worlds, have mercy on me.' This prayer should be recited also not less than one hour.

When you have learned to recite these prayer in your physical heart, you have to learn to recite them in your spiritual heart which is located in the middle of the chest, in combination with the spiritual breath.

To God, those prayers are more pleasant which are said with the words of love, according to the first commandment given by God:

'And thou shalt love the Lord thy God with all thy heart, and with all thy soul, and with all thy mind, and with all thy strength: this is the first commandment.' (Mark 12:30)

Love for the Father in Heaven can rise in the silence of the heart; the holy Theotokos can teach the believer love for God if he will plead with Her for help. For Jesus said: 'Ask, and it shall be given you; seek, and ye shall find; knock, and it shall be opened unto you: For every one that asketh receiveth; and he that seeketh findeth; and to him that knocketh it shall be opened.' (Matthew 7:7-8)

## Prayers for kindling in the heart love for God the Father

Recite the following prayers, in combination with the spiritual breath:

'Lord God, our Father in Heaven, open my heart to Thy love.'
Pronounce while inhaling and moving energy upwards: 'Lord God, our Father in Heaven.'
Pronounce while exhaling and moving energy downwards: 'Open my heart to Thy love.'

'Our Father in Heaven, Creator of all the worlds, give us Thy love.'
Pronounce while inhaling and moving energy upwards: 'Our Father in Heaven, Creator of all the worlds.'
Pronounce while exhaling and moving energy downwards: 'Give us Thy love.'

'Our Father in Heaven, Creator of all the worlds, kindle the fire of love for Thee in my heart.'
Pronounce while inhaling and moving energy upwards: 'Our Father in Heaven, Creator of all the worlds.'
Pronounce while exhaling and moving energy downwards: 'kindle the fire of love for Thee in my heart.'

'Our Father in Heaven, Creator of all the worlds, let my heart burn with love for Thee.'
Pronounce while inhaling and moving energy upwards: 'Our Father in Heaven, Creator of all the worlds.'
Pronounce while exhaling and moving energy downwards: 'Kindle the fire of love for Thee in my heart.'

A believer should turn to the message of the Twentieth Arcanum regularly in the course of his life.

The Twenty First Arcanum

## The Twenty First Arcanum. The Epoch of the Paracletus

The Twenty First Arcanum states the following spiritual truth: the Holy Spirit will gradually transform and inspire the entire Universe. The picture of this Arcanum represents the Holy Trinity; the angels with trumpets announce the coming of God the Holy Spirit, Who is symbolized by the holy elder with the Message of God the Father in his hand.

When an elder was asked what do the words of Jesus 'I am come to send fire on the earth; and what will I, if it be already kindled?' (Luke 12:49) mean, he answered: 'Jesus speaks here about the Holy Spirit, for the Holy Spirit is God's fire, which kindles the hearts and the inner of man. Through Christ we joined the Divine fire, that is 'I am come to send fire on earth'; the words 'and what will I, if it already be kindled?' proclaim the coming of the era of the Holy Spirit, for the Divine fire will gradually seize the whole earth and the entire Universe!'

When the Holy Trinity decided to save fallen humanity, God the Father, the first Person of the Trinity, appeared Himself to His elect, Moses, who had to start fulfilling the Divine plan. After that, Moses constantly prayed God the Father, and God the Father answered his prayers and appeared to Moses several times, giving him guidance and support at the crucial moments.

Then God the Father sent to mankind His only-begotten Son, Jesus Christ, Who brought mankind the Glad Tidings of God the Father and established for man the path to ascend to Him and gave man love, energy and the means to actually do it.

The time will come, and now is, when God's Third Hypostasis, God the Holy Spirit, will be even more present, and the Spirit of the living God will manifest Himself all over the earth, and the times of the universal joy and the new paths of ascending to God will come into being. God the Holy Spirit will reveal the unknown mysteries and depths of the Message of our Lord Jesus Christ. Jesus Christ had proclaimed this, for He said to the Samaritan woman: 'But the hour cometh, and now is, when the true worshippers shall worship the Father in spirit and in truth: for the Father seeketh such to worship him.

God is a Spirit: and they that worship him must worship him in spirit and in truth.' (John 4:23-24)

We know the following, which is said in the Holy Scripts about the Holy Spirit, the Comforter:

1. The spontaneity of His manifestation. Jesus said: 'The wind bloweth where it listeth, and thou hearest the sound thereof, but canst not tell whence it cometh, and whither it goeth: so is every one that is born of the Spirit.' (John 3:8)

2. The Holy Spirit carries in Him the basis of the real spiritual friendship and it helps the believers, who are open to Him, to find unity in the spiritual traditions, which lead to God, 'where there is neither Greek nor Jew, circumcision nor uncircumcision, Barbarian, Scythian, bond nor free: but Christ is all, and in all.' (Colossians 3:11)

3. The Holy Spirit reveals to His followers the Divine intelligence and the understanding of God's and man's laws. Jesus said: 'But the Comforter, which is the Holy Ghost, whom the Father will send in my name, he shall teach you all things, and bring all things to your remembrance, whatsoever I have said unto you.'(John 14:26)

And He also said: 'Howbeit when he, the Spirit of truth, is come, he will guide you into all truth: for he shall not speak of himself; but whatsoever he shall hear, that shall he speak: and he will shew you things to come.

He shall glorify me: for he shall receive of mine, and shall shew it unto you.'(John 16:13-14)

4. The Holy Spirit is full of mercy for all people, He doesn't accuse or punish, He forgives those who plead with Him for forgiveness.

## The Twenty First Arcanum

5. The Holy Spirit inspires people to do good deeds not out of fear of pain and suffering, but out of spiritual joy which belongs to His nature and which He shares with the believers.

The aeon of grievance, fear, pain and suffering will be over; the aeon of spiritual joy will begin, when the Holy Spirit descends on earth in His full Divine beauty.

After the death of the physical body the souls of the sinners will be judged by strict judges, for whom many things are sinful and the souls will be punished severely. God the Holy Spirit takes under His special protection the believers, who worked for Him, during their earthly life as well as after their death, helping them to pass the aerial ordeals without being harmed and imprisoned, so that they will continue working for Him also in their afterlife. To work for the Holy Spirit means to live according to His above-mentioned qualities.

It is described in the Gospel of John how Jesus Christ transmitted the Holy Spirit to the apostles.

'Then the same day at evening, being the first day of the week, when the doors were shut where the disciples were assembled for fear of the Jews, came Jesus and stood in the midst, and saith unto them, Peace be unto you.

And when he had so said, he shewed unto them his hands and his side. Then were the disciples glad, when they saw the Lord.

Then said Jesus to them again, Peace be unto you: as my Father hath sent me, even so send I you.

And when he had said this, he breathed on them, and saith unto them, Receive ye the Holy Ghost:

Whose soever sins ye remit, they are remitted unto them; and whose soever sins ye retain, they are retained.' (John 20:19-23)

To whom the apostles forgive sins on earth, those will be forgiven in heaven, and to whom the apostles won't forgive their sins on earth, those won't be forgiven in heaven, and they will be judged in the afterlife.

## The Epoch of the Paracletus

Christ gave to His apostles the power of the Holy Spirit to forgive sins, which is in essence the power to liberate from sins the souls of those who confessed their sins to the apostles and repented them. When the Church was created, the apostles ordained some of the believers, which means in essence that they transmitted to them the power of the Holy Spirit which they had received. Thus the priests could also forgive the sins of the believers who confessed and repented them, and carry out the other sacraments. This ritual of the transmitting of the power of the Holy Spirit, which thus has been established by the Lord, is the spiritual basis of the Church. He who hasn't been ordained, who didn't receive the power of the Holy Spirit, cannot forgive sins.

Our Father in Heaven has sent the Holy Spirit in the Name of Jesus Christ on the apostles and since then the Holy Spirit abides on earth. In the past He revealed Himself only to the saints who merited it by their ascetic life and great works of virtue. However in the epoch of the Holy Spirit, He will become accessible to the common people also. In the third millennium the Holy Spirit will increase more and more His influence on people and it will be even easier to receive Him.

However, believers should not wait passively for the coming of these times but they should start preparing their soul, for the Holy Spirit is the spiritual fire and an unprepared soul can burn down. The believer should constantly try to observe Christ's commandments and keep his heart, mind and body clean, which means a constant waging of the spiritual warfare for the purity of his soul. The essential part of this struggle is that he should learn and practise inner prayer and spiritual contemplation.

The Holy Spirit, the Comforter, will descend from heaven and He will fill our souls with God's grace. He will bring the serene, heavenly joy, life which streams incessantly, like angels' hymns. The heart will rejoice and the soul, which got tired on its way to the Kingdom of Heaven, will be consoled.

## The Twenty First Arcanum

The Holy Spirit carries in Him an unspeakable joy and He inspires the tired wayfarers to raise their heads and not to feel despondent on the way to eternal life. Blissful love will gradually seize the believer's soul and will delight the heart which grieves without God. There is nothing more delightful than the angel's hymn of praise to the Holy Spirit and there is no higher bliss than uniting with the grace which comes from the innermost of our Father in Heaven. When the believer reaches even the first stage of this bliss he immediately forgets the troubles of the world and all the suffering that he has undergone while ascending to the Kingdom of Heaven, for this suffering is nothing in comparison with the bliss of spiritual love which overflows the heart.

Therefore, believers, you who walk on the path to the Kingdom of Heaven, do not stop and do not lose heart. All your afflictions and difficulties are temporary, for God let them come on you so that your souls would become tempered and ready to meet the eternal radiance of our Lord.

Believers, who got tired on their way, do not trust the voice of sweet-singing sirens; do not burden your heart with earthly affections and do not darken it by the insatiable passions of anger, envy and earthly love. All this is transitional: therefore believers take care that you do not exchange the eternal bliss for earthly achievements, do not stop making daily super-efforts in order to carry out the prayer and contemplation exercises, do not forget God even for a moment because you are always before His eyes. Remember yourself, that is remember your intention to reach the Kingdom of Heaven; do not let yourself be carried away by the beauty and pleasures of this world for they unnoticeably poison your soul and hinder you in reaching the main purpose for which you were born. The more time you will spend with transitory things the lesser chances you have to find the eternal bliss and joy which await you in the heavenly spheres. The earthly joy is near, but the heavenly joy is more reliable for it lasts eternally, while the earthly joy lasts a moment.

Remember yourself, that is remember that you intend to find God inside your heart before your soul parts from your body. Remember yourself, that is remember that you must work on yourself every day and cleanse your mind, heart and body from passionate designs, earthly desires and the consequences of pernicious actions. Remember that in order to find God you should practise the contemplation and prayer exercises for a long while. Believer, you who are bent under the burden of wrong deeds, do not forget to perform the right actions which lead to God.

Believer, do not identify with your anger and sadness, and do not trust the advice of your pride, because everything that you have, you received from God. It is God Who gives us everything, through the people around us, and if we lose what we have, then it happens because of our self-will, vanity and pride.

It is better for the believer to gather spiritual treasures inside his soul which are, to be submissive before God, to understand the necessity to work on yourself and to resign yourself to the instructions of your spiritual mentor for he has already found God in his heart; to resign yourself to the fact that the Kingdom of Heaven can be reached only by long work and enduring inner suffering together with inner work; to resign yourself to the fact that the world will not understand you, but will mock and reject you; to resign yourself to the necessity to hide from the world that you follow the spiritual path, for when those around you will come to know this, they will reject you because you want to find the Lord while they turned away from Him, having neglected the narrow and arduous path which leads to Him. Some got exhausted on the broad path of life, their bodies, minds and hearts became old and lost their energy; others lost their hope or were felled by numerous illnesses; others lost all that they had gained in their life and are full of fruitless regret. Believer, don't be like those who do not bear spiritual fruit at the end of their lives; like those who, in a fit of pride have forgotten the Lord and came under the influence of the dark powers, which await them after their death. Do not let yourself be charmed by the songs of sweet-singing sirens, for their voices do not lead to the heavenly spheres, they lead astray from the spiritual path and the believers being charmed by the outer beauty, forget the spiritual path until the end of their days. Be like children and the gates of the Kingdom of Heaven will open for you.

In order to receive the Holy Spirit, it is necessary to observe chastity.

**On chastity**

Only the chaste can climb to the top of the ladder to heaven.

1. Chastity includes the sum of all the virtues, which are the qualities given by God to oppose the passions and to come closer to Him.
2. He who conquered only one passion cannot be considered as chaste.
3. If the believer eliminated fornication in himself, but fell into depression, he cannot be considered as chaste.
4. If the believer eliminated the passion of fornication, sadness and depression, but didn't eliminate the passion of love of money, he cannot be considered as chaste.
5. If the believer eliminated six passions and there is only one left, he still cannot be considered as chaste, for the demons can concentrate all their power in just one passion which becomes ineradicable.
6. Therefore the believer should turn to the Lord Jesus Christ and the Theotokos, pleading with them for help in his struggle with the passions, for he won't be able to win from the demons, the enemies of the human race.
7. The demons stir the passions in the believers in order to lead them astray, to confuse them and to make them stop seeking salvation for their soul and the Kingdom of Heaven.
8. Therefore the struggle with passions is in essence the struggle with demons who try to seduce the soul and make it fall.
9. That believer is chaste who eliminated all his passions and abides in contemplative conversation with God. He doesn't fornicate, doe-

sn't slander, doesn't condemn his neighbour, restrains himself in eating and drinking, doesn't seek praise from his fellow-men, is meek and humble, doesn't amass earthly riches but amasses the imperishable riches in heaven by daily work on himself, is not sad and depressed, is not greedy and observes the Lord's commandments. 10. As elders say, only few elders obtained chastity. (Philokalia, abridged)

The believer can find the Holy Spirit in his heart by reciting incessantly the following prayer: 'Holy Spirit, the Comforter, have mercy on me' in combination with the spiritual breath. In order for the believer to receive the merciful gifts of the Holy Spirit he should make a regular super-effort and remember the Holy Spirit also amidst the turmoil of everyday.

**Prayers to the Holy Spirit asking the heavenly grace**
Recite the following prayers in combination with the spiritual breath:

'Lord Holy Spirit, the Comforter, send onto me Thy joy'
'Lord Holy Spirit, the Comforter, send onto me Thy support.'
'Lord Holy Spirit, the Comforter, send onto me Thy love.'
'Lord Holy Spirit, the Comforter, send onto me Thy grace.'
'Lord Holy Spirit, the Comforter, send onto me Thy bliss.'
'Lord Holy Spirit, the Comforter, send onto me Thy protection.'
'Lord Holy Spirit, the Comforter, send onto me Thy understanding.'
'Lord Holy Spirit, the Comforter, send onto me Thy wisdom.'

A believer can merit the descent of the Holy Spirit in his heart if he will recite these prayers in his heart for two or three hours a day in combination with the spiritual breath. He might experience various states of bliss and spiritual fire. He might feel heat coming from his heart which can be so intense that it might be necessary to take a cold shower. He might see an immaterial light: it might seem to him

## The Twenty First Arcanum

at night that there is light around him, but if he opens his eyes he will find darkness. He might feel subtle spiritual states, the smell of heavenly flowers, softness of the heart, the bliss of spiritual love and similar elevated inner states as the Holy Spirit, the Comforter, is divers in His manifestations and His care for the believers. He manifests Himself not only through a spiritual, burning fire, but also through the eternally renewed beauty of the higher worlds.

A believer should turn to the Twenty First Arcanum all the days of his conscious life.

The Twenty Second Arcanum

## THE TWENTY SECOND ARCANUM. FINDING THE HOLY TRINITY IN ONE'S HEART

The Twenty Second Arcanum states the following spiritual truth: having integrated and realized the messages of the previous twenty one Arcana, a believer can find God the Holy Trinity in his heart.

We know about the manifestations of God the Trinity as three angels, visiting patriarch Abraham; as the Lord Jesus Christ, receiving baptism, the Holy Spirit descending on Him and the Voice of God the Father in Heaven; as the Lord Jesus Christ, shining with the Holy Spirit and enveloped in a dazzling cloud from which the voice of God the Father came on Mount Tabor.

God – the Holy Trinity appears to the spiritual eyes of some elders as a vast spiritual sun, shining with an unimaginable, uncreated light.

The picture of this Arcanum represents the symbolic picture of the Triune God and the elder who found the Holy Trinity in his heart. The elder is no longer afraid of death, for he has become immortal: he has full control of the outer man and he has revived the inner man. He is in constant contact with the Father in Heaven, with the Lord Jesus Christ and with the Holy Spirit; he renounced himself and he carries out the Will of the Holy Trinity.

The elder crossed the abyss about which our forefather Abraham tells the dead rich man: 'And beside all this, between us and you there is a great gulf fixed: so that they which would pass from hence to you cannot; neither can they pass to us, that would come from thence.' (Luke 16:26) The elder however has crossed, by God's mercy, this abyss and following God's Word he climbed to the top of the sacred mountain where God abides: 'I cried unto the Lord with my voice, and he heard me out of his holy hill.' (Ps. 3:4) and he found Him in his own heart.

## Finding the Holy Trinity in one's heart

The elder has realized his highest essence, his divine nature and he knows now that his true nature is the divine light. He became one in spirit with God the Father, with God the Son and God the Holy Spirit, but at the same time he didn't lose his individuality. Having become one with the Holy Trinity, he became one, in his consciousness, with all living beings, created by the Holy Trinity and he realized that in essence he is one with them, being temporarily separated from them by his transitional material shelter and his ego.

The elder found perfect inner serenity and peace; even amidst the turmoil of the worldly life he remains untouched by its temptations. He is constantly one with the Creator and through this unity he feels that he is one with the entire Creation. He sees how the Father in Heaven creates the new worlds and he can become one with the consciousness of every human being and understand the cause of its delusions because he feels himself a conscious sparkle of God's light. He has now found the radiant sun of the Holy Trinity inside his heart and he realizes that he always was one with It, but before his darkened consciousness couldn't perceive this. He realizes that God is love and that His love embraces and fills all the manifested worlds. God loves His creation and he gives His love to all, as the sun gives its light to all living beings. 'That ye may be the children of your Father which is in heaven: for he maketh his sun to rise on the evil and on the good, and sendeth rain on the just and on the unjust.' (Matthew 5:45) Therefore man comes to know God through love, and the more sincere is his love of God, the deeper the mysteries of God are revealed to him.

The elder realized that everything comes from God and with time returns to him; that God is for him father and mother, and the most beloved One, and that he can love and worship Him always and everywhere, and only if his heart is unclean he doesn't feel this love. Immediately if man gives in to worldly desires, the heart is covered with dark clouds, through which the Divine love cannot pass.

## The Twenty Second Arcanum

**Work for God**

For the salvation of fallen humanity God sent on earth the God-Man Jesus Christ, His only-begotten Son, to help people find God inside themselves and ascend to the Kingdom of Heaven.

Christ chose the twelve apostles and during three years He transmitted to them part of His knowledge: how man can gain the mercy to converse with God; how to keep the mind, heart and body clean; how to wage spiritual warfare; to struggle with the passions and with the demons which lurk behind each passion. Jesus Christ, Who, as the Son of God, truly knows God the Father and the heart of man, brought on earth new spiritual laws and the new teaching of supreme love and humility, of God's compassion, and He taught people true chastity, and He confirmed what He taught by His resurrection, three days after His death on the cross. During these three days Christ descended with His soul to hell and he liberated that part of mankind which had been languishing there, starting with our forefather Adam and the foremother Eve, to whom He brought God's forgiveness. He sent onto the apostles the Holy Spirit, so that they could continue learning from the Holy Trinity also after Jesus Christ had ascended to His Father in Heaven. Thus, in our common language, Jesus Christ has accomplished an enormous work for God the Father, Who sent Christ in the world to transmit the new spiritual Message to the fallen humanity. The apostles, having assimilated Christ's teaching so far as their soul and spirit were capable, spread the teaching all over the earth so that all peoples could grow spiritually and aspire to God the Trinity.

Jesus said: 'All power is given unto me in heaven and in earth.

Go ye therefore, and teach all nations, baptizing them in the name of the Father, and of the Son, and of the Holy Ghost:

Teaching them to observe all things whatsoever I have commanded you: and, lo, I am with you always, even unto the end of the world. Amen.' (Matthew 28:18-20)

The Apostles obeyed Jesus' command to continue His work for God and they built the Church which labours fruitfully up till now in the Lord's field helping the believers to enter the Kingdom of Heaven.

The Jews rejected Jesus Christ and His teaching, while the heathens: the Romans, the Greeks, the Egyptians and, gradually, many other peoples, adopted Christ's teaching and have become the faithful confessors of the Triune God: the Father, the Son and the Holy Spirit, as Jesus predicted it Himself: 'And I say unto you, That many shall come from the east and west, and shall sit down with Abraham, and Isaac, and Jacob, in the kingdom of heaven.

But the children of the kingdom shall be cast out into outer darkness: there shall be weeping and gnashing of teeth.' (Matthew 8:11-12)

Jesus Christ built a spiritual path to God and those, who followed Christ, grew spiritually to such an extent that they could converse, in a prayerful silence, with God the Trinity. This is the highest reward for man that is received, when the believer wins, by God's mercy and help, the spiritual warfare.

**The three stages of spiritual warfare**

1. Struggling with the passions and making the soul and the body passionless. Learning how to keep mind, heart and body clean. Regular carrying out of the prayer and contemplation exercises, up to several hours a day.

The perils of the first stage: taking illusory spiritual growth for real; accepting the visions and thoughts, inflicted by the demons, under the guise of messages of light, which leads to a fall into the depth of hell.

2. The transmission of one's knowledge and experience of ascending on the spiritual path to one's neighbours.

The perils of the second stage: growing vanity and pride in the believer, who has become or was appointed as a spiritual mentor; self-extolling to others, forgetting that all the virtues are given by God and belong to Him; secret pleasure in the power over other peopl and violence towards them which is inevitably followed by an even deeper fall into hell.

3. Having preserved faithfulness to God on the first two stages, having reached a sufficient level of spiritual growth and having merited conversation with God, be ready to work for God. The Lord Himself will indicate to such a believer what work should be done in His Name.

If the believer won't get down to the second stage, but will continue the activities of the first stage only, because of his egocentricity, he might soon lose the inspiration and support of the Lord, which is crucial for him: if the Lord supports him he is on the path to Him. The Lord supports the believer on the first stage of the spiritual warfare by giving him His love and grace and caring for him tenderly, in order to help the believer's heart to open. The Lord gives him everything, but He can also turn His face away from him, if the believer's pride starts growing at the first fruits of his prayers and exercises and he starts thinking that it was *he* who has achieved everything by *his* own efforts. Then the Lord leaves such a believer to his own lot, and his life without the Lord and His love becomes monotonously boring, resembling a voluntary imprisonment without any hope of liberation.

However, if the believer stops stagnating in his egocentricity and helps his fellow-men to grow spiritually, then the Lord will again give him inspiration, His fatherly care and love.

However if the believer stagnates in the second stage and will not carry out the work for the Lord, then the Lord will again leave him to his own lot and will not pay him any attention. The believer's life will become immediately like a torture for him, because all the light and grace come to us from the Lord, and not from ourselves.

During the first stage of his spiritual warfare Saint Seraphim of Sarov lived as a hermit for many years, even being in a monastery, until he found God inside himself. Then God laid on him the task to establish several nuns' communities and convents and be responsible for their spiritual growth. During the last ten years of his life Saint Seraphim received almost every day about two thousand men from all the social layers: clergy, members of the gentry, merchants, peasants, instructing them how to keep the orthodox faith and how to prevent falling into the abyss of hell.

The great Russian Saint, Sergius of Radonezh was for several years a hermit in a remote forest, carrying out spiritual exercises. Then the Lord sent to him a group of people, monks and laymen, who wanted Sergius to become their spiritual mentor and instruct them on their path to the Lord. Saint Sergius pleaded with God to allow him to continue living as a hermit in prayerful solitude. The Lord however, knowing that a great multitude of people would find their salvation through Saint Sergius, commanded him to accept all who came to him. Owing to the activities of Saint Sergius there appeared all over Northern and Eastern Russia in the 12th-13th centuries more than a hundred and twenty cloisters. Many people of all ranks and estates became monks in these cloisters and many of them achieved sanctity.

When Saint Theresa of Avila found Christ she had only one wish: to stay in solitary prayer to God. The Lord however laid on her the task of establishing several convents and of taking care of the spiritual growth of the nuns in these convents. Theresa of Avila didn't even have enough time to carry out her personal prayer and contemplation rule and she pleaded the Lord to free her from some of her numerous duties, but the Lord answered her that she must fulfil this work for God and help people reach the Kingdom of Heaven, and she would find her reward in heaven, after her soul parted from her body.

After their death Sergius of Radonezh, Seraphim of Sarov and Theresa of Avila were canonized and until now they abide near the Lord Jesus Christ and they continue their work for God. They help all who plead with them for help to find God, they also help worldly Christians to endure their sufferings and adversities, hoping that

## The Twenty Second Arcanum

once the fire of wanting to find the Lord in all His glory will inflame in them.

Read the fragments of the 17th chapter of the Gospel of St. John, where Jesus Christ speaks with God, His Father, about His work that He had accomplished in the Name of His Father on earth. Jesus asks His Father to care for the apostles, because Jesus has laid on them the task of working for God the Father and of bringing the Glad Tidings to all people. The time had come for Christ to return to His Father, but the apostles would continue His work and found the Church which guides and protects the believers in Jesus Christ. Jesus Christ abides in the Kingdom of Heaven but He continues His work for God the Father, and He continues to care for the Christians who aspire to Him and who follow Him, observing His commandments.

Jesus said: 'Father, the hour is come; glorify thy Son, that thy Son also may glorify thee:

As thou hast given him power over all flesh, that he should give eternal life to as many as thou hast given him.

And this is life eternal, that they might know thee the only true God, and Jesus Christ, whom thou hast sent.

I have glorified thee on the earth: I have finished the work which thou gavest me to do.

And now, O Father, glorify thou me with thine own self with the glory which I had with thee before the world was.

I have manifested thy name unto the men which thou gavest me out of the world: thine they were, and thou gavest them me; and they have kept thy word.

Now they have known that all things whatsoever thou hast given me are of thee.

For I have given unto them the words which thou gavest me; and they have received them, and have known surely that I came out from thee, and they have believed that thou didst send me.

I pray for them: I pray not for the world, but for them which thou hast given me; for they are thine.
And all mine are thine, and thine are mine; and I am glorified in them.
And now I am no more in the world, but these are in the world, and I come to thee. Holy Father, keep through thine own name those whom thou hast given me, that they may be one, as we are.'
While I was with them in the world, I kept them in thy name: those that thou gavest me I have kept, and none of them is lost, but the son of perdition; that the scripture might be fulfilled.
And now come I to thee; and these things I speak in the world, that they might have my joy fulfilled in themselves.
I have given them thy word; and the world hath hated them, because they are not of the world, even as I am not of the world.
I pray not that thou shouldest take them out of the world, but that thou shouldest keep them from the evil.
They are not of the world, even as I am not of the world.
Sanctify them through thy truth: thy word is truth.
As thou hast sent me into the world, even so have I also sent them into the world.
And for their sakes I sanctify myself, that they also might be sanctified through the truth.
Neither pray I for these alone, but for them also which shall believe on me through their word;
That they all may be one; as thou, Father, art in me, and I in thee, that they also may be one in us: that the world may believe that thou hast sent me.
And the glory which thou gavest me I have given them; that they may be one, even as we are one:
I in them, and thou in me, that they may be made perfect in one; and that the world may know that thou hast sent me, and hast loved them, as thou hast loved me.

## The Twenty Second Arcanum

Father, I will that they also, whom thou hast given me, be with me where I am; that they may behold my glory, which thou hast given me: for thou lovedst me before the foundation of the world.
O righteous Father, the world hath not known thee: but I have known thee, and these have known that thou hast sent me.
And I have declared unto them thy name, and will declare it: that the love wherewith thou hast loved me may be in them, and I in them.'(John 17:1-26)

### On the unity of the three virtues: faith in the Holy Trintiy; the hope to enter the Kingdom of Heaven; the Divine love

1. As Saint John Climacos, the Hegumen of the Mount Sinai Monastery said, God's love is like a sun, faith in God is like its ray, and hope for salvation is like its light. These three virtues are inseparable and one completes another.
2. God is love and therefore when we speak about Divine love we speak boldly about God Himself.
3. Divine love has in itself the absolute humility and absolute patience and endurance and it is the source of faith.
4. Divine love gives the sweetest delight to the one who merited it.
5. He who loves the Lord truly thinks of Him constantly feeling delight in his heart.

### Prayer to the Holy Trinity

Recite mentally, having focused your mind on your spiritual heart in the middle of the chest, the following prayer in combination with the spiritual breath: 'Holy Trinity, have mercy on me.'
This prayer should be recited for at least two hours for this is the time which the purification of your mind and spiritual heart will take, and then you can feel the warmth in your spiritual heart. When this warmth will flow all over the body it will become easy to perform the spiritual breath. Pray then to God in the language of love. The spiritual warmth of God the Trinity which will come out

## Finding the Holy Trinity in one's heart

from your spiritual heart will fill you with an unspeakable joy and serenity.

Remember that the true joy is inside you, it comes from the Holy Trinity and whether you can live in this joy depends only on the Holy Trinity and on your love of God, the purity of your heart, your persistence and your ability, which can be developed, to enter the state of inner silence.

Our Father in Heaven has created us in His own Image, and therefore He loves us and sends us His grace. However the unclean heart cannot perceive it and this is what makes inner work necessary for us. Therefore if we will sleep lazily and avoid work on ourselves we will find nothing. The gates of the Kingdom of Heaven will open only for him who knocks at them humbly but persistently for at least several hours every day of his life.

The believer should turn to the message of the Twenty Second Arcanum every day of his life.

\* \* \*

## Enclosure. Breathing techniques

Breathing techniques described in this chapter been composed by K. Serebrov on the basis of breathing techniques from Tao, Toltec and Kriya traditions. All the actions should be performed in combination with the Jesus Prayer or the prayer to the Theotokos. It is also possible to use the shortest form: 'Lord, have mercy on me.'

### Breathing technique of regaining the lost energy

1. Remember and keep in mind an acquaintance of yours, communication with whom cost you much energy.
On inhaling through the point (E) (Ill. 5) which is two fingers below the navel, draw in the lost energy from the past and bring it up the nervous channel of the spine to the point (C), that is situated in the centre between the eyebrows, and then bring the energy a metre forward. At the same time we turn our head slightly to the left. With a half exhalation we turn the head to the right and bring energy down the nervous channel inside the back of the head and the back of the 'tube' of the spine to the perineum. Then along the nervous channel through the perineum gently up to the cavity, which is situated in the centre of the lower part of the abdomen.

2. Then, while holding our breath for about five seconds, we slightly and rhythmically turn our head from right to left and back about ten times. If you do less than ten turnings, the technique will work less efficiently. It is necessary to keep the larynx open, so that the rest of the air can escape from the lungs. At the same time you push the energy of the other person out. By rhythmically turning the head you break the psychical and bodily ties with the past and you recover the lost energy of you soul, which in addition, is purified and spiritualized in the area of the spiritual eye.

You will see the results of this technique soon if you practise it daily for at least one hour.

## Breathing technique called 'spiritual breath'

A detailed description of this technique, which Konstantin Serebrov created based on the breathing technique in the Kriya tradition, can be found in his book 'The Path of the Monk. Part II: the Jesus Prayer'. We relate here an abridged form.

The nerve channel inside the spine has a diameter of 17-18 mm in men and 15-16 mm in women. This nerve channel starts at the base of the spine and runs upwards to the medulla oblongata and then further through the brain to the point between the eyebrows. During half of a year our entire life energy gradually flows upwards along this channel from the initial point in the coccyx, to the spiritual eye which is located between the eyebrows. Having made an U-turn around it, the energy flows during another half year back to the coccyx along the rear side of the 'tube' of the spine. Thus our life energy makes a natural yearly rotation from the coccyx to the spiritual eye and back to the coccyx.

The technique of the spiritual breath means that man consciously moves his life energy from the coccyx to the spiritual eye and back with the help of breathing. During the inhaling one feels that cool energy from the coccyx moves upwards along the channel inside the spine and reaches the spiritual eye located between the eyebrows. Then the energy makes an U-turn around the spiritual eye and returns into the head through the point which is about one centimetre higher than the point between the eyebrows. The most distant point of this orbit is located one centimetre before the bridge of the nose. When energy reaches this point, one starts exhaling and as said above, energy moves back into the head through the point which is one centimetre above the point between the eyebrows and it flows along the rear side of the 'tube' of the spine back to the coccyx. While energy makes the U-turn around the spiritual eye it becomes clean and warm, just like the earth is warmed by the sun. The spiritual eye is like the spiritual sun for the human organism. This is one cycle of the circulation of the bodily energy, which is then repeated.

## Enclosure

Before doing this exercise, put before you the icons of the Lord Jesus Christ, the Theotokos, the Holy Trinity and the Archangel Michael. Pray to the Heavenly Father and ask Him for help; pray then to Jesus Christ and to the Holy Spirit, also to the Most Holy Theotokos and the saints. Ask them for their intercession, guidance and support in your struggle with the passions and help in finding God in your heart: 'Heavenly Father, Creator of all the worlds; Lord Jesus Christ, Son of God; Holy Spirit, King of Heaven, the Comforter; most Holy Theotokos, the Queen of Heaven and Earth; holy Archangel Michael, our protector and the glory of God's Name and all the saints, help me to find God in me.'

Sit on a stool, covered with a woollen blanket which reaches the floor so that you can put your feet on it. You should face north or east. It is recommended to wear during the exercise woollen or silk clothes, as wool and silk protect from negative influences.

Straighten your back, shoulder blades together, hands on the thighs, and the tops of the thumbs touching the tops of the third fingers. Stick out your chest, pull in your stomach, the lower jaw should be parallel to the floor and your eyes should be closed. It is very important to keep your back straight during this exercise. The back however tends to bend after a while so straighten it again and again, otherwise you will not have good results.

Relax all the muscles and concentrate on the spiritual heart which is located in the middle of the chest.

While inhaling feel the life energy flow like gentle impulses along the channel in the spine. At the same time say the Jesus Prayer once. The life energy, being purified by the prayer, flows upwards to the spiritual eye between the eyebrows. When life energy makes the U-turn, start exhaling and say the Jesus Prayer again. At the same time the life energy flows downwards along the rear of the 'tube' spine to the coccyx.

At the beginning of the exercise you may breathe in your natural rhythm, and gradually you may try to make your breathing slower and almost imperceptible.

## Breathing techniques

Practice this prayer exercise for half an hour in the morning and in the evening before meals or at least one hour after the meal.

Having done this exercise, rest for a couple of minutes before doing something else, and try to feel how life energy flows up and down along the spine.

**Breathing technique for the transformation of sexual desire**

When sexual desire awakens in us, we can transform it into a sublimed energy that can be used for our inner or outer work. For the transformation of sexual desire, we can use the same universal method of spiritual breath, only with small variations. Sit down comfortably on a stool, and straighten the spine.

1. Focus your attention on that part of your body where you feel sexual desire.
2. On inhaling through the point, which is two fingers below the navel, draw in the energy of sexual desire and move it up along the nervous channel of the spine to the point between the eyebrows. At the same time turn your head slightly to the left.
3. Move sexual energy for about a metre straight ahead.
4. With half an exhalation turn your head to the right, bring at the same time the energy back into your head, and move it down the back of the 'tube' of the spine and then further on to the perineum. Then, without stopping, move the energy along the nervous channel on the surface of the body, and then in the body into the area approximately the size of a tennis ball in the centre of the abdominal cavity and approximately two fingers below the navel. We will call this area further in the text 'the cavity'. The energy can be preserved there for a long time.
5. Then, while holding our breath for about five seconds, rock your head slightly and rhythmically from right to left and back, taking away the energy from the sexual desire and breaking the tie with it.
6. It is necessary to repeat this cycle until you feel a vibration in the lower abdomen. It can last 15-30 minutes, depending on the intensity of the sexual excitement.

## Enclosure

7. Then it is necessary to sublime the transformed sexual energy and then saturate your brain with it. For this you need to rotate the energy during 15 seconds along the ellipse orbit: together with a short inhaling which lasts 1 second, move energy up from the perineum along the channel of the spine and the middle line of the head to the point between the eyebrows; together with a short exhaling which lasts also 1 second move energy down along the middle line of the front of the body to the perineum.

8. You should inhale, hold your breath and make 9 circular rotations with your eyes counter clockwise and then exhale. Repeat this three more times: in total 36 rotations counter clockwise. While rotating, your eyes should make a full circle, remaining open.

9. Take another breath, and while holding your breath make 6 circular rotations with your eyes in reverse direction, that is, clockwise, and then exhale. Repeat this three more times,: in total 24 rotations clockwise.

10. Focus for 3 minutes on the centre of your head, then for 5 minutes on the spiritual heart in the middle of the chest, then for 5 minutes on the point of your nose and at the same time on the area in the centre of the lower abdomen, so that the accumulated, transformed and sublimed energy will be stored there for preservation.

If you have performed the above-mentioned correctly, you will discover that the lustful desire has gone. If not, then you have to repeat the entire cycle and the lustful designs and desires will leave you alone. It is recommended to carry out this exercise daily, in the morning and in the evening, not waiting for an attack of the demon of fornication.

**Another breathing technique to overcome the passion of fornication**

1. Sit on a stool, straighten your spine and focus your attention on the perineum.
2. While inhaling move sexual energy from this point along the channel of the spine to the crown of your head and then further to a point at a distance of one metre above your head.
3. While exhaling move energy down to the point between the eyebrows and then further along the middle line of the front of the body until the perineum.
4. Go on with this breathing technique for about half an hour until all your accumulated energy of sexual desire is transferred into the channel of the spine.
5. Focus your attention on the 'cavity' for three minutes until the energy from the perineum fills it.
6. Then, after inhaling, hold your breath and make 9 circular rotations with your eyes counter clockwise and then exhale. Repeat this three more times: in total 36 rotations counter clockwise. While rotating, your eyes should make a full circle, remaining open.
7. Take another breath, and while holding your breath make 6 circular rotations with your eyes in reverse direction, that is, clockwise, and then exhale. Repeat this three more times: in total 24 rotations clockwise.
8. Focus for 3 minutes on the centre of your head, then for 5 minutes on the heart, then for 5 minutes on the point of your nose and at the same time on the 'cavity' so that the accumulated, transformed and sublimed energy will be stored and preserved there. If the sublime energy is not stored there it will be quickly wasted as it easily flows over to other people.

In both exercises all the actions should be performed in combination with the Jesus Prayer or the prayer to the Theotokos. It is also possible to use the shortest prayer: 'Lord, have mercy on me.'

ENCLOSURE

**Breathing technique to transform the passion of anger**
1. Sit on a stool, straighten your spine and focus your attention on your anger.
2. While inhaling feel that you are dragging your anger into the channel of the spine through the coccyx and move it to the crown of your head and then further to the point which is at a distance of approximately one metre above your head on the vertical line projected from the top of your head.
3. While exhaling half of the air move energy down to the point between the eyebrows and then further along the middle line of the front of the body to the perineum.
4. Hold your breath keeping at the same time the larynx open and rock your head rhythmically from right to left and back, allowing at the same time air to escape from your lungs, for about five seconds. By this you disentangle your anger.
4. Go on with this breathing technique for about half an hour until all the energy of the anger has become transferred into the channel of the spine.
5. Rotate the energy along the elliptical orbit from the perineum along the spine to the top of the head and further to the point one metre above the head and then downwards to the point between the eyebrows and along the middle line of the front of the body to the perineum during 1 minute.
7. Then it is necessary to sublime the transformed sexual energy and then saturate your brain with it. For this you need to rotate the energy during 15 seconds along the elliptical orbit: together with a short inhaling which lasts 1 second move energy up from the perineum along the channel of the spine and middle line of the head to the point between the eyebrows; together with a short exhaling which lasts also 1 second move energy down along the middle line of the front of the body to the perineum.
8. You should inhale, hold the breath and make 9 circular rotations with your eyes counter clockwise and then exhale. Repeat this

three more times: in total 36 rotations counter clockwise. While rotating, your eyes should make a full circle, remaining open.

9. Take another breath, and while holding the breath make 6 circular rotations with your eyes in reverse direction, that is, clockwise, and then exhale. Repeat this three more times: in total 24 rotations clockwise.

10. Focus for 3 minutes on the centre of your head, then for 5 minutes on the spiritual heart in the middle of the chest, then for 5 minutes on the point of your nose and at the same time on the area in the centre of the lower abdomen, the 'cavity', so that the accumulated, transformed and sublimed energy will be stored and kept there.

If the sublimed energy is not stored there it will be quickly wasted as it flows over easily to other people.

\* \* \*

## Books by Konstantin Serebrov

Trilogy "The mystical Labyrinth in Russia":
1. The mystical Labyrinth in Russia
2. The mystical Underground of Moscow
3. On the Path of alchemical Fusion

The series "Alchemical Teachings":
1. Practical Alchemy
2. Spirtual Alchemy in Words and Pictures

The series "Inner Light":
1. The Doctrine of inner Light
2. Spiritual Breath: the Practice of Kriya Yoga

The series "Inner Christianity":
1. The Path of the Monk, part I
2. The Path of the Monk, part II
3. The 22 Mysteries of the Christian Way (together with G. Gozalov)